CONCORDIA UNIVERSITY

DD93.K79   C001
GERMAN HISTORY SOME NEW GERMAN

3 4211 000023015

GERMAN HISTORY

BOOKS BY HANS KOHN

The Idea of Nationalism (New York: Macmillan, 1944)

A fifth printing appeared in 1951; the German translation, *Die Idee des Nationalismus*, was published by Lambert Schneider Verlag, Heidelberg, 1950. There are also Spanish and Italian translations.

Prophets and Peoples (New York: Macmillan, 1946)

A third printing appeared in 1952; the German translation was published under the title *Propheten ihrer Völker* by A. Franckesche Verlag, Berne, 1949. There are also Japanese and Italian translations.

The Twentieth Century (New York: Macmillan, 1949)

A third printing appeared in 1952; the German translation was published under the title *Das Zwanzigste Jahrhundert* by Europa-Verlag, Zurich, 1950. There is also an Italian translation.

Panslavism: Its History and Ideology (Notre Dame University Press, 1953)

A German translation by Dr. Helge Pross will be published in 1954.

GERMAN HISTORY
SOME NEW GERMAN VIEWS

Edited by Hans Kohn

Professor of History, City College of New York

**Library
Concordia Teachers College
River Forest, Illinois**

The Beacon Press

BOSTON MASSACHUSETTS

First published in 1954

All rights reserved

Printed in Great Britain

50525

To the Memory of
Sam A. Lewisohn

The German texts were translated
by Dr. Herbert H. Rowen

PREFACE

This book owes its origin to the two visits which I paid to Germany in the spring of 1951 and 1952. A paper which I read before the annual meeting of the American Historical Association in New York on December 29, 1951, forms the substance of the first chapter of the present book. Professor Karl W. Deutsch of the Massachusetts Institute of Technology, who heard the paper, encouraged me to enlarge it and to document it in the present book. I am grateful to Dr. Herbert H. Rowen for having undertaken the translation of the German texts. Anybody who has tried to render German writings in the *Geisteswissenschaften* into English will appreciate the difficulties of Dr. Rowen's task.

Ten German scholars are represented in this book with essays or studies written since 1945. They range in age from ninety, the venerable age reached by Meinecke, who was born before Bismarck created the Second German Empire, to his biographer Hofer, who grew up in the shadow of the Third Reich. Eight of the historians represented are German in every sense of the word. Two do not fit this description: Professor Holborn was born and educated in Germany but is now an American historian; Dr. Hofer is Swiss but has been teaching for several years at the Free University in Berlin, where he is a member of the Friedrich Meinecke Institute. Though these two are partly outsiders, their views will be found helpful in elucidating the various aspects of a complex and troubling problem.

The bibliography at the end of the volume supplements that given in the notes to Chapter One. Miss Anne Marie Reinold, assistant in the Friedrich Meinecke Institute of the Free University of Berlin, has helped in compiling this selected bibliography for which all students who wish further to pursue the discussion going on among historians in Germany today, will be greatly indebted to her.

Footnotes by the authors of the various chapters are numbered. Asterisked footnotes are by the editor for the purpose of identifying for the English-speaking student some of the less familiar names. In some of the essays a few unessential abridgements were made in the translation.

Finally, I have to thank Miss Janet Schuck for the extremely pleasant and careful manner in which she helped to prepare this manuscript for the printer.

H. K.

Cambridge, Mass.
Summer, 1952

CONTENTS

INTRODUCTION

I

Less than ten years have elapsed since the total breakdown of German national and political life in the greatest defeat which any modern power has ever suffered. In this short time the country has experienced, with Western help, an astonishing restoration of all aspects of her national and economic existence. The German Federal Republic will soon regain equality and sovereignty as a result of the contractual arrangements which she concluded with the United States, Great Britain and France. A German army will be recreated, though in the framework of a European Defence Community. The course which German and European history will take from this point on is uncertain. Thus, it might be appropriate to consider some of the forces influencing the likely further course of German development.

In modern Germany scholars, and above all historians, have always played a great role, indicating the changes in national temper and directing public opinion. Certainly, the future of Germany is being not only, and even not mainly, influenced by her historians; nevertheless, past experience reveals the symptomatic value of a study of trends in German historiography and intellectual life as a guide for gauging the nascent and dominant currents which shape and sway the people's mind. German intellectuals and scholars have carried a great share of responsibility for the anti-democratic and anti-Western attitudes of the German people in the last one hundred and fifty years. Will they now be more helpful in integrating Germany into the democratic community of the West?

Democracy is not a product of legislation or constitutions. If it were, the problem would be simple. Except for the important fact that the election of the parliament was based upon proportionate representation and party-lists of candidates putting their choice into the hands of the central party committees, the constitution of the Weimar Republic was a good constitution. It failed to prevail because it was not rooted in the way of life and the traditions of the people. It was rejected by many of them as an importation from the West and therefore as unsuitable for the German mind and conditions. The deep anti-Western feeling of the Germans was a poor soil for allowing democracy to take root.

In recent times democratization has become even more difficult by the fact that lately the government has been assuming more and more vital tasks for everyday life which were formerly left to private initiative and private organization. For that reason, too, it may be salutary that Germany after 1945 was organized on a federal basis with as little centralization as possible, allowing a large measure of autonomy and responsibility to the various states and communities, where individual participation is much easier and where not everything is left to a distant and aloof bureaucracy. The future of Germany will largely depend on whether the Germans will retain and expand this federalization or whether they will turn, as the Weimar Republic unfortunately did, to an ever-increasing centralization under the name of 'unity' and the guise of 'efficiency'.

The next years will also reveal whether Germany has shown her true face during the last seven years. From 1945 to 1952 many voices were silent—by the shock of defeat and the force of occupation—which now will be heard more freely. For the old Germany has naturally preserved much of her hold over people's heart and mind; it has been encouraged lately by, what some observers think, a premature start of rearmament. But there is the hopeful sign, that since 1945 many German historians and scholars have seriously begun to revise the picture of German history, which has predominated for the last one hundred years, in an endeavour of avoiding the wrong turns which German development has taken in the nineteenth and twentieth centuries. They have tried to revive more ancient trends of German-European thought which had been submerged in the later part of the nineteenth century by the onrushing Germanophile nationalism nurtured by anti-Western thought and by Bismarck's success. Will these thinkers and teachers, who are still in a minority, be strong enough in their convictions and courageous enough to stand up against the whole background of popular beliefs and emotions, which are by now deeply engrained in the German mind? Fortunately, they seem to have at least part of the younger generation on their side—one of the most encouraging facts in the present picture of Germany—among whom one finds much willingness to *Selbstbesinnung*, to a searching self-criticism, looking on recent German history with open eyes, no longer closed to any light which may come from the West. To listen to these critical voices revising the evaluation of recent German history will be helpful not only to the Germans but also to the American and British students of German-European affairs, for up to the rise of Hitlerism many of them shared the admiration for Bismarck and the prejudices and illusions of the majority of German scholars about Germany and her role in contemporary Europe.

Even in recent years voices could be heard in Germany interpreting the National-Socialist period in a manner exonerating the German people and thus precluding the hope of a re-evaluation of the recent German past. They excused the German aggression against the Soviet Union in June 1941, as a move of German self-defence, or as a move on behalf of European civilization.[1] In  reality, Stalin did everything to avoid the war with Hitler, though he was probably eager to reap the benefit from a long and protracted war between Germany and the West which would have left both parties completely exhausted. In 1941 such a danger of exhaustion was far remote as far as Germany was concerned. In fact, Germany was then seemingly at the zenith of triumph and power, after having destroyed European civilization all over central and western Europe (with the exception of Great Britain, Sweden and Switzerland) and having helped Stalin to destroy European civilization in Poland and in the Baltic republics. Rarely has so spurious a claim been put forward as the proud pretence of National-Socialist Germany having defended Europe against barbarism and totalitarianism. It was Hitler's pact with Stalin of August 1939, which destroyed the barriers which kept the horrors of Bolshevism away from Europe. It was the German wanton invasion of Poland which wiped out, in co-operation with the Communist Politburo, a Christian people and removed a protective shield for Germany against Russian attack. It was Hitler's long-planned and unprovoked aggression against the Soviet Union which brought Stalin and his régime into the centre of Europe. The American and British armies had to invade the Continent to restore at least western Europe and large parts of Germany herself to civilization and to the Western tradition.

The growth of this legend of Western 'responsibility' for Stalin's expansion into the centre of Europe and of Germany's

---

[1] See, for instance, Hans Günther Seraphim, *Die deutsch-russischen Beziehungen 1939–41* (Hamburg: H. H. Nölke Verlag, 1949), and for a more realistic picture, Walther Hofer, 'Zur Geschichte des Dritten Reiches und des zweiten Weltkrieges', *Schweizer Monatshefte*, xxxi (September 1951), pp. 378–83.

role or attempted role as 'saviour of civilization' is one of the danger signals in the present picture of Germany. Another is the attempt to present the rise of National-Socialism as an event within the context of 'objective historical necessity', to which moral categories are not applicable. Some German publicists and historians expound the thesis that National-Socialism was not primarily a German movement but the result of general trends common to all Western peoples. Hitlerism is presented as something which could have happened anywhere and which happened in Germany only as a result of some tragic circumstances for which the Germans are in no way responsible. Thereby, Hitlerism is divested of all specific German traits and is explained as a result of Western trends, of the radicalism of the French Revolution, of the Industrial Revolution, of the upsurge of the masses, and of theories of racial superiority, which developed above all in the Western lands and penetrated from there to the Germans. Such an attitude not only leaves entirely unexplained why modern industrialism and industrial civilization did not produce fascism in Great Britain or why, in spite of Gobineau and the Dreyfus Affair, the racial theories never dominated the French mind. In England industrialism strengthened democracy; in France the liberal forces won—in spite of national defeat and a desire for revenge—against MacMahon, Boulanger and the anti-Dreyfusards. There are dangers in modern civilization and in human nature in general, and the Western peoples should be clearly and painfully aware of them. Blind smugness would be not only morally but also practically disastrous. But only in Germany (and partly in Spain and Italy)—owing to specific circumstances and traditions, to an anti-Western intellectual resentment and pride and a pre-democratic social structure, to political inexperience and an inclination to venerate emotional 'depth' and 'lofty' self-adulatory 'ideals'—have these trends and conditions grown to the frightening dimensions, which they assumed in the twentieth century but which were prepared by the developments of the nineteenth century. The troubling problem is not the personality of Hitler nor the phenomenon of mass civilization, but the fact that the Germans in their overwhelming majority fell for their worst features. It is the task of German intellectual leaders today to clarify and explain the specific German traits responsible for Hitlerism and its roots in the German soil and tradition. Nothing could be more disastrous for the mental and

moral future of Germany than if the responsibility for the rise of
Hitlerism would be laid to outside causes or to Hitler alone, who
is being regarded as an Austrian bohemian lacking any real roots
in Germany. Yet a tendency is growing in Germany today to
exonerate as far as possible the German people and the German
tradition and to find scapegoats in the non-German world. If
German historians and intellectuals should refuse to face squarely
the question of German responsibility for Hitlerism and to guide
the people towards its recognition, little hope exists for a new
Germany in a new relationship to Europe.

II

It has become customary to ascribe the wars of Germany and
Europe to the triumph of Prussia. There is a large truth in this
contention. Prussia rose as a power in the eastern marches of
Germany by an almost total concentration on a Spartan way of
life. On January 18, 1701, the Elector of Brandenburg, a four-
teenth-century march in the originally Slav lands east of the Elbe,
assumed the title of King of Prussia. He did it in Königsberg, a
city outside the territory of Germany, surrounded on all sides by
Slav and Lithuanian lands, conquered by the military fanaticism
of the Teutonic Knights. One hundred and seventy years later,
on January 18, 1871, the King of Prussia was proclaimed German
Emperor in his army camp outside the besieged capital of the
vanquished foe, the French. Today Prussia, which survived the
catastrophe of 1918, does not exist any longer. Königsberg has
become Kaliningrad.[1]

It will always remain a debatable issue, how far the Prussian
tradition survived into recent times. Perhaps its faults proved
of greater vitality than its undeniable virtues which hardly
survived 1870. Frederick II, an eighteenth-century rationalist
and cosmopolitan king of Prussia, Bismarck, a nineteenth-century old-fashioned Prussian militant statesman, and Hitler, the
twentieth-century German mass-man, have little in common. But
Hitler could rightly regard himself as the heir of the policy of
Frederick II in 1740 and of Bismarck in the decade beginning with

---

[1] On January 18, 1951, in commemoration of the 250th anniversary of the
foundation of the Prussian kingdom, Hans Joachim Schoeps delivered an address
at the Bavarian University of Erlangen, *Die Ehre Preussens* (Stuttgart: Friedrich
Vorwerk Verlag, 1951).

1862. The example of their methods of conquest and of their success was a heavy mortgage on all later German history. The deep and growing impression which these three men and their very temporary successes (Frederick's and Bismarck's work collapsed twenty years after their respective deaths, Hitler's millenary Reich lasted twelve years) made upon the German people has more fundamental causes than the demoniac power of their personalities or the glamour surrounding them at the height of their achievements. 'Adolf Hitler would never have come to power, if he had not found the soil well prepared among the German intellectual class. This class everywhere influenced the course of political life, and it does not make any difference, whether it participates in it actively and has a decisive direct effect or whether it abandons itself (as in the case of Germany) to unrealistic ideas. Such unfulfilled and unfulfillable hopes, frustrations, negations or attitudes of indifference, leave a vacuum. This vacuum affords an opportunity to the demagogue to fill it by using one or the other of these hopes or frustrations to flow into it.'[1]

Prussia was a unique kind of state which exercised a power of attraction on non-Prussian German intellectuals. It was based upon an over-estimation and idolization of power. In a way unknown to the English-speaking nations, 'reason of state' (*raison d'état*, *Staatsräson*) governed not only the political but the moral and intellectual life of Prussia. The concept originated with the Italians and French in early modern times, but in Prussia it lost its rational, utilitarian and limited functions and was raised into an all-embracing philosophy. It stipulated priority for the 'higher' interests of the state, a supreme consideration for its own supposed necessity, without due respect to the rights of the citizens within or other nations without. The state became an 'organic' being, a super-personality, the centre of all values. That was a development in strict opposition to the teachings of the greatest German philosopher, Kant, who in his native Königsberg was a true and proud son of the Enlightenment and its individualist and universalist morality. Nor was Prussia consistently 'Prussian'. Frederick William III and Frederick William IV were kings to whom the State-Machiavellianism of Frederick II and Bismarck was entirely alien. In the decisive years in the

[1] Friedrich Glum, 'Ideologische und soziologische Voraussetzungen für die Entstehung von Nationalismus und Nationalsozialismus', *Die Neue Rundschau*, 1952, Heft 1, p. 64.

second half of the nineteenth century, Frederick III promised to
become such a monarch, too, if a fate, cruel to Germany and
Europe, had not cut short his life. On the other hand, even liberal
German intellectuals succumbed to the lure of Prussia's power
concept. They tried to harmonize 'power' and 'spirit' (*Macht und
Geist*), and in that attempt the *Geist* always succumbed to the
Macht. Max Weber, certainly one of the most prominent German
liberals, declared in his inaugural lecture 'Der Nationalstaat und
die Volkswirtschaftspolitik' (1895): 'We have not to bequeathe
to our descendants peace and human happiness, but the eternal
struggle for the preservation and up-breeding (*Emporzüchtung*) of
our national character (*unsere nationale Art*). . . . The power-
political interests of the nation are, when they are involved, the
final and decisive interests in the service of which its economic
policy has to be placed. . . . The national state is for us the secular
power-organization of the nation and the 'reason of state' of this
nation-state is for us the ultimate value and yardstick also in
questions of economic policy.'[1]

It was the tragedy of Germany that there were so few liberals
in the Western sense of the word among its intellectuals or its
political and economic leaders. There were few intellectuals, if
any of importance, who continued the tradition of Kant and
Goethe. In the eighteenth century, as in the Middle Ages,
intellectual Germany formed an integral part of the West. Its
greatest son, Goethe, who lived through the war of 'Liberation'
from the Napoleonic and French 'yoke', remained faithful to the
German ideas of the eighteenth century. In his conversations
with Eckermann, in his last years, he always stressed how much
he owed to the French and how highly he regarded their intellectual and moral civilization. He warned his sovereign, Duke
Karl August of Saxony-Weimar, against joining the anti-French
alliance. 'Whether Prussians or Frenchmen, it did not make much
difference to Goethe; he thought that the Prussian allies behaved
much worse than the enemies. He also held the Prussians
responsible for the fact that that had attracted Karl August to
their side and thus brought unrest and war, instead of tranquillity and peace, to Saxony-Weimar. . . . He knew war, and he
preferred peace under Napoleon's rule to a war under any other
commander. The ideal of a free fatherland and similar things

---

[1] Max Weber, *Gesammelte politische Schriften* (Munich: Drei Masken-Verlag, 1921),
p. 20.

2

were without interest for him; to him they were only phrases which meant marching armies and misery for hundreds of thousands.' Goethe not only faithfully admired Napoleon, he remained entirely indifferent to the enthusiasm for the war which swept much of the German intellectual youth. 'For he did not foresee a unification of Germany and regarded it, rightly, as impossible and ineffectual. That, too, was a legacy of the eighteenth century. The following centuries threw it away much too hastily, together with the Enlightenment and with the old Reich—for that very reason Germany lost, out of sheer romanticism, its political and cultural integrity.'[1]

The patriotic struggle of 1812, incited by the intellectuals and to which Goethe remained aloof, sets the example for the fateful development of nationalism in many central and eastern European, and later among Asiatic, peoples. It was animated by a fervent and self-righteous rejection of the West, of the Enlightenment, of rational reasonableness and universalist objectivity. It identified the nascent German nationalism with boundless hatred of the French and the alien.[2] From this first 'up-rising of the German folk' (*Aufbruch des deutschen Volkes*), from the youth movement of the *Turnerschaften* and *Burschenschaften*, a straight line leads to the second 'up-rising of the German folk', which the German youth celebrated with a reason-defying and death-defying enthusiasm in 1933. Karl Adolf Menzel (1784–1855), a German conservative, saw in 1820 clearly the dangers involved: 'This hostile fury to which you strive in the midst of peace to excite the hearts of the youth against a whole people, these truly cannibalistic war-songs which you make the young sing, this lamentable doctrine that God will not abandon his Germans . . . all this is not Christian and German but pagan and Jewish, Jewish in the worst sense of the word.' The irrational and semi-religious adoration of the German people and their mission in the war against the West dominated many German minds even before 1848, long before Bismarck and Hitler. Heinrich Heine bore witness to it negatively; a prolific writer like Wolfgang Menzel (1798–1873), for many years before 1848 the leading literary

---

[1] Heinrich Meyer, *Goethe, Das Leben im Werk* (Hamburg-Bergedorf: Stromverlag, 1949), pp. 444f, 448. See also p. 630.
[2] See Hans Kohn, 'Arndt and the Character of German Nationalism', *American Historical Review*, LIV, 4 (July 1949); 'Father Jahn's Nationalism', *Review of Politics*, XI, 4 (October 1949); 'The Paradox of Fichte's Nationalism', *The Journal of the History of Ideas*, X, 3 (July 1949); 'Romanticism and the Rise of German Nationalism', *Review of Politics*, XII, 4 (October 1950).

critic of Germany, was one of the many who bore witness to it positively.[1]

More and more, as the nineteenth century neared its close, the German intellectuals oscillated between eschatological and un-fulfillable hopes on the one hand and a deep despair of civilization and politics on the other. These moods were supported by the politically backward structure of the Prussian-German state. 'For the German state of the nineteenth century could rely neither on a politically alive nobility nor on a bourgeoisie serving as a positive basis for the state, and it had . . . no parliamentary tradition at all. For this reason . . . it was thrown back, more than any other European state (with the exception of Russia) on the twin pillars of army and bureaucracy, established in the eighteenth century.'[2] When the twentieth century began, some German thinkers pointed to the danger of Germany's alienation from the Enlightenment and from the West. 'Must we not regain some of the ideas of the Enlightenment which we have abandoned?' Wilhelm Dilthey asked. And Wilhelm Windelband insisted that 'in many ways we are today in a situation in which we must resume the fight for the achievement of the Enlightenment in clarity and liberty of life, perhaps a more difficult struggle than that which the Enlightenment successfully waged'.[3]

These warning voices went unheeded. The war of 1914, the enthusiasm in the August days intensified the feeling of a German mission in the rejection of, and struggle against, the West. No other books bear better witness to it than Thomas Mann's *Betrachtungen eines Unpolitischen* (Thoughts of a non-political man) and Werner Sombart's *Helden und Händler* (German Heroes and Western Shopkeepers), the voice of two truly representative and to a certain degree world-minded German intellectuals. The unexpected defeat of the 'better' side in 1918 fanned among German scholars, writers and youth leaders the fires of anti-Westernism. The German mind has produced, especially in the period from 1760 to 1830, when there was no unified and powerful Germany, marvellous creations in many fields, above all in

[1] See Erwin Schupper, *Der Burschenschafter Wolfgang Menzel* (Frankfurt a. M.: Schulte-Bulmke, 1952). On the modern German youth movement see Eduard Spranger, 'Fünf Jugendgenerationen 1900–49' in his *Pädagogische Perspektiven* (Heidelberg: Quelle & Meyer, 1951).

[2] Rudolf Stadelmann, *Moltke und der Staat* (Krefeld: Scherpe Verlag, 1950), pp. 414f.

[3] Dilthey, *Das Erlebnis und die Dichtung* (Leipzig: Teubner, 1912), p. 174; Windelband, *Die Philosophie im deutschen Geistesleben des 19. Jahrhunderts* (Tübingen: Mohr, 1909), p. 94.

philosophy, in music and in literature. There are certain qualities which, when controlled, enhance the productivity of the mind. When they are given free rein, however, they can grow to dimensions destroying human measure. The German mind seems to prefer often 'becoming' to 'being', the infinite to the finite, the measureless to the measured. German romanticism glorified these sides of the German mind and rejected the control by the French sense of the measure or by the English sense of the reasonable and useful. The Austrian poet, Grillparzer, warned in 1842 in a poem dedicated to Mozart, in which he stressed these dangers of the German inclination to the measureless in hopes and fears, in expectations and rejections.

> . . . Nennt ihr ihn gross? er war es durch die Grenze.
> Was er gethan, und was er sich versagt,
> Wiegt gleich schwer in der Wage seines Ruhms;
> Weil nie er mehr gewollt, als Menschen sollen,
> Tönt auch ein Mass aus Allem, was er schuf,
> Und lieber schien er kleiner, als er war,
> Als sich zum Ungethümen anzuschwellen.
> Das Reich der Kunst ist eine zweite Welt,
> Doch wesenhaft und wirklich, wie die erste,
> Und alles Wirkliche gehorcht dem Mass.
> Dess seid gedenk, und mahne dieser Tag
> Die Zeit, die Gröss'res will, und Klein'res nur vermag.

(You call him great? he was it by accepting a limit. What he did, and what he renounced to do, weighs equally on the balance of his glory. Because he never willed more, than human beings should will, there is a harmony in everything he created. He preferred to appear smaller than he was, than to grow beyond human measure. The world of art is a second world, real like the first, and all reality is subject to measure. Remember that, and may this day warn a period which aspires to something very great and yet can do only little.)

III

German romanticism and historicism, fusing with Prussian concepts of the authoritarian power-state, coloured much of German thinking in the War against the West, which started around 1812 and reached its climax after 1933. The break with the standards of Western liberal thought occurred in the first half of the nineteenth century, when many of its foremost thinkers like Ranke were still under the influence of the common European tradition.[1] There were Prussian conservatives then who opposed the cult of material success and the nation-centred outlook which triumphed in the era of Bismarck. Ludwig von Gerlach (1795–1877) belonged to them. He founded the Prussian Conservative Party and its organ, the *Kreuzzeitung*, but in 1866 his party and paper refused to go along with him, and from that time on he was an entirely isolated, lonely figure. The anti-Western attitude dominated not only German radical thinkers like Jahn and Marx, it was as characteristic of the Right. It was the tragedy of modern Germany that there was not only very little liberalism in the Western sense of the word, there were also too few conservatives who wished to preserve the heritage of the West by adapting it to changing circumstances. Germany had become the vanguard of the revolt against the West, from the 'socialist' Left as well as from the 'nationalist' Right.[2] Both fused in Hitler's National-Socialism, prepared by German intellectuals and supported by German 'conservatives'.

From Bismarck on, the German conservatives were ever-willing to use the appeal to revolutionary forces. In the years between the two wars, there was much talk in Germany of a 'conservative revolution'.[3] Its leaders—among whom were Ernst Jünger, Carl Schmitt, Martin Heidegger—prepared the way for Hitler's triumph. Western conservatives are men with a deep respect for slow and organic growth, for moderation and restraint, profoundly conscious of the limitations of man and of his

[1] 'According to Ranke, every nation has a right to follow its own logic, of politic as well as of any other phase of national life. His theory therefore was limited not only to Germanophilism. The original break with the standards of Western liberal thought was carried forward . . . in a destructive but inevitable chain reaction into Slavophilism, Sinophilism, Indophilism, Turkophilism, et cetera. Wherever the standards of the most advanced Western nations clashed with local traditions, a similar ideological revolt was the logical consequence of local nationalism. The Prussian and German revolt was the first one. It supplied the essential guides of thought for all subsequent ones.' Theodore H. von Laue, *Leopold Ranke, the Formative Years* (Princeton University Press, 1950), p. 100.

[2] See on Gerlach, Hans Joachim Schoeps, *Das Andere Preussen* (Stuttgart: Friedrich Vorwerk Verlag, 1952). Schoeps also discusses there the historian, Heinrich Leo (1799–1878), who in his open exultant militarism and rapacious annexationist appetite was much more typical of modern German conservatism. This pious Christian ridiculed 'the poison of sentimental humanitarianism' and found the harshest terms for the glorification of violence and for the vilification of Germany's enemies.

[3] See Arnim Mohler, *Die conservative Revolution in Deutschland 1918–32* (Stuttgart: Friedrich Vorwerk Verlag, 1950), and the excellent review by Professor Michael Freund, 'Conservatives Harakari', *Die Gegenwart*, January 15, 1952.

power. The conservative revolutionists in Germany were the antithesis of this type. A disturbing factor in the present situation in Germany is the immense respect, paid by so many to the work of Heidegger or Jünger.[1] A new war against the West is being launched in some circles and this, as it was often under Hitler, in the name of a new Europe, of the true Europe, which only German leadership, at the moment at least spiritual leadership, can create. Hans Zehrer, who as editor of the monthly *Die Tat* was before 1933 one of the most prominent leaders of the conservative revolution and of the war against the West, has now become editor of the Protestant *Sonntagsblatt*. There he published on June 16, 1952, a long article, 'Das abendländische Volk', (The people of the Occident). In it he wished to protect Europe equally against Eurasia (Russia) and the Atlantic (the United States); he found Europe not in France or England, Switzerland or Holland—these are to him old and past people—Europe's hope, according to him, rests with three young people, the Spaniards, the Italians, and the Germans. To them belongs the task of forming the new Europe. In this triad, the Germans will by necessity exercise leadership. Shades of 1940—of Hitler, Mussolini and Franco! Naturally these three leaders are not named, but there is a clear appeal to the Germans to regard themselves as *the* people of the Occident, who must liberate themselves from the 'burden of modern times', from all the Western influences, under which they had to suffer for so long. This in many ways typical article is the more remarkable on account of the organ in which it was published. Similarly, Hermann Rauschning, who warned the world against the revolution of nihilism which he and his friends had helped into power, wrote in 1950: 'What could help us is not that which appears right and reasonable, shrewd and understanding, practical and useful in the bourgeois sense, but only the saving tragic, mortal leap into the consuming divine fire, into which despairing man plunges like Empedocles into the Aetna. Only as they go under, do men and nations experience rebirth.'[2]

How far are these voices dominant? What Germany needs

---

[1] See on Heidegger, Karl Löwith, 'M. Heidegger: Denker in dürftiger Zeit', *Neue Rundschau*, LXIII, no. 1 (1952), pp. 1–27, and Alexander Lernet-Holenia, 'Die Sprachzauberer', *Die Neue Zeitung*, July 31, 1952, and for an English criticism, G. L. Arnold, in *The Twentieth Century*, CLII (August 1952), pp. 161 f. On Jünger and his most recent book, see Max Rychner, 'Fahrt nach Godenholm', *Die Tat*, Zürich, June 14, 1952.

[2] Rauschning, *Deutschland zwischen West und Ost* (Berlin-Hamburg-Stuttgart: Christian Verlag, 1950).

above all, is the very thing which Rauschning rejected. It needs greater emphasis on Goethe than on Hölderlin, or Kant than on Nietzsche. Germany stands between the East and the West, open to both. In helping her to decide for the West—not to lead a 'young' Europe against the West but to reintegrate herself with the old and ever-new West which is truly conservative and truly revolutionary—German historiography can make an important contribution. It can show how Germany formed an integral and important part of the West, living out of a common heritage and enriching it by her contributions. It can show how the 'War against the West' formed a revolutionary break with the best German traditions. It can confront utopian and self-adulatory hopes and nihilistic denunciations of civilization with critical insight and a measured outlook. Some German historians are doing it and are rendering thereby Germany and Europe a great service. Of some of these attempts the following pages wish to tell.[1]

---

[1] It is interesting to note that the Soviet historians have lately tried their best in Germany, to revive the anti-Western enthusiasm of the war against Napoleon. See Leo Stern, 'Gegenwartsaufgaben der deutschen Geschichtsforschung', *Neue Welt*, VII (July 1952), pp. 1684–1709, an appeal to the *sanctus amor patriae* and to the spirit of Scharnhorst, Clausewitz, Jahn, Fichte, Arndt, Heinrich von Kleist and the brothers Grimm. The *Tägliche Rundschau* of July 5 and 6, 1952, rediscovered 'a little-known chapter of Russian-German friendship', the *Russisch-Deutsches Volks-Blatt*, which Kotzebue edited in 1813. There, too, Jahn is glorified. *Neues Deutschland* of June 1, 1952, carried a long article by Fritz Lange, 'Über die Notwendigkeit, aus der eigenen Geschichte zu lernen. Das Beispiel des grossen deutschen Patrioten Neithardt von Gneisenau' (On the necessity to learn from our own history: the example of the great German patriot Gneisenau). The article asks to organize the national resistance against 'the Adenauer gang' in the language of Gneisenau, Arndt, Jahn, Heinrich von Kleist, of these 'best men of Prussia'. Thus, in Communist-dominated Germany the tradition of Prussianism and nationalist enthusiasm is being revived in the lands which historically formed its core. See Harry Pross, 'Deutschnationale Aspekte in der jüngsten SED. Publizistik', *Ost-Probleme*, IV, no. 39 (September 27, 1952).

CHAPTER ONE

RETHINKING RECENT GERMAN HISTORY

by Hans Kohn

Friedrich Meinecke, the Dean of German historians, celebrated in October 1951, the month of his eighty-ninth birthday, the fiftieth anniversary of his appointment to a full professorship. In his reply to an address by the Freie Universität Berlin, of which he is one of the founders and Ehrenrektor, Professor Meinecke called our time great because of its concern with the 'highest and most sacred values of mankind, the liberty, honour, right and dignity of the individual', a struggle which draws 'all the vital forces of Western civilization' closer together, labour and the middle class, Catholics and Protestants.[1] This emphasis on individual liberty and on the unity of Western civilization has rarely been heard among German historians. Perhaps Meinecke's personal evolution is one of the hopeful signs in Germany. For he came from the strictest conservative Old-Prussian background: his upbringing was satiated with anti-liberalism, anti-semitism and a fervent Bismarckism.[2] In his younger years he praised the German 'ascent' from the cosmopolitanism of a Kant or Goethe to the nation-state of a Ranke and Bismarck. As an old man he began to ask himself whether Ranke had not misled German historiography and the German intellectual development. As far back as 1924, in an introduction to a new edition of Ranke's *Politisches Gespräch*, he pointed out that Ranke's concept of the powerful states as the embodiment of God's thoughts and ideas ennobled and sanctioned their elemental struggle for power. This glorification of the state became even more dangerous when later German historians abandoned the objective idealism and religiosity of Ranke's time for the voluntarism of the period after 1848.[3]

[1] The address is reprinted in *Colloquium*, Zeitschrift der Freien Studenten Berlins, v (1951), no. 11.

[2] See his autobiographical volumes, *Erlebtes 1862–1901* (Leipzig: Koehler & Amelang, 1941) and *Erinnerungen: Strassburg, Freiburg, Berlin 1901–19* (Stuttgart: K. F. Koehler, 1949).

[3] Meinecke, *Vom Geschichtlichen Sinn und vom Sinn der Geschichte*, 3rd ed. (Leipzig: Koehler & Amelang, 1939). See on Ranke, Theodore H. von Laue, *Leopold Ranke, the Formative Years* (Princeton: Princeton University Press, 1950) and on Meinecke the comprehensive study by Walther Hofer, *Geschichtsschreibung und Weltanschauung. Betrachtungen zum Werk Friedrich Meineckes* (Munich: Oldenbourg, 1950). In his well-known *Die Deutsche Katastrophe* (Wiesbaden: Brockhaus, 1946) Meinecke suggested for Germany a return to the objective realism of the Goethe period.

In 1948 Meinecke compared Ranke, for whom power is the manifestation of a spiritual essence, an original genius which leads its own life (*In der Macht an sich erscheint ein geistiges Wesen, ein ursprünglicher Genius, der sein eigenes Leben hat*), with the solitary individualist, Jakob Burckhardt. Ranke saw in organized religion and even more in the powerful state the highest manifestation of civilization; Burckhardt, therein much nearer to Kant, placed civilization high above state and religion for the very reason that it does not claim a power of enforcement (*Zwangsgeltung*) but allows freedom and spontaneity. Meinecke asked himself whether Burckhardt should not become more important than Ranke for German historians. 'What we lived through in the last fourteen years, forces us to accept entirely new perspectives and problems in the evaluation of our past. We must relearn (*umlernen*) in many ways.'[1]

This process of rethinking the German history of the last one hundred and fifty years is an encouraging sign in present-day Germany. After the First World War, German historians, instead of re-examining the foundations of the Bismarckian Reich and of the Ranke tradition, set their hearts on the vindication of the past and on the fight against the 'war-guilt-lie'. In a surfeit of self-pity and self-justification, many German intellectuals viewed the world situation as if it had begun with the Allied 'crime' of Versailles. Even leading representatives of the typical German national liberal trend like Hermann Oncken, the biographer of Ferdinand Lassalle, failed lamentably in that respect and put all their talents into the service of the nationalist attack upon the consequences of the German defeat. Many Germans today seem equally inclined to excuse the past by reference to the 'criminal stupidity' of the Allies in 1945. New legends—of Hitler's Germany as the bulwark of Christendom and the West against Communism and of a stab in the back by the Allies and by the resistance movement of July 20, 1944—are growing. Many writers[2] attempt to show that

---

[1] F. Meinecke, *Ranke und Burckhardt* (Deutsche Akademie der Wissenschaften zu Berlin, Vorträge und Schriften, no. 27. Berlin: Akademie Verlag, 1948).

[2] The memoirs at present published in Germany by former high officials like Otto Meissner and Ernst von Weizsäcker or former officers like Gen. Guderian or Admiral Kurt Assman largely serve this purpose. An example of books capable of misguiding the Germans is a collection of talks, delivered by Hitler before officers in his headquarters in 1942–43 and published as *Hitlers Tischgespräche* (Bonn: Athenäum Verlag, 1951). Though there are some passages on genocide in the German occupied Soviet territories which reveal the true Hitler (pp. 44, 73, 115–17) the book can serve, as it was intended by Hitler, to obscure the true character of the man and his movement. More promising are books by younger authors like Heinrich Graf

the pernicious trends in modern German history were common
to European civilization as a whole. Totalitarian terror was fore-
shadowed in the 'democratic' nationalism of the Jacobins; the
racialist theory of Count Gobineau influenced Richard Wagner;
the Nazi creed of '*Blut und Boden*' was anticipated in Maurice
Barrès' *La terre et les morts*; and not a few American or English
soldiers and writers were impressed by power. But isolated trends
in Western nations became dominant ideas in Germany. Kings,
diplomats and demagogues, who succumbed to the demoniac
lure of power, existed elsewhere; but the inclination of the
majority of the German people and of German intellectuals to
accept them uncritically is the troubling problem. Instinctive
reactions to concrete situations were sanctified and absolutized
in Germany by philosophical reasoning which absolved individual
conscience from responsibility. Nationalism was in the Western
lands primarily a product of the Enlightenment, a demand of
citizens for the right to criticize and limit governmental power:
in Germany (and in Russia) nationalism rose out of the spirit of
romanticism; it turned to self-glorification and lacked sober
appreciation of moral and material forces without. The underlying concepts of German historiography which made the uncritical acceptance of the Bismarckian Germany possible alienated
Germany from Europe. The powerful auto-suggestion of having
been wronged by history—in comparison with the Western
nations—created a sense of living in a unique situation which
justified unique measures. Thus a reinterpretation of German
history is not a question of new facts or documents but of a new
perspective, of a different frame of values.[1]

The breakdown of Bismarckian Germany in the Second World
War created the psychological conditions for such a rethinking. In
his war diary *Strahlungen*, Ernst Jünger, a writer much respected
by German youth today, noted on April 11, 1945: 'From such a
defeat one does not recover any longer, as peoples formerly
recovered after Jena or after Sedan. Such a defeat marks a
turning-point in the life of nations, and in such a transition not
only innumerable human beings must die but also much that
moved us in our very depths.' In 1945 the Germany created in

von Einsiedel, *Tagebuch der Versuchung* (Berlin & Stuttgart: Pontes Verlag, 1951).
Einsiedel, a great-grandson of Bismarck, a fighter pilot in the Second World War,
was in 1939 eighteen years old.
[1] See also Walther Hofer, 'Über das Problem einer Revision des deutschen
Geschichtsbildes', *Schweizerische Hochschulzeitung*, XXI, no. 1 (March 1948).

1866, not the short-lived Hitlerian milleniary empire, collapsed. Hitler's *Grossdeutschland* was only an extension of Bismarck's *kleindeutsch* solution, an even greater Prussia which included the Austrian lands and made Berlin (not Vienna, Frankfurt or any other historical German city) the centre of all German life. Was the past which made Berlin the capital of Germany, Prussia its core and the Iron Chancellor its hero, definitely buried in the ruins of the Siegesallee? Would the centre of German life return from the north-eastern semi-colonial marches to the old seats of civilization in the west and south-west and would Germany find the way back to the common Western tradition which had been opposed by so many German trends after 1812? In his *The German Catastrophe*, Meinecke called National-Socialism 'an astonishing deviation from the main lines of European development'. But this deviation started long before Hitler. As Meinecke himself points out, German nationalism and socialism had 'a wholly peculiar character' and were consciously anti-Western. 'Specifically Prussian and militarist characteristics', unknown as such in the West, were stamped on Bismarck and Bismarck's work.[1]

In his *Die Dämonie der Macht*,[2] Professor Gerhard Ritter points out that National-Socialism was made possible by 'the separation of German political thought from western European thought, a separation which led from Fichte and Hegel through Ranke and his disciples to Treitschke.'[3] Though Professor Ritter deplores

[1] Meinecke's book has been translated by Sidney B. Fay (Cambridge: Harvard University Press, 1950). Meinecke believes that 'the desire to become a world power has proven to be a false idol for us' and sees the German future similar to that of the other Germanic states like Holland or Sweden.

[2] The sixth printing appeared in 1948, Munich: R. Oldenbourg. The first printing under the title *Machtstaat und Utopie* appeared in 1940. See also by Ritter *Das Sittliche Problem der Macht* (Bern: A. Francke, 1948) and *Europa und die Deutsche Frage, Betrachtungen über die geschichtliche Eigenart des Deutschen Staatsdenkens* (Munich: Bruckmann, 1948). See there the characteristic passage pp. 144f., and Hans Barth, 'Deutsche Vergangenheit und Zukunft in Deutscher Perspektive', *Neue Zürcher Zeitung*, June 3, 1950. Against Gerhard Ritter's conservative nationalist interpretation see Otto B. Roegele, 'Gerhard Ritter und die Geschichtsrevision', *Rheinischer Merkur*, December 16, 1950, and Johann Albrecht von Rantzau, 'Individualitätsprinzip, Staatsverherrlichung und Deutsche Geschichtsschreibung', *Die Sammlung*, May 1950. The controversy is carried on in Ritter, 'Nationalismus und Vaterlandsliebe', *Frankfurter Allgemeine Zeitung*, February 2, 1951, and Rantzau, 'Politische Geschichtsschreibung und Patriotismus', *ibid.*, March 16, 1951.

[3] *Die Dämonie der Macht*, p. 153: 'Loslösung des deutschen Staatsdenkens vom westeuropäisch-insularen, die von Fichte und Hegel über Ranke und seine Schüler bis zu Heinrich von Treitschke führte.' On p. 106 Ritter stresses that the Western political religious revolution of the seventeenth century has deepened still more the difference between insular and continental (in any case German) thought. ('Den Gegensatz zwischen insularem und kontinentalem, jedenfalls deutschem, Denken noch erheblich vertieft.')

the aberrations of the Machiavellian acceptance of power in German fascism and though he writes in his preface of 1947 that the whole future of Western civilization depends on overcoming the old differences between German and Western political thought, his book will appear to many readers as a by no means reluctant appreciation of the 'immanent power-drive and vitality' of great states, of the conflicts of interest between nations which appear inevitable like a natural law (*Immanenter Macht- und Lebensdrang grosser Staaten, naturbedingte Interessengegensätze der Nationen*). Ritter contrasts the Machiavellian *Machtstaat*, which he regards as typically continental European, with the utopianism of Thomas More in which the demon of power 'hides its true face behind the mask of justice'. Professor Ritter shows little appreciation of the essence of democracy, its acceptance of fair play and of the spirit of compromise. He apparently is impressed by Carl Schmitt's political philosophy which proclaimed the extreme friend-foe relationship as normal and fundamental and which reduced the will to truth of the philosopher and the will to justice of the jurist ultimately to a naked will to power.[1]

Ritter's identification of Machiavellianism with continental thought is much too broad. The Germanic Dutch and Swiss incline much more to the 'insular' attitude which in reality is the general Western attitude. In Germany, too, critical voices were raised against Machiavellianism even when its policy appeared successful and when it was embodied in great personalities like Frederick II or Bismarck. The solitary genius of the Prussian king was rooted in the rationalism of the Enlightenment and in a non-nationalist and non-Germanic civilization. What his admirers among later German historians accepted from him was his unrestrained reliance upon *raison d'état*, his faith in aggressive wars, his refusal to share responsibility with his subjects. The leading minds of his own generation, men like Herder and Winckelmann, rejected the barbarism of Frederick's militarism as void of all ethical or humane principles. The young Herder advocated the dismemberment of Prussia for the happiness of its peoples and prophesied that Frederick's work would remain sterile and his

---

[1] See *Die Dämonie der Macht*, pp. 57, 167. On the other hand, see the excellent passages pp. 135–38, 154, 159. The reappearance of Carl Schmitt in 1950 is certainly remarkable. See Friedrich August von der Heydte, *Hochland*, XLIII, 3, 288–94; Hans Barth in *Neue Zürcher Zeitung*, June 9, 1951; Eduard Rosenbaum in *Rheinischer Merkur*, November 25, 1950.

50525

empire disintegrate.[1] Many people everywhere succumbed to the
demoniac temptations of power; but German historians surrounded this acceptance with the halo of a philosophy which they
extolled for its 'deep' understanding of the forces of history and
nature. It is gratifying to find a contemporary German historian
putting the differences between the West and Germany on a
simpler basis: 'In the Western concept man sins by the abuse of
power; in the German Lutheran concept man sins by revolting
against power.'[2]

Ernst Troeltsch who grasped the difference between Germany
and the West with clarity and courage, wrote once that 'we
Germans have no gift for democracy or for politics, and we have
been badly prepared for them by our history. The old Germany
possessed in its towns a living republican and democratic spirit;
and Switzerland and the Netherlands, which split off from the
main body of Germany, have developed this spirit strongly. We
should be able to achieve it as well as they and must learn to
achieve it under all circumstances, though we may have to learn
through suffering, pain and much trouble.' The German historians are now at least partly fulfilling Troeltsch's hopes. At
their meeting after the war in Munich in September 1949,
Professor Ritter in his opening address discussed their future task.
He warned them against their traditional concentration on diplomatic history and foreign policy. While the West emphasized
individual liberty and regarded wars as destructive misfortune,
German historians in their 'often enthusiastic affirmation of the
state' (*überschwengliche Staatsfreudigkeit*) had educated the Germans
to accept wars as a contest of moral energies. German historical
thought had turned away from rational natural law and the
universal ideals of the eighteenth century and had, following
Ranke, conceived universal history as the progressive differentia-
tion of the peculiar character of each nation. Many of Professor

---

[1] See Hans Kohn, *The Idea of Nationalism* (New York: Macmillan, 1944), pp.
356–69, and Friedrich Meinecke, *Die Idee der Staatsräson in der Neueren Geschichte*
(Munich: Oldenbourg, 1929), pp. 340–424; especially p. 357.

[2] 'Für die westliche Welt (liegt) die sündhafte Möglichkeit des Menschen im
Missbrauch der Macht, während für die deutsch-lutherische Welt die sündhafte
Möglichkeit des Menschen in der Auflehnung gegen die Macht liegt.' Fritz Fischer,
'Der Deutsche Protestantismus und die Politik im Neunzehnten Jahrhundert',
Historische Zeitschrift, CLXXI (May 1951), p. 475. Gerhard Ritter, *Luther, Gestalt und
Symbol* (Munich: Oldenbourg, 1925), p. 154: 'One has discussed much recently
whether Luther belongs to the Middle Ages or to the modern world. Much more
important seems to us the question whether we ourselves belong or wish to belong
to the modern world, if one understands by it the spirit of the Anglo-Saxon or Latin
Civilizations.'

Ritter's conclusions show the earnestness with which new perspectives are being sought for the rethinking of German history. Though Professor Ritter rejects National-Socialism and rightly denies its claim to be the necessary outcome and logical fulfilment of preceding German history, he is today the foremost spokesman for the vindication of conservative German nationalism and for a warm though not uncritical appreciation of Bismarck and his work. National-Socialism is attributed to the penetration into Germany of 'Western' nationalist ideas, of the spirit of 'mass-democracy' which originated in the French Revolution. But it was the former ruling classes of Germany or rather perhaps of Prussia and their historians who developed the political philosophy which alienated Germany from the West, who defended the social structure which differentiated Prussia from the middle-class countries, and who cultivated that *Untertanengeist*, that enjoyment of obedience and dislike of political life, which facilitated the rise and rule of Hitler. For all this Bismarck —though by origin, character and inclination the very opposite of the National-Socialist 'élite'—can be held largely responsible. The present process of rethinking German history centres rightly around the appreciation of Bismarck's work.

As has been the case with the contemporary German critics of Frederick II, the opposition to Bismarck has not been exclusively the product of hindsight and defeat. Many Germans protested against Bismarck's goal and methods during his lifetime. The success of 1866 did not blind them nor did it silence their objections based on considerations of ethics and principle. Among the opponents of Bismarck's Prussian policy were some of the foremost German historians of the time, Johann Friedrich Böhmer (1795–1863), Georg Gottfried Gervinus (1805–71) and Onno Klopp (1822–1903). The courageous and farsighted words written by Gervinus in 1871 have been amply vindicated: 'The German Confederation was created for the very purpose of forming in the centre of Europe a neutral state which would by its federal organization guarantee peace. By the disruption of the Confederation in 1866, two-thirds of the German territory has been transformed into a warrior-state ever ready for aggression. It is not wise to disregard, out of patriotism, the fact that the events of 1866 have revived for the whole continent and for the whole epoch the dangers of a system which was generally held to be disappearing, and have immeasurably magnified them.' He foresaw the distrust which Bismarck's policy would of necessity create; to avoid it he proposed the decentralization of Germany and the transfer of its capital from Berlin to a city which would symbolize a peaceful German civilization. He warned against intoxication with a success which was too easily attributed to inborn national virtues but which might be due to the chances of a passing situation and to the unique skill of exploiting it. Klopp predicted that Bismarck's success would result in great misery for Germany and Europe; he regarded Prussia in its origins and history as irreconcilably opposed to true liberty and to the interests of the Germans to whom it would bring above all increased military burdens.[1]

The opposition to Bismarck from a federalist point of view has been renewed in recent years. It was strengthened by the revival of the almost forgotten conservative Christian thinker, Constantin Frantz (1817–91), a Prussian, the son of a Protestant pastor, and of late highly regarded by South-German Catholics. 'The Christian state is unthinkable without the Christian League of Nations', he wrote. 'Then the patriots will find their glory not in the cultivation of the peculiar character of their nationality but in leading their nation to concern itself with the great common tasks of mankind.'[2] Frantz is a controversial figure and some of his attitudes and opinions will appear of very doubtful value. But at a time when governmental centralization and unprincipled nationalist egotism gained ground rapidly in Germany, he upheld, for moral as well as for political reasons, a federalism which would satisfy the legitimate demands for self-government and the rational need for a universal order. It was Europe's misfortune that in the middle of the nineteenth century, when the roads to a federal solution seemed still open, the nation-state idea triumphed. The federal idea in Germany can claim historical roots in the mediaeval empire; the lectures which Julius von Ficker, the Innsbruck historian, delivered in 1861 on *Das deutsche Kaiserreich*

---

[1] See G. G. Gervinus, *Hinterlassene Schriften* (Vienna: W. Braumüller, 1872), pp. 21–23, 73, 92, 95, 97; and Wiard von Klopp, *Onno Klopp: Leben und Wirken*, ed. by Franz Schnabel (Munich: Schnell & Steiner, 1950).

[2] 'Der christliche Staat ist ein Unding ohne den christlichen Völkerbund. . . . Nicht in der Pflege und Verherrlichung des eigentlichen Wesens ihrer Nation werden dann die Patrioten ihren Beruf finden wollen, sondern darin, ihre Nation hinzuweisen auf die grossen Anliegen der Menschheit.' From an article, 'Überwindung des Nationalismus' in *Bayreuther Blätter*, 1885. Most of the many writings of Frantz are inaccessible today. A selection of his works under the title *Der Föderalismus als universale Idee* was edited by Ilse Hartmann (Berlin: Oswald Arnold, 1948).

in seinen universalen und nationalen Beziehungen insisted on these foundations in the past.

This harking back to the Reichs-tradition was dangerous whenever it became subservient to modern nationalism, to the justification of the predominance of one ethnic or linguistic group over others. Writers and politicians in Germany, Hungary and Poland, inflicted much misery upon the peoples of central Europe by confounding the supra-national dynastic, religious or nobilitarian state of former times with the modern nation-state. Bismarck was free of this mediaeval Reichs-imperialism; Prussia had risen to greatness in opposition to the Reich and its universal-traditional foundation. Later German historians, however, reinterpreted Prussian history as the fulfilment of German historical trends and needs and waxed enthusiastic about the German Reichs-mission, under Berlin's leadership, in central and eastern Europe. They claimed for German nationalism the right to lead and order the central European area. The Austro-German historian, Heinrich Ritter von Srbik, welcomed the annexation of Bohemia by Germany in an article in the *Völkischer Beobachter* of March 19, 1939, entitled 'Deutsche Führung—der Segen des Böhmischen Raums'. But the federal or Reichs-idea, in spite of its nationalist abuse, contained in its pre-nationalist stage promising seeds for a possible post-nationalist development. One year after Ficker's lectures, Lord Acton showed in his essay on 'Nationality' that in a multi-national state based on freedom, nationality could become not only a limit to an excessive growth of state power but also a bulwark of self-government. 'Liberty provokes diversity, and diversity preserves liberty by supplying the means of organization. It is a firm barrier against the intrusion of the government beyond the political sphere which is common to all into those departments which escape legislation. Intolerance is sure to find a corrective in the national diversity. The co-existence of several nations under the same state is a test as well as the best security of its freedom.'[1] The Bismarckian nation-state was founded four years after Acton's warning. As a result of its very foundations, it was obsessed during its short life by fears of enemies of the state within and hostile alliances without, and thus was not a propitious soil for the growth of liberty and tolerance.

---

[1] The essay, published in July 1862, was reprinted in Lord Acton, *The History of Freedom and other Essays* (London: Macmillan, 1907), pp. 270–300.

In the federalist rethinking of Bismarck's achievements Professor Franz Schnabel of Munich has assumed leadership by the breadth of his views and the philosophical depth of his approach. In his essay 'Das Problem Bismarck' he characterizes Bismarck as the last great master-mind of the old school of diplomacy whose life and work fell into an epoch and a situation demanding the search for new goals and the employment of different methods. Bismarck aggravated the crisis by the temper which he brought into the traditional suavity of diplomatic craft and art, a temper which corresponded to the more primitive social structure of Prussia east of the Elbe. 'Nobody will deny that the habit—of sharp attitudes (*des schneidigen Auftretens*) towards the supposedly weak and of the use of strong language which, with a quick gesture of the hand, stigmatized an ever larger part of the German people as enemies of the Reich—was introduced by Bismarck and William II into politics.'[1] Bismarck's habit of acting in a summary and short-tempered way (*nicht viel Umstände zu machen*) and of speaking with a contemptuous cynicism was not confined to domestic affairs. He employed the same methods in foreign policy. The wish to change the arrangements of 1815 was widespread when Bismarck came on the political stage; that the changes came through annexations and militarism was his work. 'By such methods one could only succeed, in the old fashion, by violating rights and finally by breaking definitely all historical relationships. The German people got only too easily accustomed to moving in this direction, moving far beyond what Bismarck had wished, wanted, and expected.'[2]

Professor Schnabel regards the concept of a German nation-state under Prussian leadership as an unhistorical concept in German life, without roots in the German people or tradition. It was first put forward around 1840 by scholars and writers. Its greatest shortcoming was its concentration on power in theory and on German power in practice. The nationalism of other peoples was also marked by that force without which political life is impossible; but at the same time it carried some universal generous message, the promise of freedom of conscience or of individual rights, of human equality or of greater social justice.

[1] 'Das Problem Bismarck', *Hochland*, XLII, no. 1 (October 1949), *pp. 1–27, p. 14*. See also Schnabel, 'Bismarck und die Nationen', in *Europa und der Nationalismus*, Report of the International Meeting of Historians in Speyer, October 1949 (Baden-Baden: Verlag für Kunst und Wissenschaft, 1950), pp. 91–108.

[2] 'Das Problem Bismarck', *op. cit.*, p. 24.

It sought its justification—without hypocrisy—in some moral order, in an appeal to the heart and minds of humanity. Bismarck's solution was devoid of any faith in a higher universal order. This basic criticism has been raised against Bismarck not only from the federalist point of view stemming largely though not exclusively from Catholic and non-Prussian sources, but also by Prussian Protestants and liberals. This opposition could claim to continue an attitude expressed during Bismarck's successes and represented even in the highest Prussian court circles. This protest of conscience, that voice of deep human concerns, has never been entirely silent in Germany. At the end of a long life of scholarship devoted in an uncompromising love of truth to the study of the sources of Prussian history, Max Lehmann (1848–1929)—a man of notably Prussian background and upbringing—the famous biographer of Scharnhorst and of the Freiherr vom Stein, editor of the political testaments of the Hohenzollern princes and Prussian state archivist and instructor at the Prussian War Academy before becoming a university professor—tried to reinterpret Bismarck's work before his students in Göttingen. These lectures[1] were only recently published. Their value as an original contribution to history may not be great; their significance as a human and German document can hardly be overstressed. This septuagenarian, who personally witnessed the development from 1866 to 1918, wrote his book with astonishing forcefulness, ethical warmth and psychological penetration. His 'Western' point of view proves, if proof be needed, that the human spirit is not determined by origin or upbringing. The old man had freed himself from all captivity to the fascination of success, from all belief in the supposed Machiavellian necessities of political life and of the moral autonomy of the *raison d'état*. 'The historian should not only try to understand success and victory,' he wrote, 'he fulfils his high task completely only if he makes an effort to do justice to the vanquished, too.' He shows how Bismarck's successes were made possible by the personal insufficiency and by the mistakes of Francis Joseph and Napoleon III and he castigated Bismarck's policy in 1866 as a Machiavellian masterpiece.[2] Though Lehmann wrote several years before

[1] Max Lehmann, *Bismarck*, ed. by Gertrud Lehmann (his daughter) (Berlin: Oswald Arnold, 1948). The short book deals only with the period to 1871. An English translation would be desirable.

[2] *Bismarck, op. cit.*, pp. 135, 154, 160. On Bismarck's policy in 1866 see O. Becker, 'Der Sinn der dualistischen Verständigungsversuche Bismarcks vor dem Kriege 1866', *Historische Zeitschrift*, CLXIX, no. 2 (August 1949), pp. 264–98, which approaches

Hitler's name became known, the reader of his book will be impressed by the similarities in methods—though naturally not in goal or underlying outlook—between Bismarck and Hitler and in the reaction of the Germans to the achievement and appeal of these two leaders despite their unbridgeable differences in origin and personality.

Lehmann's lectures have received little attention. The liberal rethinking of Bismarck's era found its best expression thirty years later in a book by a German émigré in London, Erich Eyck, a standard work which Gerhard Ritter called 'the first great biography of Bismarck based on critical research in the sources'.[1] It is interesting to note that the most scholarly and comprehensive biography of Bismarck so far has not been produced by a professional historian in Germany but by an 'outsider' living in a country where the great biographies of leading historical figures were generally done by writers with an understanding—not on the whole granted to German historians—of history and of the moral and social issues involved through a closer familiarity with political life. Eyck deplores Bismarck's triumph because it marked, in a period of general advance of liberalism and humanitarianism, a fateful victory of the contrary forces in Europe's key country. Nor was Bismarckism the pre-ordained way to the

the problem from a pro-Bismarck point of view and believes that Bismarck wished to secure Prussian hegemony peacefully if possible by Austria's yielding, by war for which Prussia prepared if necessary. 'Bismarck wollte Österreich so weit matt setzen, dass es sich zu den Opfern gezwungen sehe, die es freiwillig nicht zu leisten gedenke', p. 271. A more critical attitude is taken by W. Lipgens, 'Bismarcks Österreich-Politik vor 1866', Die Welt als Geschichte, x, no. 4 (1950), pp. 246–62. Bismarck's only goal was the increase of Prussian power and to this goal he was ready to sacrifice everything. 'Dass die nationale Einigung jedenfalls bis 1866 bestimmt kein Leitgedanke seines Handelns war, dass er vielmehr ununterbrochen seinen Spott über die nationalen Gefühlsduseleien der Nationalliberalen . . . ausgegossen und als ein etatistisch Denkender ausserdem ständig ein Bündnis mit den Tuillerien erwogen hat, ist seit der Jahrhundertwende eindeutige Erkenntnis der wissenschaftlichen Forschung gewesen.' The liberal opposition against Bismarck shows its understanding of the situation also in four new letters by Franz von Roggenbach, published by Walther Peter Fuchs, 'Zur Bismarck-Kritik Franz von Roggenbachs', Die Welt als Geschichte, x, no. 1 (1950), pp. 39 ff.

[1] Erich Eyck, Bismarck: Leben und Werk, 3 vols. (Zürich: Eugen Rentsch, 1941–44). A much abbreviated version was published in English under the title Bismarck and the German Empire (London: Allen & Unwin, 1950). See on the Bismarck controversy the important article by Gerhard Ritter, 'Das Bismarckproblem', Der Merkur, IV (1950), no. 6, pp. 657–76 and 'Grossdeutsch und Kleindeutsch im 19. Jahrhundert', in Schicksalswege deutscher Vergangenheit, Festschrift für Siegfried A. Kaehler, ed. by Walther Hubatsch (Düsseldorf: Droste Verlag, 1950); Hans Rothfels, 'Problems of a Bismarck Biography', The Review of Politics (July 1947); Heinrich Ritter von Srbik, 'Die Bismarck-Kontroverse. Zur Revision der deutschen Geschichte', Wort und Wahrheit (Vienna, December 1950), pp. 918–31; Erwin Hölzle, 'Die Reichsgründung und der Aufstieg der Weltmächte', Geschichte in Wissenschaft und Unterricht, II, no. 3 (March 1951), pp. 132–47.

achievement of German unity. A younger German historian, recently lost to scholarship by a premature death, pointed out that if the Germans had shown moderation and restraint in the Schleswig-Holstein controversy in 1848, Britain would have been willing to help create a German nation-state in conformity with the prevailing liberal attitude of the nineteenth century and not in opposition to the *Zeitgeist*.[1] German historians are right in stressing that Hitler's rise to power was in no way the necessary outcome of German history or of German character. Some of them might now be willing to see that Bismarck's rise to power was not at all the necessary outcome of the German situation one hundred years ago.

Even Bismarck's critics have directed too much of their attention to Bismarck's personality and motives; thus they risk the danger of establishing his personal responsibility as the dominant factor in recent German history. Too little consideration has been paid to the prevailing intellectual and moral climate and the social structure of modern Germany. These made possible the enthusiastic acceptance of the leadership of Bismarck and William II. Research and study should be extended into the sociological causes and deepened into the ideological roots of the German catastrophe. Otherwise Bismarck or Hitler will be erected into convenient scapegoats. The arrogant alienation from the West started before Bismarck. His victory sealed for a long time the character of German nationalism by making triumphant one of its trends which was fundamentally different from Western nationalism. This trend, in Professor Ritter's words, would create a nation-state 'less for the sake of the liberty of the individuals to protect them against governmental arbitrariness (*obrigkeitliche Willkür*) than for the sake of the growth in power (*Machtverstärkung*) of the state itself', a purpose which demanded the mobilization and activization of the people.[2] There were,

[1] Rudolf Stadelmann (1902–49), *Soziale und Politische Geschichte der Revolution von 1848* (Munich: Münchner Verlag, 1948), pp. 109 ff. 'Die äusseren politischen Voraussetzungen für einen massvollen deutschen Verfassungsstaat waren also nicht ungünstig, und wenn dieser deutsche Nationalstaat nicht geboren wurde, so werden wir die Ursachen nicht in feindseligen europäischen Voraussetzungen, sondern im Innern der Revolution selbst zu suchen haben' (p. 115). On the newest researches on 1848: Karl Griewank, 'Ursachen und Folgen des Scheiterns der deutschen Revolution von 1848', *Historische Zeitschrift*, CLXX, no. 3 (October 1950), pp. 495–523.

[2] *Schicksalswege deutscher Vergangenheit*, *op. cit.*, p. 184. See also the work of another German 'outsider' and émigré, Werner Richter, *Kaiser Friedrich III* (Zürich: Eugen Rentsch, 1938), a book equally remarkable for the fairness of its views and the brilliancy of its presentation. A translation of this book into English would be desirable.

however, other trends and traditions in German life which were overshadowed or silenced by the triumphs of Bismarck but which may come to life again.

In spite of their different approach, the federalist and the liberal attempts at the re-evaluation of nineteenth-century German history are heirs to a common ethical outlook, which predates Hegel and Ranke, the spiritual fathers of German modern historiography.[1] Perhaps today more Germans will be ready to recognize that they have followed for the last eighty years a will-o'-the-wisp. The utopianism of Thomas More is much less utopian than the Machiavellian power-state; and moral forces, though they never appear in history in anything approaching perfection, help to shape history more enduringly than military successes. The Germans of Friedrich Schiller's generation knew that well:

> The great swift deeds of might,
> The amazing powers of the moment—
> These do not make people happy;
> Their creation does not endure in quiet strength.[2]

The federalist tradition is today—even after so many years of centralization—alive in the German lands.[3] Nor was the liberal point of view ever unrepresented. It may be argued that for the last eighty years the prevailing trend of German historiography, dominating even the southern German universities, obscured to the outside world the strength of German doubts about the validity of the Hegel-Ranke-Bismarck concept of history.

The process of rethinking recent German history is still in its infancy. The old trends are still most powerful. A lecture, delivered at the foundation meeting of the Union of German Teachers of History on September 15, 1949, may illustrate an

---

[1] 'Nur von Hegel und Ranke her ist die Eigenart deutscher Geschichtswissenschaft bis in unsere Tage zu verstehen.' Gerhard Ritter, 'Deutsche Geschichtswissenschaft im 20. Jahrhundert', *Geschichte in Wissenschaft und Unterricht*, 1, no. 2 (May 1950), p. 82.

[2] Die grossen schnellen Taten der Gewalt,
Des Augenblicks erstaunenswerte Wunder,
Die sind es nicht, die das Beglückende,
Das ruhig, mächtig Dauernde erzeugen.

[3] The literature in this field is little known. See on Hannover, H. H. Leonhardt, *Der Weg preussischer Vorherrschaft und das unsichtbare Reich der Welfen* (Hannover: Culemannsche Verlagsanstalt, 1949); and on South-west Germany, Otto Feger, *Schwäbisch-Allemannische Demokratie* (Konstanz, 1946). A good survey from the federalist point of view is offered by Wilhelm Röpke, *Die Deutsche Frage* (Zürich: Eugen Rentsch, 1945), translated into English, *The Solution of the German Problem* (New York: G. P. Putnam's Sons, 1947).

attitude representative not only of the circle addressed: 'Everywhere in the world we see power politics, nationalism, imperialism at work. The hegemony of the others has spread mightily and by forceful means (*gewaltig und mit gewaltsamen Mitteln*), and right is being abused by undisguised or badly disguised might. But the doctrines which have played such a fateful role in our intellectual and political development, do not come from us Germans and have not been formed in Germany; they were a poison which came to us from the general European intellectual development. ...Without the petty, tricky and short-sighted policy of the victors of the First World War our people would not have been driven to listen to the temptations and the agitation of Hitler. The mission of National-Socialism with us was to unmask the world of illusions (*das Scheinwesen*) in which we had lived until its rise. No especially keen observation is needed to understand that the other people are ensnared in the same world of illusions. There too, as formerly with us, material desires, vitalistic urges, the same vitalistic concept of one's own nation's right to live at the expense of other nations, especially the German nation, direct the policy. Only a thin veil of morality, humanitarianism and Christianity disguises the materialistic core of their political action.'[1] Such German-centred and nationalistic views can be heard even in some book reviews in the *Historische Zeitschrift* which resumed publication in 1949, though many of its contributors are critically exploring recent German history. Yet there are many people in Germany who doubt the need of rethinking former attitudes. This still strongly entrenched attitude explains the great popular success of books like Ernst von Salomon's autobiographical *Questionnaire*. Similar nationalist outpourings and resentments are naturally found among all peoples; but they have been in recent decades fatefully dangerous to the Germans with their misunderstanding of political life, their inclination to a self-centred nationalism and their antipathy to Western democracy. It is characteristic that a typically nationalistic standard work of popular German historiography, Johannes Haller's *Die Epochen*

[1] Ernst Wilmanns, 'Geschichtsunterricht, Weltanschauung, Christentum', *Geschichte in Wissenschaft und Unterricht*, I, no. 2 (May 1950), pp. 77f. The same periodical published a highly critical and excellent review of Ernst von Salomon, *Der Fragebogen* (Hamburg: Rowohlt, 1951) by Theodor Eschenburg, 'Bilanz eines konservativen Revolutionärs', *ibid.*, II, no. 10 (October 1951), pp. 617–20, where the reviewer says: 'Der unpolitische Deutsche mit seinem Hang zum Nationalismus und seiner Antipathie gegen alles Demokratische könnte in diesem Buch einer beglückenden Bestätigung seiner eigenen Empfindung gewahr werden.'

der deutschen Geschichte, reappeared in a new edition in Germany in 1950.[1] But it is equally characteristic that its republication was opposed by leading German historians. 'While the German historians are trying hard to rethink German history,' writes the reviewer in their representative organ, 'the old concepts are being served up again. It is like meeting a ghost.'[2] Unfortunately, some of the old ghosts seem still full of life.

When Haller's book was written, in the period of the Weimar Republic, the Bismarckian tradition was still so strong that a rethinking of German history could not take place. Few of the German historians or intellectuals became National-Socialists, fewer still were liberals or had a sympathetic understanding of the West. Without identifying themselves with National-Socialism as a political party, or with the social or intellectual culture pattern of the National-Socialists, they shared much of its general outlook and its anti-liberal and anti-Western feeling of a crisis in which the German spirit was called upon to save Europe. The historical vision of Oswald Spengler, the philosophy of Martin Heidegger, the theology of Karl Barth, all seemed to confirm this trend of thought.[3] Words like *Verhängnis, Schicksal* and *Krisis* assumed a meaning justifying German anti-Western 'depth' and the pathos of self-justification. When these intellectuals became disillusioned with the realities of National-Socialism and above all fearful of its consequences for Germany's welfare and power, they turned

[1] Characteristically it was this very book which was published in an English translation in 1930 and used in a number of college courses in the United States. The book sold in its eight printings, 125,000 copies in Germany. The printing of March 1939, proclaimed Hitler as the fulfilment of German history. The new edition appeared in Stuttgart: Port Verlag, 1950. It was not changed in tone or contents.

[2] 'Während sich unsere Wissenschaft um die Erneuerung des geschichtlichen Bildes müht, wird hier ein retouchiertes altes als "völlig modern" angeboten. Man glaubt einem Gespenst zu begegnen.' L. Dehio, *Historische Zeitschrift,* CLXXII, no. 2 (October 1951), p. 325. Gerhard Ritter spoke of this and similar books as works 'deren nationalistischer Grundton uns heute unerträglich dünkt'. And at the end of 1951 Erich Marck's enthusiastic *Bismarck, eine Biographie 1815–51* which, except for an addition covering the years 1848–51, appeared first in 1909, was republished. One can read at the same time in *Geschichte in Wissenschaft und Unterricht,* I, no. 6 (September 1950), p. 330, in an article on eastern Germany: 'Wie auch immer geartetes Renegatentum ist verwerflicher als Überbewertung des eigenen Volkstums.'

[3] It might be recommended to re-read today books like Walther Vogel, *Das Neue Europa und seine historisch-geographischen Grundlagen,* 2nd ed. (Bonn: Kurt Schroeder, 1923), and Moeller van den Bruck, Heinrich von Gleichen, Max Hildebert Boehm, eds., *Die Neue Front* (Berlin: Gebrüder Paetel, 1922). A liberal voice in the Weimar Republic was that of Johannes Ziekursch, *Politische Geschichte des neuen deutschen Kaiserreiches,* 3 vols. (Frankfurt: Societäts-Druckerie, 1927–32), while A. O. Meyer, *Bismarck, der Mensch und der Staatsmann* (Stuttgart: Koehler, 1949) represents perhaps the best monument, erected by nationalist-conservative scholarship under the Weimar Republic, to its hero. Though the book was written under Hitler, it belongs really to the preceding period.

characteristically to the Prussian officer corps as the possible
saviour and patron of the 'better' Germany.[1] But the events of
1944–45 not only destroyed National-Socialism but also the
Prussian army. Thereby the stage for a radical rethinking of
German history has been set. There is no doubt that a serious
effort has been made, during the last five years, to bridge the gulf
between German and Western thought. New directives have
been drawn up for the teaching of history in German schools.
While similar directives for Prussian schools in 1925 proclaimed
as their goal the rooting of 'young men strongly in the native
soil, in the German folk-tradition (*Volkstum*) and in the state',
the directives in Hessen in 1949 demanded that the problem of
man and of human history (*die Frage nach dem Menschen und dem
Menschlichen in der Geschichte*) be made the centre of teaching.
'The young generation should learn from history the human
responsibility for life and welfare, for reconciliation and peace,
for the world of the spirit and the mind.'[2] The teaching of history
becomes part of the humanities in the common tradition of
Western civilization.

The second meeting of the German historians after the Second
World War, which took place in Marburg in September 1951,
marked a further step in liberation from the state-centred and
German-centred historical concept of the Bismarckian and Weimar
generations. The direction of a new approach was best indicated
by Franz Boehm, professor of law and economics and recently
rector of Frankfurt University. He remarked before an international conference of social scientists in 1951 that power conflicts should no longer fascinate historians; they should instead
recognize, as the great task of history, the study of the social
process in its unfolding, with a minimum of emphasis on power.
The interest of the Marburg meeting in German thought and

---

[1] A criticism of the development in Prussia, based on Christian ethics and recalling
the non-Frederician tradition in Prussia which was strong before Bismarck's
triumph—one is reminded of Ernst Ludwig von Gerlach's opposition to Bismarck's
annexation in 1866 and to the *Kulturkampf*—can be found in Otto Heinrich von der
Gablentz, *Die Tragik des Preussentums* (Munich: Hanfstängl, 1948) and *Geschichtliche
Verantwortung. Zum christlichen Verständnis der deutschen Geschichte* (Stuttgart: Ernst
Klett, 1949).

[2] *Richtlinien des Geschichtsunterrichts in allen Schulen im Lande Hessen* by Ida Maria
Bauer (1949). See also *Die Sammlung*, March 1950, and 'Richtlinien für Geschichtsunterricht an höheren Schulen im Land Nordrhein-Westfalen', *Geschichte in Wissenschaft und Unterricht*, 1, no. 4 (July 1950), pp. 219–34. Very useful is also the survey
of U.S. attitude towards Germany 1945–50 in Fritz Ernst, 'Blick auf Deutschland.
Ausländische Stimmen zur neuesten deutschen Geschichte', *Die Welt als Geschichte*,
x, no. 3 (1950), pp. 192ff.

trends before 1866 and in the history of the various Länder, was as auspicious for the process of rethinking as was the address by Ludwig Dehio, one of the two editors of the *Historische Zeitschrift*. It was a farewell to the period in which Germany tried to become the dominant world power and resumed, on a broader canvas, the theme set five years before by Meinecke in his *The German Catastrophe*.[1]

Professor Dehio sees the two world wars of the twentieth century as one attempt on the part of Germany to establish itself as the dominant power. Though Charles V and Philip II, Louis XIV and Napoleon had tried before to overthrow the European balance, the new attempt was different because Germany entered upon it after being formed by the unique traditions of the Prussian power-state. Prussia owed its peculiar kind of greatness to its faith in the triumph of will power, audacious leadership, systematic military preparation and a disciplined soldier people. The first struggle for world hegemony was lost by the Germans because their intellectual formation made it difficult for them to understand the moral and material resources of the Anglo-American nations. Unfortunately, the defeat did not open German minds; they persisted in their delusion and infatuation and refused to weigh soberly the true reason for their defeat. 'We pondered the defeat to prove to ourselves that it was unjustified instead of trying to understand its justification.'

The situation was made even worse because the defeat did not leave Germany exhausted as Spain had been at the beginning of the seventeenth and France at the beginning of the nineteenth centuries. True to the dominant character of its nationalism, Germany directed its unbroken energies not into revolutionary but into restorative channels, authoritarian within, power-conscious without. This new German will-to-power was favoured by the fact that the catastrophe overtaking Germany in 1918 created at the same time alluring possibilities for the resumption of the German attempt at world hegemony: the isolation of France

---

[1] The lecture, published in the *Historische Zeitschrift*, CLXXIII (February 1952), pp. 77–94, was a continuation of the author's *Gleichgewicht oder Hegemonie, Betrachtungen über ein Grundproblem der neueren Staatengeschichte* (Krefeld: Scherpe Verlag, 1948). Dehio also published an essay, 'Ranke und der deutsche Imperialismus', *Historische Zeitschrift*, 170, no. 2 (September 1950), pp. 307–28. See also Carl H. Müller-Graaft, *Irrweg und Umkehr, Betrachtungen über das Schicksal Deutschlands* (Stuttgart: Reclam, 1948): 'The majority of Germans see today in Hitler a terrible destroyer of their country. But if we seek a better way we must learn to understand fully that the destruction started with Bismarck's work and that the Wilhelminian epoch externally so glamorous contained the seed of death.'

which was abandoned by its Anglo-American allies; the disintegration of the Habsburg Empire and the balkanization of
central-eastern Europe; the bolshevization of Russia which was
regarded either as a hopeful ally against the West (Seeckt,
Brockdorf-Rantzau, Dircksen, Niekisch) or as an enemy to be
conquered (Ludendorff), in any case as a means to the goal of
world hegemony. Practically all German parties after 1918 strove
to expand Germany by changing the eastern frontiers and by
including Austria, thus creating an unprecedented strong continental basis for the second attempt at hegemony.[1] This attempt
was again frustrated by the moral and material resources of the
Anglo-American nations which as the result of their doctrinaire
political philosophy, the Germans—and the Russians—have per-
sistently misunderstood and underrated.

In view of the ruin brought to Europe by the two German wars,
Professor Dehio tried to answer this question: why had these wars
been so infinitely more destructive for Europe than former great
wars? The campaigns of Philip II, Louis XIV, Napoleon had not
been merely destructive. As knights of the Counter-Reformation,
as models of a universal aristocratic culture, as bearers of the
achievements of the French Revolution, they had inspired Europe;
and even the struggle against them had its invigorating and constructive aspects. The Germans, on the other hand, appeared in
their struggle for domination as a naked demoniac force without
any supra-national message or any constructive or cultural compensation. Thus the two wars may at present impress contemporaries as a total waste. Perhaps the future will find compensation for all the destruction in a possible renaissance of the Western
spirit and in a better organization of the Western political community. Will Germany participate in this new life of the West?
Five years ago Meinecke demanded as a preliminary condition the
renunciation by Germany of the ideological power concept and
the material power complex. In the intervening years Germany
has made an astonishing economic recovery and the old nationalism, with its ideological misconceptions and infatuations, is

[1] Rudolf Pannwitz, *Die deutsche Idee Europa* (München-Feldafing, 1931, now
Verlag Hans Carl, Nürnberg) has some excellent pages (29–32) on the proposed
German-Austrian customs union of 1931 which are very worthwhile re-reading
today not only for Germans but also for Anglo-Americans. Remarkable are the
opening sentences of the book: 'The historical moment has come when Germany
must be integrated into Europe. Germany did not wish it: in world politics and in
world economy it wished to be as independent as the United States or Britain. . . .
Through this delusion Germany has allowed itself to be misguided into an anti-
European direction and has misunderstood itself and its task.'

reappearing. But like Meinecke in 1946, Professor Dehio in 1951 regards as the only possible creative German reaction to the events of the last half century the 'inexorable recognition of the frightful role which the Germans played in them as the last and thus the most demoniac dominating power of the old European continent in its decline'. The German historians from Ranke to Treitschke have helped to shape the German character and destiny in a way which contributed, by opposing Germany to the West, to the recent catastrophe of Germany and through it of Europe. There are some hopeful signs at present that several German historians are seeking ways which will help to integrate the Germans into the West and thus provide a new opportunity for their creative contribution to a common civilization based on a common heritage.[1] Whether they will be strong enough to stand up against the still widespread popular beliefs of the Bismarck era, and whether they will find disciples capable of supplying the detailed research and the general surveys needed to solidify and to popularize the new trends of rethinking German history, may be one of the factors deciding Europe's future.

[1] A very promising *Institut für europäische Geschichte* was founded in 1951 in Mainz. The section on universal history (*Abteilung Universalgeschichte*) is directed by Prof. Martin Göhring, author of a new history of the French Revolution, *Geschichte der Grossen Revolution*, 2 vols. (Tübingen: Mohr, 1950–51).

CHAPTER TWO

THE *VIA DOLOROSA* OF THE CIVILIAN SPIRIT IN GERMANY

by Karl Buchheim

Karl Buchheim was born in Dresden in 1889 and received his doctorate of philosophy in Leipzig in 1913. After his participation in the First World War, during which he was seriously wounded, he taught history at a secondary school in Saxony until, with Hitler's rise to power, he resigned. From 1945 to 1950 he was a lecturer of history at the University of Leipzig, and from 1946 to 1950 a member of the Saxon Diet where he joined the Christian Democratic Union. In 1950 he was called to the Institute of Technology (*Technische Hochschule*) in Munich as associate professor of history. He is the author of a number of books among which is a history of the *Kölnische Zeitung* (1930) and a text-book on the history of the world from 1814 to 1950 in the collection 'Erbe des Abendlandes' (The Heritage of the Occident) (Düsseldorf, 1952). Other of his works, like *Wahrheit und Geschichte. Zur Begegnung von Glaube und Wissenschaft* (Leipzig, 1935) and *Das messianische Reich. Über den Ursprung der Kirche im Evangelium* (Munich, 1948), deal with the problems of religion and history, theology and science.

In 1951 he published a short book, *Leidensgeschichte des Zivilen Geistes oder die Demokratie in Deutschland* (Munich, Kösel-Verlag, 1951), from which the following pages are taken.

The civilian, rather than the military, habit of thought failed to take hold in the political life of Germany during the last century and a half. One essential barrier in its development was the widespread belief that in Germany the character of the people and the culture was unlike that of Western Europe, and that the German should, therefore, guard against patterning the political forms of his country on those of the West, lest he lose his soul. In this respect, many Germans indulged in an ideology akin to that of the Russians. The term 'Westernizers' for those whose thinking had become uprooted, who imitated the foreigners, was not unknown in German history, though it was not as current as in

Russia. For proof of this, we need only recall Thomas Mann's *Betrachtungen eines Unpolitischen*, written in the war year of 1918. In any case, the appearance of an anti-Western movement in Germany is astounding. For, in the thousand years of its history, our country was as much an integral part of the Christian West as was France or England. If we think of the age of the Enlightenment from the second half of the seventeenth century, we will hardly be able to establish any essential cultural and political opposition between Germany and Western Europe. The Enlightenment was then the great spiritual power determining the principles of politics in all great countries.

But, in dwelling upon the Enlightenment, we have come to the decisive problem. Mark the failure of the Enlightenment to have any political effect in Germany comparable with that in the West. In France and in the American colonies of Great Britain, it led to the outbreak of great revolutions. To be sure, there was no political overturn in Great Britain, but she did undergo a powerful influence from the very developments abroad she had helped to generate. Furthermore, at about the same time she went through the Industrial Revolution. In Germany Lessing, Kant and Fichte turned the Enlightenment toward idealist metaphysics. The vast revaluation in moral philosophy which resulted often seemed weird to Western Europeans, but it did not lead to a political transformation. Only a few monarchs like Frederick II of Prussia and Emperor Joseph II made a revolution 'from above'. The French Revolution may be viewed as a great political experiment of the Enlightenment, but, with the many levels at which it worked, it was much more than that. Strong social tensions, untenable distribution of land, the immense public debt, and the repeated failure of the French monarchy in foreign affairs —these belong among the causes of the Revolution as much as the rationalist spirit, decisively as it did influence the course of politics. This same power, even if more coloured by British tradition, speaks out in the Declaration of Independence of the United States. This shared spirit of the Enlightenment laid the foundation for the political affinity of the three countries.

In Germany, on the other hand, no political revolution of the Western kind took place. The bearers of the French Revolution bestowed upon the Germans not freedom but foreign imperialism, just as today the Russians' satellite states have the benefit only of the distorted Communism of Muscovite power politics. It was then that the great majority of Germans grew suspicious of Westerners bearing political gifts. Foreign rule did least of all to make the German people ripe for revolution. Instead, as in Spain after 1808 and in Russia after 1812, foreign rule drove the German people to expand much of its energy in the cause of counter-revolution. It is very significant that this was the time when the leading thinkers of the German nation began to turn away from the Enlightenment. The force which soon began to control politics was romanticism. Anti-Westernism in Germany also has roots in the abysmal Francophobia which developed under foreign rule. It was soon magnified into rejection of what the West calls 'civilization'. A writer like Fichte, at first a supporter of the French Revolution, later championed the thesis, in his *Addresses to the German Nation*, that German culture was more primal and fundamental than Western civilization. Out of this notion, disregard for the values of civilian life could develop only too easily. Fichte also averred that it was 'unquestionably equivalent to have character and to be a German'. What a disastrous chasm of misunderstanding this opened wide! Thereafter, and for a long time, it became difficult to introduce Western political practices and institutions into Germany. Subsequently, the principal demand made upon German liberalism and constitutionalism was to have a different look than liberalism and constitutionalism in the West. These circumstances aided political and social reaction in Germany to claim that its forms and ideas were inherently German.

Not surprisingly, since the Prussian state came to play so important a role in German history, Prussian militarism, in its opposition to democratic institutions, was able to present itself to patriots as the quintessence of German character which ought never to be sacrificed to democracy on the Western model. Because the army and democracy became antithetic factors in Germany the whole problem of German democracy can be understood only by a critical analysis of Prussian militarism.

From its beginnings, the army of Brandenburg-Prussia was not subordinated to the natural needs of the country. It was an instrument of power having its own purpose. With this army as the means for casting off Polish and Swedish suzerainty, the Great Elector [Frederick William, 1640–88] created a sovereign state for himself, outside the German Empire in the duchy of Prussia, once the land of the Teutonic Order. However excessive the numbers of these military forces, once they were in being, they were available to the Emperor, in exchange for subsidies or political concessions, to use against Turks and Frenchmen, but they were also available, for similar financial or political payment, to the King of France to use against the Empire. Elector Frederick III, the Great Elector's successor, received as such compensation the Emperor's consent to take the royal title of Frederick I in Prussia. King Frederick William I organized the entire civil administration to meet the requirements of the army. Upon his peasant subjects, he placed the obligation of a regular tax in men for recruits. King Frederick II completed the grant of social privileges to the military. He made the officer corps identical with the class of the squirearchy and landlords who ruled the villages. While the French crown transformed the rebellious landlords of the provinces into the court nobility of Versailles, the King of Prussia overmastered feudal opposition by transforming the squires (*Junkers*) into a military nobility. This amalgamation of the feudal squirearchy with the autocracy of military command was the origin of what must be called the 'militarist' system. In Prussia, military uniform was exalted as court dress; the King himself wore a uniform to set an example for all noble society. The royal office was changed into the post of 'Supreme War Lord', for all to see, becoming, in truth, the 'Soldier King'. The landlord was similarly turned into the officer. For Frederick II to prohibit the appointment of any commoner as an officer, except in some technical units, was consistent with this policy. This was the only way he could successfully complete militarization of the landed nobility. It became a Prussian principle to rule by militarizing society.

Just as this principle was applied in the eighteenth century to the squirearchy, it was used in the nineteenth century on the representatives of the bourgeoisie who had risen to social influence. After Roon's reform of the army in 1860, the institutions of a corps of reserve officers and of one-year voluntary service were successfully employed to deprive the bourgeoisie of its self-confidence. German academicians and businessmen in the period of William II, the Weimar Republic and the Hitler government, were often far prouder of their rank as reserve officers than of their civilian qualifications. Thus in Prussia the military became the basic element of social order; 'militarism' arose as a result. The Prussian army incorporated into its organization the harsh caste differences between the landlord, on the one hand, and the peasantry, with its traditional subjection, on the other. The equivalent class difference between officer and enlisted man belonged to the essential distinguishing marks of the old army. A social abyss opened between the soldier's barracks and the officer's clubhouse; to rise from enlisted ranks into the officer corps was not normally permitted. In Prussia, the private soldier and the non-commissioned officer never carried 'a marshal's baton in his knapsack'.

Unless these social realities are taken into account, a satisfactory definition of the fundamental nature of 'militarism' cannot be given. To call any and every policy of war and conquest 'militaristic', or to define militarism as a policy 'giving priority to technical military considerations',[1] is to see external symptoms and nothing more. It amounts to obfuscating our understanding of Prussian militarism by losing it in generalities. Our real problem is to keep clearly in view the specifically Prussian characteristics underlying the concept of militarism, even though the fundamentals of militarism may exist elsewhere. Seldom do we make historical categories clearer by making them more general, for it is of the essence of things historical to happen once and never really to recur. The exact content of the concept of 'militarism' arises out of the specific social reality in Prussia; it is not just the formation of a large army or any policy of conquest. Wholly unmilitaristic peoples and governments may find it wise or necessary to maintain a strong army as an essential element in their policy. To be sure, it is quite in character for a militarist government to be arming constantly, to over-estimate the viewpoint of the military expert, and to favour a policy of conquest. But it is quite possible for militarists to advise against such a policy. Thus, after the victory over Poland and France in 1939–40, the leaders of the German army would have gladly called a halt to conquests. They had no wish whatever for the war against Russia which Hitler started in 1941. They feared not only an interminable war of conquest, but also wished to stand by the old Prussian tradition of seeing Russia as ally rather than as an enemy. But, most of all, they were opposed to any conquest that might further alter the social structure of Germany and thus endanger their own social position.[2] Militarists, it thus turns out, may well oppose a policy

---

[1] Gerhard Ritter, *Die Dämonie der Macht* (Munich, 1948), p. 148.

[2] H. R. Trevor-Roper, *The Last Days of Hitler* (London: Macmillan & Co., Ltd., 1946), p. 9. (German edition, Zürich, 1946, p. 19.)

of conquest. They are solely concerned with defence of a social structure in which the officer is assured of his traditional social pre-eminence.

Only social reality can really explain democracy in Germany, just as it was the only explanation of militarism. German historians formerly tended to base their definition of democracy upon constitutional forms, and to consider the principle of popular sovereignty as decisive. They treated safeguards against the absolutism of the majority as characteristic of the constitutional state-under-law (*Rechtsstaat*), and sought to establish a fundamental distinction between constitutionalism and democracy. They said, too, that constitutionalists or liberals were concerned with the ideal of freedom, and democrats with the ideal of equality. No doubt the French Revolution had proclaimed both ideals, but it does make a real difference whether you give individual liberty to each citizen and therefore limit the power of the state, or you subject the citizen, for the sake of equality, to any and every uniformity that has been approved by a majority of the people. By such considerations, German historians such as Erich Brandenburg expatiated on the difference in the essentials of liberalism and democracy.[1] I think that the Swiss, Gonzague de Reynold, is right when he writes, contrariwise:

Liberalism and democracy were born together. Liberalism is the spirit, democracy the form. They can only be divided artificially, by confusing the meaning of both words and distorting history.[2]

Veit Valentin's proposal to characterize the great conflict which governed so much of the history of the nineteenth and twentieth centuries as the clash between 'democracy' and 'autocracy', seems quite to the point.[3] This places liberalism within democracy, while autocracy receives its sharpest expression in militarism. When the military is the social class in control of society, there is a necessary trend towards the autocratic form of government, for the military commander has an autocratic attitude. Frederick II of Prussia was the only commander of his

---

[1] Erich Brandenburg, *Die Reichsgründung*, 2nd ed. 1 (Leipzig, 1924), pp. 125 ff. Brandenburg's conception is expressly rejected by Ludwig Bergsträsser, the leading specialist in the history of German political parties, *Geschichte der politischen Parteien in Deutschland*, 6th ed. (1932), p. 32.

[2] Gonzague de Reynold, *Die Tragik Europas* (Lucerne, 1935), p. 119.

[3] Veit Valentin, *Geschichte der deutschen Revolution 1848–49*, p. 323. Cf., on the concept of democracy, the discussion on p. 480.

state. Like a military commander, he had only subaltern cabinet councillors to assist him. He looked upon and treated the high officials of his government as menial helpers.

Baron vom Stein attacked this militaristic autocracy. It is therefore fundamentally correct to call him a precursor of German democracy. That he was conservative in many things, does not matter. From their standpoint, the Prussian Junkers were quite right in calling him a 'Jacobin'. Although local self-government, the essential goal of his policy of reform, was not carried through, for the most part, the very fact that Hardenberg, Stein's successor, exalted the bureaucracy at the expense of the autocracy, meant some limitation upon Prussian militarism. In the first half of the nineteenth century, Prussia was on the road to becoming a more civilian country. The Prussian bureaucracy, with their Kantian and Hegelian education, were to some extent forerunners of the democratic movement. It is not impugning Bismarck's genius to see in his system a disastrous reversion to autocracy. After Bismarck autocracy continued its course in the form of the 'personal rule' of William II, the dictatorial 'Supreme Army Command' of Ludendorff during the First World War, and the authoritarian 'presidential power' of President Hindenburg. The last stage of autocracy came with 'Führer' Adolf Hitler, whose every 'command' was an 'order' that all obeyed, blindly confident or impotently carried along by the tide, till they were led into unparalleled catastrophe. This very continuity of militarist autocracy gave rise to the continuity of democracy in Germany, which includes every effort, for more than a century, to assist the victory of a civilian order of society in Germany from the Prussian reform movement to the Weimar Republic.

Baron vom Stein, though minister of the Frederician state, became the opponent of the Frederician system. He quit office in severe conflict with this system. It was an admission of bankruptcy when Frederick William III recalled him with broad powers after the Peace of Tilsit. He then compelled the King to renounce government by his personal cabinet, which had been the instrument of autocracy.[1] The agrarian edict of October 1807, prepared by the East Prussian reformers, especially von Schön, repealed the Frederician distinction between the classes. Abolition of serfdom was intended to clear the way for elimination of manorialism. The municipal ordinance of November 19,

[1] Karl Buchheim, 'Steins Vaterland', *Hochland* (1941), pp. 371 ff.

1808, granted self-administration to the citizenry at least in the towns. It was hoped that local autonomy would train broad strata of the population in political maturity. A direct reference to Frederician militarism was made by the author of the basic draft of the municipal ordinance, the director of police in Königsberg, Johann Gottfried Frey, who had personally suffered from interference by the military in municipal affairs.[1] He wrote in his introduction to the draft ordinance, 'In general, our expectations of awakening among us the civic spirit of the English and French will be utterly vain unless we place upon the military those limitations which they may not trespass in any country where the community rules.' Stein wished to make the bourgeoisie and the peasantry the active agents of the reorganization of the state. The establishment of a property qualification for the suffrage ought not be regarded as a limitation upon the trend to democracy. It was still the time when the owners of a stable business in the towns or a farm in the countryside, not proletarians without property, were counted as the 'people' in the political sense. It is wrong to explain the preference shown to property in the grant of political rights by motives of Mammonism or bourgeois class egoism. Much more controlling was the idea that property was the material side of freedom. When the powers that be, high and low, try to make things go their way, you can say 'no' only if you have some material independence. If you live from hand to mouth, you may have to do their bidding. Healthy democracy does not start with misuse of the mass of the propertyless by plebiscites, but rather when free men owning land in town or countryside and having adequate training and education win political influence. A democracy which gives preference to the propertyless because they are propertyless, is neither 'pure' nor 'social', but only sick. It is in constant peril of falling into chaos and then under the rule of military force. Democracy does not mean that all are made equal by sharing in the lack of property and rights, but that all have the same opportunities to get and keep property and rights. Upon this fundamental principle de Tocqueville developed the conception of democracy for France in opposition to pre-revolutionary absolutism and, most of all, to Bonapartism. Politics, he held, should not be directed to the might and fame of the statesman, but to the development of 'the happiness of the

---

[1] Heinrich Heffter, *Die deutsche Selbstverwaltung im 19. Jahrhundert: Geschichte der Ideen und Institutionen* (Stuttgart, 1950), pp. 93 ff.

little man'.[1] The Jacobins still took this task seriously, although they allowed themselves to be diverted into terrorism. De Tocqueville and Stein shared this understanding as well as support for local autonomy.

Hand in hand with civil reform went reorganization of the military forces by Scharnhorst. It is wrong to see in his reforms a step towards the expansion and consolidation of militarism. The idea of general military service originated in the French Revolution. The Landwehr later organized by Boyen was intended to be a militia of the citizenry, corresponding to the French National Guard created by Lafayette. Hence, when militarism was revived after the wars of liberation, it felt that the Landwehr was not at all flesh of its own flesh, but a foreign body. In general, it was decisive for the military as well as civilian aspects of Prussian history in the nineteenth century that the Hohenzollern state did indeed draw from the labours of the period of reforms the energies to bring about the rising of liberation in 1813 and to reconquer its previous position as a great power, but that the reorganization of the social order was prevented and the militaristic system, with Junker domination, the Supreme War Lord, and general subordination in town and countryside, was re-established. The convocation of a popular assembyl was promised not less than four times before the final defeat of Napoleon, and a law of 1820 provided that no new loan would be raised without the participation and advice of the Estates. But after Hardenberg's death there was no more talk of it. The government of the Prussian state preferred to forego any new credits for decades rather than fulfil its promise of a constitution. Frederick William III believed that by convoking eight provincial assemblies organized upon the basis of the traditional estates, he had done enough in making his word good.

The Hambach Festival of 1832 has epochal importance in the history of the civilian spirit in Germany. At last democracy became self-confident. It was backed by the people at least in South-west Germany. Its spread to other parts of Germany was only a question of time. Henceforth German democracy possessed its historic habitat, opposed to the habitat of militarism in Prussia. The formation of a democratic habitat thereafter was a force in German history, not only in the movement of 1848, but also in the

[1] Ludwig Bergsträsser, 'Alexis de Tocqueville, Kritiker und Verteidiger der Demokratie', *Der Monat* (1950), pp. 609 ff.

politics of the German Empire under William II, in the transition to the Weimar Republic, and in the struggle for its preservation. Until now too little attention has been paid by historians to the existence of this habitat of democracy, in which democratic ideas were accepted by public opinion and the general pattern of life was quite unlike Prussia's. Historians should not forget it because of Prussia. While the Prussian power-state was unifying Germany, the rise of the bourgeoisie, the development of industry and the formation of a working class in Germany were taking place according to their own laws of growth. The National Assembly in Frankfurt was strongly influenced by the democratic south-west in the way it sought to unite Germany.

The democratic forces in Germany also found support in political Catholicism. One may look on political Catholicism in Germany as the core of an 'old German conservatism west of the Elbe', which sometimes supported and sometimes opposed 'old Prussian conservatism'.[1] But it should also be recognized that the essential impulse of European political Catholicism consists in a democratic and liberal aspiration, freedom of the Church. Political Catholicism in the nineteenth century arose from resistance to the exaggerated claims of the state power, such as the Gallican Caesaropapism of Napoleon. It is a movement of resistance opposing this danger to spiritual freedom. Hence, after it was born, it became a brother to bourgeois liberalism and the socialist labour movement.[2] This can be best observed on German soil by study of the political movement in the Rhine province of Prussia before the outbreak of the Revolution of 1848, when the trends of Catholicism, liberalism and socialism worked parallel and almost without distinction between 1830 and 1848, and the boundaries seemed completely fluid.

To be sure, the attitude of political Catholicism on individual matters was often conservative, but this should not be reason to misconstrue its importance for the rise of democracy. As a matter of fact, it promoted the formation of political purposiveness among the masses of the people more strongly than did liberalism, particularly in the Rhineland, where the liberals early became the representatives of businessmen and could maintain only incomplete contact with the broad circles of the people. In South-western Germany, upon the soil of Hambach, liberalism

---

[1] Arthur Rosenberg, *Die Entstehung der deutschen Republik* (Berlin, 1928), p. 18.
[2] Karl Buchheim, 'Grundlagen und Anfänge des politischen Katholizismus', *Frankfurter Hefte* (1947), pp. 1224 ff.

remained more something of the people's. In the Rhine province the Prussian government could easily crush a liberal mass movement by its own resources. Against a Catholic movement, they would not suffice.

On March 19, 1848, it seemed that militarism had lost mastery over Prussia in open and bloody struggle. Democracy was triumphant. It does not matter that we cannot help but realize that the fighters on the barricades could hardly have won out had the troops continued to fight without thought of consequences. The King of Prussia did not dare to send them into action so forthrightly. This was a moral victory of the democracy. Of course, how long the victory would last was not yet decided.

From the first hour, there were determined spokesmen for the military who did not dream of abandoning their position of power because of the King's supineness. The occupant of the Prussian throne was thereby revealed to be an autocrat less as king than as supreme war lord. If he failed in this function, they were determined to act without him. This was the experience of Frederick William IV, as it was later of William II. Bismarck's report on how the officers of the royal guard, openly violating military discipline and courtesy, made their wrath clear to the King, is very impressive.[1] In reactionary circles, plans were immediately laid for dethroning the King. Apparently on behalf of Prince Karl of Prussia, Bismarck himself, on March 23, 1848, went to Princess Augusta, the wife of Prince William of Prussia, who had fled to England, to ask her approval for the transfer of the crown to Prince Frederick William, her son, who was still not of age. She never forgave Bismarck this atrocious request to conspire against her own husband. It was the source of the enduring hostility of the later German empress against her husband's chancellor. Frederick William IV retained his throne, but soon he, too, felt that his submissiveness toward the Revolution had been a serious mistake, or indeed a sin. Throughout the country the conservative party rallied. For the Junkers and militarists soon realized how advantageously they could employ the techniques of the Revolution, popular propaganda and a free press, on behalf of their own interests. Late in June 1848, they established their own effective organ, the *Kreuzzeitung*. The counter-attack against the victors of March 19 could start.

Democracy in Germany faced the task of getting the better of

[1] Otto von Bismarck, *Gedanken und Erinnerungen* (Volksausgabe), I, p. 44.

militarist Prussia. Only if it could do so, could it triumph. If it kept the goal clearly in mind, it could seek to create a strong centre of power in South-west Germany. The beginning of a shift away from Prussia was made by the convocation of the National Assembly at Frankfurt. It was also possible to set up an executive power. Archduke Johann of Austria was elected imperial vice-regent and was joined by a parliamentary ministry. This was a defeat for Prussia. Popular opinion in South-west Germany remained anti-Prussian. But the formation of a real power around parliament and the federal government, able to match the real power of the Prussian army, did not take place. The forces of the people were split and dissipated.

At the time, of course, many supporters of democracy believed that they had won Prussia itself for their cause after the victorious barricade struggle in Berlin. But this proved to be an error of the gravest consequences. It rested upon the lack of social-political awareness at the time, which for the most part did not bear in mind that democracy can only triumph if the realities of society offer the prerequisites for such victory. A victory had been won upon the pavements of Berlin. But nothing had been altered in the power of the landlords in the provinces, the Junker officer corps in the army, the personal influences in the court of Frederick William IV. To be sure, alongside the German National Assembly in Frankfurt, a second Prussian National Assembly in Berlin was convoked to decide upon a democratic constitution for Prussia. Thus there was a representative body for a Prussia making itself a democracy. This meant fundamentally strengthening Prussia as a separate state. Two capitals were rising in Germany which easily could enter into conflict with each other.

The Frankfurt régime was not in the position to effect its policy in the face of separate Prussian policy. But at the same time democracy was evidently in decline in Prussia. To maintain its victory of March 19, it had to succeed in democratizing the spirit of the army. But the spirit of the army remained fundamentally repugnant to democracy. After a sharp clash between the garrison and the town militia in Schweidnitz, a deputy to the Berlin National Assembly, Stein, proposed that the war minister issue a decree ordering the officers to mingle socially with the civilians, so that they would show 'that they wish to collaborate sincerely and devotedly in the establishment of constitutional legality'. On this occasion, another democratic deputy, Waldeck, demanded the abolition of special military tribunals. The deputies appealed to the spirit of the unity of army and people by which the victory of 1813 had been won. The army, however, felt that it had been hit in its innermost nature and injured in its honour. It wished to remain what it had been—a separate body with its own law and its own concept of honour. It wished to have nothing to do with the bourgeoisie. The acceptance of Stein's proposal by the National Assembly merely led to the departure of Hansemann's government from office and the appointment of a general as premier. When this general turned out to be ready for compromise, he was followed in a few weeks by Count von Brandenburg, the 'saviour'. General Wrangel became 'commander in chief in the Marches' (Brandenburg). In November his troops entered Berlin and disarmed the militia. The National Assembly was transferred to the small provincial town of Brandenburg and then, when it refused to approve the taxes, dissolved. On December 5, a constitution was 'granted' to Prussia.

Then, with all the techniques of propaganda which men had learned to use during the year of revolution, militarism was made popular throughout Prussia. A *Treubund* (Loyalty League) was established in order to cultivate loyal feelings toward 'King and Fatherland'. It was not forgotten to set up a women's auxiliary. The principal thing was to reawaken confidence in the army. *Gegen Demokraten helfen nur Soldaten!* (To make democrats fail, only soldiers avail!)

The period of reaction in Prussia, which developed similarly in other German countries, lasted until Prince William took over the regency in the Fall of 1858. It constituted a nadir in the domestic political development of Germany, which proved disastrous for a very long time. Domestic politics therefore never wholly freed itself of a certain spasmodic convulsiveness in its development, which finally led into the great catastrophes of the two world wars. The so-called 'New Era' in Prussia opened a deceptive prospect for new liberal achievements. The military and revolutionary events in Italy since 1859 caused the proponents of the national unification of Germany to think of making Prussia the German Piedmont, without realizing that the Prussian military state would play out this role quite differently. The difficulties which arose in the Prussian mobilization during the war danger of 1859 led to the introduction of an army bill in which one seeks all in vain for any concession to the civilian spirit. It was, far more, a turning away from what was left of Scharnhorst's army reform. The army bill of war minister Roon put an end to the Landwehr of the wars of liberation. In the midst of the 'New Era' came, unmistakably, refusal to permit even the slightest beginning of democratization of the Prussian army. The active leaders of militarism, Roon and the chief of the military cabinet, Edwin von Manteuffel, worked to overthrow the Prussian government, which had the support of a majority of the chamber of deputies. Roon and Manteuffel wished to re-establish a purely conservative and militarist Prussia and to thrust aside the constitution just then coming into greater honour. Principal resistance was offered to giving any detailed indication of military expenditures in the budget, in order to exclude any parliamentary control. In March 1862, a motion was brought in by deputy Hagen to demand such itemization, and parliament was then dissolved. When the new election resulted in another very strong liberal majority, King William, upon Bismarck's advice, decided to govern without a budget. Little attention was paid to the constitution, and Bismarck, as premier, did his best publicly to snub the chamber of deputies.[1] Discussion of the budget became an empty formality, since it was clear beforehand that the government would pay no heed to decisions adopted. As if the era of absolutism had returned, the conception prevailed that the army was the exclusive affair of the king and that any limitation of his power by the budgetary powers of the deputies was intolerable. War minister Roon carried on his task apart from his colleagues in the 'New Era' cabinet. He acted as the advocate of the military which felt itself to be, under the command of its supreme war lord, the one and only class upholding the state in Prussia. Disdain for parliament was finally carried to the point of an effort to repress freedom of speech for deputies. Early in 1866 the superior court of Berlin issued a judgment making deputies responsible under the penal code for what they said in parliament.

What Bismarck accomplished principally by this policy was to make himself indispensable to the king. Retreat was no longer possible. A change of the system would mean a change in sovereigns. Bismarck had to be indispensable so that he could drag his monarch along with him in his revolutionary foreign policy. By such means, he overcame all legitimist resistance. After

---

[1] Johannes Ziekursch, *Politische Geschichte des neuen deutschen Kaiserreichs* (Frankfurt-a.M.), I, pp. 101 ff.

the Danish war, he succeeded in starting war with Austria and then in violently breaking up the German Confederation. For Bismarck, victory at Königgrätz (Sadowa) meant victory over the Prussian popular assembly as well. The military glory just won by the army silenced the arguments of the opposition. The progressive deputy Franz Ziegler admitted, 'Where Prussia's banners wave, there beats the heart of Prussian democracy.' The remark demonstrates that Bismarck had successfully shattered the moral basis of those who wished to make Prussia a democracy. To be sure, the Prussian opposition did not wish to deny its liberal conscience. But the nub of the problem was that the conscience of persons like Ziegler did not speak out against Bismarck's policy of conquest. They were themselves in the grip of the daemon of power. On the Left of the chamber of deputies then sitting, there were many outspoken annexationists. Thus, for instance, old Waldeck was from the beginning in favour of the incorporation of Schleswig-Holstein, at a time when almost the whole public opinion of Germany still supported the rights of the Duke of Augustenburg. In any event, Waldeck was later among those who opposed the Indemnity Bill, by which Bismarck in September 1866 sought the delayed approval of the Chamber of deputies for the budgetary bill it had previously refused. Bismarck thus formally re-established constitutional peace in Prussia. The chamber of deputies could not but be delighted that it was conciliated at least in this form. But it was a fact that it had been defeated; for a long time, this defeat was a decisive blow against German democracy. For the second time since 1848, the effort to deprive the military caste of its privileged position in the Prussian state had failed, at the very time when that state was called upon to have the principal hand in shaping the existence of the entire German nation. An impediment was erected in the way of transforming public life along civilian lines as the spirit of the age urgently required. Germany was more strongly isolated than before from Western Europe. The policy of a single statesman of undoubted genius served to open an artificial path of separate development which, decades later, continued to bring disaster.

Uhland's* assertion, 'No prince will rule over Germany unless he has been anointed with a full drop of democratic oil', was heard far and wide in Germany in 1849. It now proved itself to

---

* Johann Ludwig Uhland (1787–1862), famous German Swabian poet and democrat.

be false prophecy. In the actual establishment of the new Empire in 1871, any participation of the civilian forces was carefully excluded. Bismarck twisted the imperial idea, which not only had deep roots in old German history but also many democratic overtones, until it fitted the supreme war lord of the Prussian military state. The overwhelming majority of the political public and the entire people were ready to accept its mutilation. The new Reich necessarily took on the character of a military state, and democracy could at best look to winning influence in it only after it had been established.

The destruction of the German Confederation, the expulsion of Austria, the annexations of 1866, naturally led those elements, democrats as well as Catholics, which feared suppression by the predominance of Prussia, to form a closer alliance. By 1868, Bismarck was dissatisfied with the elections to the customs-union parliament in southern Germany. The alliance of democracy and 'Jesuitism' seemed especially dangerous to him. The rise of a man like the Hanoverian Windthorst to a leading position in the Centre party was held by Bismarck to be an indication of its attitude of 'hostility to the Reich'. The anti-papal attitude of liberal opinion, which took papal declarations from the dogma of the Immaculate Conception of 1854 to the dogma of Papal Infallibility of 1870 as a challenge to science and all modern progress, had little impact upon Bismarck then. He was moved to the *Kulturkampf* by the claim of the church for freedom in the face of the omnipotence of the state. He considered the prospect of a great party gathering around this demand for freedom, which could simultaneously include the federalist opposition to Prussia and the democratic traditions of the German West and South, to be a threat. He feared that it could attack the courtier-military basis of his imperial structure, which he knew excluded many vital forces.

However much Bismarck aided Prussian militarism to establish its rule over all Germany, he was personally not a recognized representative of the military caste. Prussian kings themselves shared the feelings of the military men. The military inevitably took severe offence at Bismarck's position as the real ruler of Germany, which detracted from the prestige of the supreme war lord. It was a decisive error in Bismarck's policy that he did not use the position of power he held for decades in order, with the help of parliament, to limit militarism. He had come to power with the support of militarism. But after victorious wars and the establishment of his own unique authority as a statesman, it was well within his power to do so seriously with the collaboration of the liberals and all the democratic forces of Germany. None the less, he would not have forfeited his position with William I, for he would have found backing from the Crown Prince and Princess which should not be under-estimated. Bismarck employed his immense political skill and vigour in order to keep down the 'party of the Crown Prince' artificially, instead of making its vital energies come to fruition. He scorned the goodwill of the Crown Prince, the liberals and so many others, and was able to perceive only evil forces in those he considered his enemies. The creative forces of German democracy would have been available to him, but he was not ready to give up an iota of power. Bismarck himself said that in order to determine the true quality of a statesman, one must always subtract his vanity from his ability. With Bismarck we must subtract his mad lust for power, which led him to thwart the natural growth of the democratic forces in Germany so thoroughly that in the end the courtier-military autocracy had no difficulty in throwing him overboard.

Bismarck made use of the legend that in the wars of liberation and at the Congress of Vienna the diplomats purportedly lost what the soldiers had won for the fatherland on the field of battle. This legend, which used to be quite common in Prussia, was believed by many patriots. It contributed largely to hampering the democratic development of Germany and strengthening the military autocracy. Bismarck claimed that his handiwork in 1866 and 1870 was 'the glorious accomplishment of the Nation', with the majority of the Reichstag representing anti-national 'partisan spirit'. In this way, the Chancellor stabilized his autocratic rule. In any event, he never ceased to demand in principle the right of decision for the crown. Hence he had no real cause for complaint when William II finally decided to act seriously upon this principle and used it against the Chancellor himself. Only Bismarck had not anticipated such an attitude on the part of the new monarch. While Frederick III was reigning briefly, William, then heir to the throne, in a speech on Bismarck's birthday in 1888, called the Chancellor the standard-bearer of the Reich, 'from whom we expect all things'. He exclaimed, 'Let him go forward, we will follow him!' We note with horror the similarity between these words and the Hitlerite slogan, 'Führer command, we follow!' Thus we see the fateful continuity of autocracy.

During the First World War many of the bourgeoisie permitted themselves to be misled into the general failure to perceive the true seriousness of the military situation. Sanguine hopes of great German conquests, and hence, newly strengthened sympathy for militarism were aroused in them. They became supporters of ruthless war (the 'unlimited submarine warfare') and 'peace by victory' (*Sieg frieden*). The antagonism between the adherents of 'peace by victory' and 'negotiated peace' had very little to do with foreign policy. It was almost solely concerned with domestic policy and duplicated, in fundamentals, the antagonism between parliamentary democracy and the military autocracy.

Meanwhile an important development began within Social-Democracy. The communist separated from the democratic elements. The process of severance was not started just by the Russian Revolution, but began somewhere around 1915.[1]

On August 29, 1916, the most popular military leader, Field-Marshal General von Hindenburg, was named supreme commander of the forces in the field, and General Ludendorff was appointed his 'First Quartermaster-General'. Together they now constituted the 'Supreme Army Command'.

The man actually in control was Ludendorff. He had not aspired to this position, and no constitutional change resulted. But in actuality, along with total military authority, political power fell into his hands almost automatically, and, it must be said, with the approval of the German people. Public opinion expected that Hindenburg and Ludendorff, the victors of Tannenberg, would be able to bring the war to a victorious conclusion. Chancellor von Bethmann-Hollweg resisted Ludendorff, for he saw clearly that the General was incompetent in foreign affairs. But he was in no position to reject political demands by the supreme army command which Ludendorff and Hindenburg supported by arguments on their military responsibility. The power by Ludendorff as against the Emperor rose so high that in January 1918, he successfully demanded the dismissal of von Valentini, chief of the civilian cabinet, who enjoyed the special confidence of William II. As in the time of Bismarck, the person of the monarch was again pushed into the shadows, but this time not by a surpassing statesman, but, we might say, by the chief engineer of the war machine, which operated as an end in itself. The civil administration had

---

[1] A complete account of the split within the German Social-Democratic party before the influence of the Russian Revolution was felt is given by Carl Severing, *Mein Lebensweg* (Cologne, 1950), I, pp. 198 ff, 206 ff.

to do its part supinely. In foreign policy, the supreme army command on its authority initiated unlimited submarine warfare and thus brought America into the war. The supreme army command also bears responsibility for the mistaken policy towards Russia after the fall of Tsarism. On Ludendorff's orders, Lenin was permitted to return from Switzerland to Russia. Already by the summer of 1917 it was becoming evident that the hope of making England ready for peace by means of the submarine war was illusory. In the new situation, the Reichstag tried to strengthen its influence on political decisions.

Because the Prussian military state had triumphed over the civilian opposition and established the German Empire upon courtier-military foundations, the doctrines of a violent proletarian revolution took a broad and lasting hold within the German Social-Democratic movement. It is no accident that these doctrines finally attained their world historical position in Russia, where Tsarism had ruled and no bourgeoisie of real importance had existed. In Germany, an alliance of the working class with the numerous bourgeoisie and peasantry would have been more natural than the class antagonism preached by the Marxists. At bottom, this was how the workers felt. Their principal demands until the end of the First World War were for negotiated peace, the abolition of compulsory labour, the lifting of the state of siege and the censorship, general equal suffrage in Prussia and in all federal states, towns and townships. These are democratic and not at all communist demands. No particular zeal developed for the abolition of the monarchy. Chiefly for reasons of foreign policy the person of the emperor had become impossible, and in domestic affairs he had himself done most to undermine his own prestige and authority. In the final analysis, all the German princely courts identified themselves so completely with the militarist system that when it fell, they were swept along into extinction.

Soon it became clear that the most dangerous opponent of the young democratic Republic was in fact not Left radicalism, whose forces were inadequate to do more than play upon the stupefaction and confusion of its first months, but the Rightist opposition. The Right, weakly represented as it was in the Weimar National Assembly, still had more deputies than the revolutionary Left. Socially, it remained as strong as ever. The position of the Prussian Junkers in the eastern provinces was unshaken. Big industry was very soon able to win back its influence. The patriotic bourgeoisie whose great certainty of victory Ludendorff had been able to maintain until the summer of 1918, was hurled so precipitately into defeat that it thought devilry and deception had been at work. At the moment of the collapse, the leader of the conservative party, von Heydebrandt, had called out in despair, 'We have been duped by lies and fraud.' Very soon, however, the disillusion was explained not by the old rulers having lured patriotic hope to destruction by a Fata Morgana, but by obscure forces which had prevented victory. The legend of a stab in the back grew up. Jewish, Jesuit or Masonic machinations were invented which were purported to have crippled the will to resist and shattered combat morale Soon there were many who no longer believed that Ludendorff had lost the war, but now thought that Erzberger, when he signed the armistice and accepted conditions which alone made Germany defenceless, had been a traitor.

In 1932 the general assault upon the Republic began. At first Brüning was able to beat back the attack. In the April elections for the presidency, Hitler was defeated and Hindenburg re-elected, this time by the votes of the democratic parties. Now the attack was directed against the Chancellor personally. The first blow was struck by the Reichswehr. Its spokesman was the so-called 'chief of the Wehrmacht office', General von Schleicher. He felt capable of winning a huge political gamble. This was disastrous self-over-estimation, by which he prepared, first, his own personal destruction and, then, that of the Wehrmacht as the bearer of the tradition of Prussian militarism. When, after the presidential election, General Groener, Brüning's minister of interior and defence, banned Hitler's stormtroopers, Schleicher attacked his superior officer behind his back and declared to Hindenburg that Groener no longer held the confidence of the army. Of course, it was in no wise the function of the army in a democratic state to refuse its confidence to a responsible minister. In Schleicher's declaration lay a reversion to Ludendorff's methods and hence the decision of militarism to take over power again in Germany. It was Hindenburg's constitutional duty to dismiss Schleicher at once. But it was not Schleicher he dismissed, but Groener. A few weeks later Brüning, too, fell. The new chancellor, von Papen, was the man in whom the reactionary circles placed their confidence. His first action was violent abolition of the still existing government of the Weimar coalition in Prussia on July 20, 1932. The executive power of the largest German state was handed over to General von Rundstedt. Once more the old military caste of Prussia took over leadership. Twelve years later it was slaughtered in a bloody debacle by Hitler, whom it had looked upon in 1932 as an ally. By a curious coincidence, this also happened on a July 20, the day of its own undoing prepared by some two centuries of the power of Prussian militarism.

CHAPTER THREE

THE BISMARCK PROBLEM

Franz Schnabel

Franz Schnabel is today the leading spokesman of what might be called
the non-Prussian German historiography, which represents Catholic
southern German traditions. Born in 1887, he was, before the war,
professor of history at the Institute of Technology in Karlsruhe. Since
1947 he has occupied the chair of modern history in Munich. There
he lectures, as Treitschke did in Berlin under Bismarck, to overflowing
gatherings of students in the largest auditorium of the University, but
the spirit in which he presents modern history differs from that of
Treitschke. Schnabel's monumental history, *Deutsche Geschichte im
Neunzehnten Jahrhundert* (4 vols., 1929–36), is an attempt to present the
subject covered by Treitschke in a new light.

The ensuing article deals with the central problem in the re-
evaluation of German history, the problem of Bismarck. It was first
published in the Munich periodical, *Hochland*, for October 1949.

The Empire which Bismarck founded lasted half a century. When
it fell, historians centred their interest upon the personality and
life work of this man who, more than any other, put his own
stamp upon the second half of the nineteenth century. What was
written before 1918 on this great problem must now be considered
for the most part obsolete. After the collapse of the German
Empire and the monarchies in the middle and small German
states, the archives were opened and a profusion of important,
unknown documents brought to light. The events which took
place in Germany between 1918 and 1945 were such, moreover,
as to make men question what Bismarck did and said, what he
was and what he wanted. Or, they made men change what he
brought about. One after another, all Bismarck's opponents have
risen again; once more they have borne testimony against him.
The multitude of those who in his lifetime heaped praise upon
him, citing the success of his endeavours, were too hasty in their
conclusions. Men had to learn from experience, like those before

them, that only a much later age can pass final judgment on success in history—the Empire which began so brilliantly stood but for fifty years. There were times, to be sure, when Bismarck himself spoke with profound pessimism of the durability of his achievement. After his dismissal, domestic and foreign difficulties in fact continued to multiply. But dominant public opinion brushed aside any suggestion that the course along which Bismarck had directed German and European history was responsible for this state of affairs. The more painfully obvious were the short-comings of his successors and the emperor under whom they served, the easier it seemed to bring forward the founder of the Reich in edifying contrast to them.

After the first catastrophe in 1918, however, the spiritual descendants of the earlier German liberalism and democrats took the field. They established Bismarck's responsibility for the predominance of the policy of 'Blood and Iron'. They voiced regret that ever since Bismarck the people and the parties had always played the role of followers or opposition, but not of participants in responsibility in the 'authoritarian state' which bore the impress of the Prussian system. Bismarck was also criticized for having over-estimated the vitality of the Austro-Hungarian monarchy and neglected therefore to bring about *Anschluss*. Thereafter, as cupidity increasingly took the place of concern for the state and political life as such, as the masses ceased to think of the interests of the state, which guaranteed law and order, and should have provided their rational guide to action, as nationalism and neo-romanticism, literary scribblings (*Litera-tentum*) and theories of the 'folk' (*Volk*) gained the upper hand, Bismarck's reputation began to decline correspondingly. Though once, in an exchange of opinions with Gottfried Kinkel,* he drew a distinction between his soul, the 'soul of a diplomat', and the heart of the patriotic leader, the heart of a poet, men at that time began to draw closer again to the patriots of the period when unification was being prepared. They were extolled because they wished to unite all 'folk comrades' (*Volksgenossen*) and 'bring home' the *disjecta membra* into the empire for which they strove, and because they wished therefore to reorganize Europe upon the basis of folk membership (*Volkstum*) and tongue. In this way, men knew, the old princely policy of territorial incorporations

---

* Gottfried Kinkel (1815–82), German revolutionary poet, professor at Bonn; aided to escape (1850) from prison by Carl Schurz.

could be continued by a new, folkish policy of incorporations; but they did not gladly have their attention drawn to the fact that it was the doctrines of German romanticism which first really brought the nationalities of eastern Europe into movement. But, in the twentieth century, the national state conception reached a complete *reductio ad absurdum*; it brought incalculable disaster upon millions who were driven from their homes because of the language they spoke and the people to which they belonged. Not surprisingly, therefore, men found reason to re-examine critically the entire national state movement since 1815, which had resulted in endless disorder, two world wars, and catastrophe; nor was it surprising either that they called up again those opponents of Bismarck who combated his power-permeated concept of the state, his alliance with the German national state idea, and who condemned the division of Europe into national states and demanded a European federal structure.

Thus the age of Bismarck lies today concealed in profound obscurity. We do have the documents at hand, but interpreting them is difficult because, living in devastated lands, we find it hard to attain that lofty and far-off vantage point where the historian must take his stand. In earlier ages, when historical awareness had not yet been formed, men came quickly to their own aid in explaining things. Among us, too, resentment will bring about simplification. States and empires, it is said, decline for the same reasons by which they rise. Thus an effort has been made to find a single trace that goes from Bismarck to Hitler, from the 'Iron Chancellor', the man in cavalry boots, to the National-Socialist policy of violence. But this means forgetting the popular and revolutionary forces which had been at work ever since 1815. To remember where we must seek in German history for the spiritual ancestors of modern demagogy, of explosive ideologies, of the extolling of violence, we need merely read the sentences written in 1833 by Heinrich Heine in which he drew the outlines of the future German revolution. At that time Lorenz Oken,* the philosopher of nature who has been lauded as the 'great revolutionary', tried to start a movement of revolutionary enthusiasm among the youth in Germany and was expelled from the University of Jena, on Goethe's decision, as a 'Catilinarian'. As always, things were expected to take place

---

* Lorenz Oken (1779–1851), German scientist and philosopher, leading philosopher of nature of the romantic period.

faster than they actually occurred. But, under the immediate impact of the Hambach Festival of 1832 which J. G. A. Wirth* organized, Heine felt so bold as to prophesy:

Kantians unwilling to hear of any piety in the phenomenal world either, ruthlessly upsetting the foundations of our European life, will make their appearance. Armed Fichteans unwilling to be hampered by aught in their fanatic wilfulness will take the stage. But most terrible of all will be the philosophers of nature, unleashing the daemonic forces of the German pantheism of yore and thus awakening that battle passion which fights not to win, but merely to fight. . . . To some extent, Christianity has mitigated that Germanic battle passion. But once the Cross is broken, then the clangour of that wildness of which the Nordic poets sing and speak so much will be heard again. . . . But when you hear such a crashing and clanging as was never before heard in the history of the world, then a drama will be played out in Germany, alongside which the French Revolution will seem but a harmless idyll. To be sure, things are still quiet among us; we do not as yet know whether the Crown Prince of Prussia or Dr. Wirth will come to power in Germany. But do not believe that one day to come these will appear upon the scene as the real actors. They are only the curs running about in the empty arena and snarling at each other, before the hour comes when the troop of gladiators enters who will fight for life and death. And that hour will come! The peoples will gather round Germany, as if seated upon the banks of an amphitheatre, to see the great battle-play.†

It must be admitted that in the procession of such antecedents there is no place for Bismarck. It is still our task to define his position in the history of Europe, and to determine what were the opportunities that were then open to him and to other, positive forces in German history, as well. These were opportunities which he hampered or destroyed. During the last war a valuable start in this task was made by Erich Eyck. His three-volume biography of Bismarck was written and published outside of Germany. It is a work of high scholarly standing. Based upon knowledge of all the German and European sources, it is well written and to the point. It is, in fact, the first large, rounded biography of Bismarck. None the less, its description of Bismarck cannot be accepted as definitive. The discussion already under way over this important work must be continued; it can become

* Johann Georg August Wirth (1798–1848), German democratic leader; organizer of the Hambach Festival of revolutionary youth, May 27, 1832.
† Tempel ed. (Leipzig, n.d.), VII, pp. 424–26 (modified).

fruitful and contribute to solving the problems which we still find in understanding Bismarck, the man, and his life work. We must frankly say that Eyck was able to write an imposing and easily understood work because he examined the play of opposing forces from a fixed position. But unfortunately, in taking this position, Eyck did not rise above the times. He stayed down amidst the embattled political parties. True, the author, thanks to his great skill as a writer, was able to leave the polemics of those strife-filled decades far behind him. Only a few presently current turns of phrase hinder the flow of the narrative here and there. The personal greatness of Bismarck is recognized, and the author, when he comes up against the weaknesses of Bismarck's foes, does not keep silence about them. But Eyck is convinced that the national-liberal movement of the sixties was on the right track, that it could really have established the German national state in conformity with its own ideals. Eyck belongs among those opponents of Bismarck who may be called 'German Whigs'. They included persons in the highest reaches of society, including the royal family and the liberal princely courts. For the new Bismarck biographer, Gladstone is the lofty ideal of a statesman. Eyck, who lives in England, has written a fine monographic study on Gladstone. Bismarck, the great hater, held no other statesman of his time in such scorn as 'the Grand Old Man' who let his policy be guided by humanitarian and even pacifist ideals, opposed the advance of imperialism, approached the Irish nationalist movement in an accommodating spirit, and extended the suffrage for the British parliament. According to Eyck, Bismarck's interference with the development of conditions for the rise of a statesman like Gladstone in Prussia and Germany was the source of all the evil to come for Germany and for Europe.

By now the reader will have realized that Eyck accepts without further ado the position that the isolated national state with centralized institutions was the only correct and possible solution of the 'German question', the only one corresponding to the strivings of the German people for unity. He directs his criticism just at the methods which Bismarck employed. In Eyck's opinion, if Bismarck had given more consideration to the ideals of his liberal allies, the internal structure of the new Reich would have met the needs of that day better and would have been more durable as well. Moreover, it would have been possible to found the Reich without using the violent methods which Bismarck did.

Eyck voices most profound regret that the new state was born with the flaw of lawbreaking and violence, and that German liberalism developed from a party of law and order into a service group of success worshippers.

Certainly, this is not a new train of thought. There were always at least a few liberal and democratic writers in Germany, during and after Bismarck's imperial chancellorship, who held firm to ideals of freedom and humanity, deplored their loss in Germany when it came under Prussian control, and therefore remained at all times critics of Bismarck. But they produced no major historical work. They were not able to distinguish and correctly to evaluate, upon the basis of detailed research, the various streams within the liberal and democratic movement. They had no importance compared with the specialists, from Sybel down to Erich Marcks, who did the valuable scholarly service of refuting the claims which the reigning monarch [William II] made on behalf of his grandfather [William I, 'the Great']; but these erstwhile leading historians took part in the movement of liberalism into Bismarck's camp, they defended it and found it to be in conformity with the needs of modern times. Eyck is the first person who has managed to put forward the position of the liberal opponents of Bismarck in a large, well-supported analysis. Since Eyck's work is becoming known in Germany at a time when, after a lapse of almost half a century, the spiritual and political ideas of Western European liberalism are again acceptable, there is a danger that the old myth, which justified and praised Bismarck as the 'Realpolitiker' will now be replaced by a new historical myth. All the more must our thanks go to Eyck for his analysis, which affords us a reason for examining in a fundamental way the problems of Bismarck's achievements and establishing the facts in the matter.

Hans Rothfels, now of the University of Chicago, has set down in a far-reaching critique, 'Problems of a Bismarck Biography', the principal points which must be made against Eyck's approach. Not only did he carry the analysis forward, he also greatly simplified it. The assumption that the goal which Bismarck and the liberals shared—the little-German (kleindeutsch) national state under Prussian leadership—could have been achieved without the methods employed by Bismarck, and that Bismarck brought the kleindeutsch Empire into ill repute by his methods, is one which cannot be proved. All the evidence we have supports the position that the powers accepted only unwillingly the formation of a new national state in the heart of Europe. Either, like Napoleon III, they wished for 'compensations', or they were surprised by Bismarck's procedure and did not have time to prepare themselves spiritually and materially to counter it. All the virtuosity of Bismarck's manipulation of the rival powers, his skill in the handling of men and his daring as well, were required to achieve the goal. It was not alone the extension of Prussian power which the other states disliked. They did see with misgivings that the traditions of Frederick the Great had been taken up again, that the old policy of rounding-off the borders of Prussia and conquering new territories which at an earlier time had been directed against Saxony, now led to the annexation of Schleswig-Holstein and the kingdom of Hanover. But the programme of establishing a national state, which at the outset had nothing to do with the Prussian drive for expansion and a Frederician policy, gave the powers no less reason for anxiety and interference. Whether or not German nationalism became an ally of Bismarck, the liberals would have come into conflict with Europe. As early as the Hambach Festival of 1832, when most of the participants were wholly under the influence of the French revolutionary spirit and of Franco-German fraternization, the speakers could not refrain from rejecting France's claim to the left bank of the Rhine, and J. G. A. Wirth dared openly to express the view that the desired unification of Germany 'very probably' would also have as a result the return of Alsace-Lorraine to the ancient homeland. The executive committee of the festival then eliminated this phrase from the official minutes, 'in deference to the friendly French people', and there were many who took amiss the speaker's 'slip'. But the *furor teutonicus*—as the favourite catchword of the Bismarckian period ran—burned brightly precisely after 1859, and without Bismarck's intervention. The *kleindeutsch* patriots were scarcely ready to grant compensations to Napoleon III and to renounce the left bank of the Rhine. The German variety of nationalists in St. Paul's Church [where the National Assembly met in Frankfurt in 1848] had thrashed it all out! How many times had the verse '*So weit die deutsche Zunge klingt!*'* ('Where'er is heard the German tongue!') been reiterated within its walls, as the basis for far-reaching claims! Amid great applause a speaker in the National Assembly at Frankfurt declared that one could not

* A famous patriotic poem, *The German's Fatherland*, by Ernst Moritz Arndt.

draw the sword for the Germans in Schleswig and at the same time abandon South Tyrol. It became evident at St. Paul's Church that there were *irredenta* in many parts of Europe; the courts and governments of the powers agreed that to treat status as a people (*Volkstum*), nation and national state, as mutually equivalent expressions, was a 'Germanism'. They saw it as a great error which, as Ernest Renan expressed it in 1882, 'if it came to dominate, would hurl Europe into immense wars and destroy its civilization'. As a matter of fact, the governments feared the ideology of the German liberals and democrats more than the ambitions of the Prussian statesman. True, the *kleindeutsch* programme was limited to strict boundaries, but once released and given wing by its first success, the movement would necessarily develop its latent tendencies and would then be able to make use of Bismarck's power methods. We need merely to recall the great interest which was given to the question of the 'Germans in the outside world' at the festivals of gymnastic, rifle, singing and Schiller societies since 1840. After 1859 this element of national ambition kept emphatically to the front; even the *Kleindeutschen* could not remain free of it. It was expected in the European courts after 1871 that a period of pan-Germanic expansion would begin, and there was astonishment and a return to calm feelings when it was seen that such plans were far indeed from Bismarck's mind.

But the movement of folk groupings was the very force which, as soon as it could attain freedom for development, had to bring disorder and war upon Europe. Among the peoples of Europe, ambitious to make their own states, the belief in humanity and the solidarity of free nations, each developing along its own lines, did not prevent an embittered struggle from breaking out at once over the frontiers of provinces and folk groupings. Though still in vain, Robert Blum,* together with the leaders of the nationalities of eastern Europe, had already sought to bring about the dismemberment of the Habsburg Empire, in order to split away the Germans of Austria from all the other nationalities, bringing the Germans into a centralized unified Republic. This goal was not abandoned. Yet its achievement would have brought European chaos, as Metternich and Grillparzer in Vienna, the midpoint of many nations, had predicted. In our own day, we have experienced its terrible results. The beginnings of a secular

---

* Robert Blum (1807–48), German political leader; head of Left at Frankfurt Assembly; executed (November 1848) by Austrians for part in Vienna uprising.

nationalist 'revivalist movement' were already quite strong in
1848. Blum, it is true, did not become the 'leader and arouser of
the people', and no one in Germany was called upon to play the
role which was enacted in Hungary by Louis Kossuth; to a remarkable degree the German movement on behalf of a national
state ran an anonymous course. Then Bismarck, having brought
the liberals both into alliance and into subordination, took the
rudder; thereafter there was no place for a patriotic leader like
Gottfried Kinkel. Bismarck held fast to the traditions of the old
statecraft, and thereby placed the German movement under the
command of the state-centred conception. He maintained it in
the form of a constitutional monarchy, in correspondence with
the relationship of forces which existed within Germany after
almost all German states had received such constitutions. The
wars which he waged were in their own way wars for unification.
They were not organized as people's wars, but were conducted
in the strict forms laid down in the armies of the kings, and with
strict, wholly political aims. We must always recall to our
memories the sentence which proved such breadth of vision and
which has received such frightening confirmation: 'What ought
to be placed in that part of Europe which is at present occupied
by the Austro-Hungarian monarchy? New creations in this soil
could only be of a revolutionary character.'

This—and just this—was the decisive course of events. Bismarck thwarted not only the beginnings of a liberal and democratic movement, but he restrained the development of [Central]
European nationalism in general, which for specific, historically
verifiable reasons had arisen in close relationship with the liberal
and constitutionalist conception, but, where it could develop,
ended in dictatorship, the centralized unitary republic, and unlimited expansion. How Louis Kossuth, Mazzini and Daniele
Manin were extolled in the democratic journals of bourgeois
democracy, *Didaskalia* and *Gartenlaube*, although they were
certainly not liberal and constitutionalist politicians; one wished
to extend Hungary to the crest of the Carpathians, the other Italy
to the Brenner frontier! Even Ferdinand Lassalle had entered
upon a similar path, though he started from a different point of
departure; he was a fervent patriot, and he would have favoured,
in fact, a *grossdeutsch* socialist centralized republic. The extent to
which the liberal upper bourgeoisie could construct a barrier from
its own resources is very questionable. They could not bring

forth, and could not desire, an arouser of the people. Into the gap stepped the statesman who had nothing in common with the dictators of the nationalist period, but had his origin in classic diplomacy and statecraft.

For historical science it is a question of assigning to Bismarck his correct place in the historical sequence, not of justifying him or 'vindicating his honour'. He had naught to do with the doctrines of folk and living space (*Lebensraum*), with the old imperial idea, or with what Eichendorff* so ironically called 'modern patrioteering' (*moderne Vaterländerei*); the patriots and national heroes, as they arose everywhere in the wake of nationalism, were of different stamp. In his old age he permitted himself to take pleasure in popularity and noisy hero-worship, which were foreign to aristocratic times. But he did not owe his successes, certainly, to the 'Third Estate' or to the masses, but rather to the mastery with which he controlled the rules of the older diplomacy. Actions and transactions involving the courts and states had been developed to a high level of science and art in the chancelleries of the Italian Renaissance and the absolute monarchy of the French type. European unity was smashed to bits upon this mosaic pattern of politics, and Machiavellianism came into practice. After the kings and their counsellors had brought this to pass, nationalism pushed them aside, took over and further developed their methods and works, and adapted them to the needs of the masses who were coming into prominence. The history of the rise and decline of classic diplomacy has still to be written, however rich the sources available for it; we have only fragments from the hands of experienced diplomatists. Bismarck is the last great representative in the line of classic diplomats, which begins with the famed Venetian ambassadors and the papal nuncios of the sixteenth century. He did not in any way create a new type, but rather acted out to the full an old and strong departmental tradition. Even in his time diplomacy was in the process of becoming a bureaucratized profession with a strict course of training and a caste-stratified pattern of promotion. When Junker Bismarck, then only the squire of Schönhausen, still on the lowest rungs of his career as officer and jurist, entered their caste as an outsider, those who had served according to the rules were discontented. While he had deserved well of the crown in his service as a deputy, he had made his way into diplomacy

---

* Joseph, Freiherr von Eichendorff (1788-1857), German romantic poet.

by the detour of parliament. But he soon acquired the gentlemanly training of the international high society of Europe, to which stratum he belonged by origin and effort; his first assignment to Frankfurt as Prussian envoy to the Federal Diet gave him an opportunity to acquire experience and develop his abilities. His memoirs still give us today a direct impression of the way in which, in the style of the old diplomacy, he evaluated the forces at work in every situation which confronted him, and tested, and to some extent calculated through, all possible combinations one after another. Thus he was a 'member of the guild' with Choiseul, Kaunitz, Talleyrand and Metternich, all of whom left us their memoirs; however different were the states and interests which they represented, politics was for each of them an exact science concerned with calculable magnitudes. We may let the question rest whether there is a difference of spiritual rank between Bismarck and his great predecessors, and it has been observed of his manner of negotiating that he had been in the habit of peddling his wool on the market square in Stettin. Talleyrand and Metternich, the bishop of the Gallican church and the Rhenish nobleman, had still absorbed the lofty intellectual culture of the *ancien régime*. But, in the last analysis, the East Elbian Junker had belonged to the exclusive student *Korps* at the University of Göttingen, educated himself in the world of society, and always maintained a French recess in his mind.

To be sure, Bismarck, as minister of a constitutional monarch, had to count no longer only with potentates, courtiers and favourites. He had to play not only in the 'concert of Europe', but also on the instrument of parliament as well. And here then was to be seen the limits beyond which the old classic diplomacy did not reach. The great transformation which was taking place in that period of the awakening of nationalism and its democratic concomitant, consisted precisely in the fact that it was no longer the governments which led the peoples, but the peoples which decided for the governments. Thereby an element was introduced into politics which escaped all calculation. So long as Bismarck had dealings only with the Tsar and Gorchakov, with the Empress and the ladies of the court, that is, with the great ones whom someone who knew people well could see through to some extent, his diplomatic art could hew to the old methods which earlier had been formed under the world dominance of mathematics and mechanics. But, with the rise of Panslavism, all

calculations became uncertain. Bismarck took German nationalism into custody and utilized it, subordinated it to the state conception and made it available for diplomatic craft. It was a very
unequal alliance which was concluded then—a true *societas leonina*,
for the Prussian state received the lion's part; the nationalist movement had to permit limits to be drawn to its activity, with regard
to domestic freedom as well as to 'pan-German' tendencies. For
the time being, Bismarck was the master; and the world in which
he felt at home and moved with complete security was the grand
world of the courts and aristocratic society. There he sought for
the decisions, exactly as had been done in bygone times in the
manner depicted in the historical writings of Ranke. Bismarck
and Ranke, the contemporaries, belong together most intimately
from this point of view as well, and everything, furthermore,
which was common to them—the objective comprehension of
reality, the conviction of the primacy of foreign policy, the doctrines of the power-state and the legitimacy of political action—
came out of the school of the old diplomacy. Following the same
pattern, Bismarck and Ranke both fundamentally looked upon
the state from the top downwards, while the patriots saw it as
their task in politics and science to judge public affairs from
below, upon the basis of the rights and requirements of the
people. This celebrated formulation, which fixes the difference
between the enlightened-absolutist and the democratic conceptions of public life, was first coined by Arndt; Treitschke took it
over from him and misunderstood it. Even in his later life
Bismarck limited the labours of the statesman and the diplomat
to governments and courts; he was always foreign to the newly
developing diplomacy which had to devote its energies to the
fatiguing tasks of directing large staffs and studying the peoples
and the economic and social phenomena of distant lands. Bismarck
was not equal to working in the new world of the popular forces
which had come into movement—consider the fiasco of his
domestic policy after 1871! In just the same way the historian
Ranke did not judge correctly those parties in the past in which,
alongside the diplomats and court theologians, primal forces from
below forced their way. Bismarck never did learn, as Napoleon
did, to flatter the crowd. He was gripped by narrow class
prejudices as was another leading statesman of his time. Hence
he inaugurated his social policy principally for considerations of
power politics and preferred such solutions as were, in his view,

adapted to strengthening the state. Even when he desired, he was unable to negotiate with deputies and party leaders as skilfully as with ambassadors and ministers of other powers. He always looked upon Windthorst* as just the former minister of a defeated royal house who only sought revenge in gathering the Catholics around himself; he never even made the effort to achieve an understanding of the endeavour of the Catholic portion of the population to help shape the inner structure of the new Reich. And he made just as little effort to develop in August Bebel† and his party a willingness to co-operate upon the basis of even the slightest concession. There is no doubt that his narrow and unchanging horizon served to strengthen his national-liberal and conservative allies in their lack of understanding for the Christian and Social-Democratic labour movement.

Thus Bismarck is to be understood as a historical phenomenon only upon the basis of the old statecraft, with its lofty intellectuality and self-sufficiency, in which the people played no part. He created the German national state within the framework of the old state system and with the old methods; after him, it went into decline. One has to look at Hindenburg and Ludendorff and compare them to the earlier leaders of German destinies in order to realize that Germany used to live more decently. The charge has often been made, and is emphatically repeated by Eyck, that Bismarck took no care to provide for the new generation, and tolerated no independent persons of quality around him. His collaborator in St. Petersburg, Leopold von Schlözer, always called him 'the Pasha'. But yet it was rare for him to encounter in the government departments such fine and upstanding personalities as Schlözer himself; when he did meet them, he did not withhold his respect. Furthermore, not only in the chancelleries and governments, but in the other domains of life in the era of rising nationalism, with the entry of the masses into history, noble personalities were forced into the background behind robust and servile characters.

In the old classic diplomacy to which Bismarck belonged, it was true that the principles and methods which are included under the name of Machiavellianism had been in long use; it remains to

---

* Ludwig Windthorst (1812–91), German political leader; minister of justice in Hanover (1851–53, 1862–65), leader of Centre Party in the German Reichstag after 1870.

† August Bebel (1840–1913), German political leader; founder and leader of German Social-Democratic Party.

be seen whether, in this respect, Bismarck acted without restraint
to an unusual degree. Where it is required by reason of state,
Machiavelli considers anything to be permissible. He recom-
mends lying, breaking treaties, deceit, violence; one must be a
lion and a fox at the same time, and success justifies the most
outrageous villainy. But, on the other hand, as the sagacious and
honourable Johann Jakob Moser* taught in the eighteenth
century, the small state cannot build upon force; therefore it must
build upon law and justice. But it is obvious that the 'minor
powers', when they became involved in the affairs of the world,
have been the most perfidious, while the great powers maintained
their strong positions and no longer had to pursue a shifty course.
The Prussian state was the most recent and smallest of the powers.
This is the explanation of many of the acts of treacherous behaviour which are to be found so frequently in the history of
Prussian policy. But Talleyrand, too, who certainly had a great
power behind him, was never squeamish, and in Bismarck's time
Prussia was so great a military power that it did not need small
expedients. But Bismarck always applied the methods of deceit
or violence which seemed useful to him, without meditating upon
them. A statesman who saw his state as incomplete, he was
moved by ambition to make it larger; moreover, the increase of
power by all means was a personal necessity for him. He brought
about three wars with complete deliberateness, as he frankly
admitted afterwards. He dragged the King of Hanover into war
in order to drive him from his throne, confiscated his property in
violation of an agreement, and then had parliament forbid him
to make restitution. He concluded the Reinsurance treaty with
Russia against Austria and carefully concealed this fact from his
ally. It is not possible and not necessary to enumerate here all the
misdeeds or improprieties of his foreign and domestic policy.
Even at the time they were brought to light of day by those
affected, and were vigorously discussed by contemporary public
opinion; but when he was successful, his power became so great
that all who were dependent by function or character, bowed
their heads and worshipped his genius. It was an ill harbinger of
things to come that these were the leading intellectuals; previously
humanitarian or liberal in attitude, they wished to remain on top
as time passed, whatever came to pass. Eyck has carefully brought
out in the course of his narrative every instance of violation of

* Johann Jakob Moser (1701–85), German juridical scholar and teacher.

law and justice, of violence, of unfair conduct of affairs on the
part of Bismarck; we now know much more of what he did than
contemporary polemists knew at the time. We possess for no
other statesman, not even for Talleyrand, so elaborate a register
of his sins. Bismarck had the additional misfortune of finding a
historian who pursued the old sinner through every twist and
turn of his career.

But, what is more, the picture of Bismarck was drawn even
more unflatteringly because of his personal idiosyncrasies. Words
exist to conceal ideas, went the celebrated paradox coined by
Talleyrand. Such behaviour was not to Bismarck's taste. Though
he was able to watch his step, he did not find it easy. He carried
over into political controversy the coarse language he had used
as a member of a student *Korps* at the university and as a reserve
officer in the army. He never acquired the self-control which one
learns in the chancellery of state or *salon* society. For him at least,
parliament was not the best school at which to prepare for
diplomacy. Furthermore, he tended to make his criticism too
slashing. He took delight in witty conversation, which he spiced
with the kind of merry tale and unexpected jest his adversaries
would then turn against him. He did not scruple to speak his
mind. He said openly that he would not be balked by trifles.
Other cynical turns of phrase from his lips soon became public
knowledge. Such cynicism, also, set his successors a bad
example. His imitators mimicked his cynicism, but not his
honourable traits. The time was not far off when the reigning
monarch, in his overbearing arrogance, hardly cut the figure of a
prince or nobleman. In a world of rapidly growing wealth and
splendour, William II was more the *parvenu* than the aristocrat.

No one will deny, therefore, that Bismarck and William II
introduced into politics the habit of acting harshly toward
ostensible weakness, and the use of strong words, so that ever-
larger sections of the German people were summarily stigmatized
as enemies of the Reich. Such conduct was foreign to the despots
in previous times, because they sat, lonely and silent, upon the
thrones in their Escorials. To be sure, many a cynical, blunt
remark ('a crime, but not a mistake') has come down to us from
Napoleon, who was dependent upon the crowd. However, he
too adapted very easily to the new opinions taking form among
the people; what is more, he too failed. Like Hegel, the 'Prussian'
in philosophy, Bismarck inculcated in the German Empire the

belief that one 'shouldn't be squeamish' ['*Nicht viel Umstände zu machen*']. The role which the Junkers from east of the Elbe were now called upon to perform was, perhaps, particularly appropriate to them. Every reformer, from Freiherr vom Stein down to the liberals of the pre-Bismarck period, was indeed convinced, of course, that Prussia would have to renew herself upon the basis of the forces and institutions of Rhenish and Westphalian Germany. As a matter of fact, despite Bismarck, the centre of gravity of the German national movement in the nineteenth century did lie in the West, where the Rhenish economic leaders were at home and democracy had roots in the life of the people. In northern Germany the liberal movement won influence only in the cities. In that area, the authentic Prussia of old, which was Bismarck's homeland, his methods were quickly adopted and imitated. Freiherr vom Stein and his collaborators had not worked wholly without success in Prussia; Berlin in the time of Schinkel,* and Königsberg in the time of Theodor von Schön, the Kantian and Prussian reformer,† gladly put a long distance between themselves and Frederick's Prussian system. But now, by Bismarck's example, anyone who had any power whatever to use found himself encouraged to act more abruptly. Only where constitutional courts were able to exercise effective control was there any safeguard against utter disregard of law and justice. This flouting of right under law was frankly proclaimed at the time in the form of the right of necessity, as was done in 1914 in the invasion of Belgium.

We may be surprised, therefore, that the leaders of the Prussian-German state adopted such methods when they had ceased to be customary among legitimate monarchies after Napoleon's fall. We must ascribe to Bismarck a large individual share in promoting this development. In Prussia itself professional diplomats looked amiss at these methods. Bismarck was, after all, not only an outsider, but a man out of the ordinary, from whom one could look for a *coup d'état*; he was, therefore, of the same ilk as the men of 18th Brumaire and 2nd December. We forget too easily how deep an impression was made by the reappearance of Bonapartism at a time when the nineteenth century was becoming more and more bourgeois, in an age of liberalism and belief in progress. It

---

* Karl Friedrich Schinkel (1781–1841), German architect and painter, particularly active in Berlin.

† Theodor von Schön (1772–1856), Prussian statesman; took liberal role in East Prussia in war against Napoleon.

was a stupendous phenomenon which aroused misgivings lest the means and resources of liberal democracy prove inadequate in the difficult and hard time just beginning. If anything encouraged Bismarck to enter upon the path of violence, it was certainly the conduct of Prince Louis Napoleon. There is reason, furthermore, to investigate more deeply the extent to which he also felt encouraged by Cavour's example; the Piedmontese was a great 'realist' who also drove many princes from their thrones and yet did not become dependent upon extremism. But, beyond doubt, many aspects of Bismarck's life work trace back to the French Second Empire. That is all just history now. It would be difficult to find threads which extended from that time into the twentieth century. The general character of Caesarism or dictatorship as such, exemplified in the Renaissance and once again brought into being by Napoleon I, was such a thread. The twentieth century, on the contrary, did not find its exemplars in the great realists and proponents of reason of state, but rather in the theory and practice of violence as created by the nationalists of eastern Europe and Italy. Kossuth, Mazzini and Garibaldi mobilized the youth of their nations and led them in hosts, again and again, to destruction. They aroused men's instinctual passions. In general, they were demoniac in character for they adopted chimerical goals, used the most extreme methods, and remained relatively indifferent to success, which neither they nor their imitators met. Bismarck had no part in all their doings, not even when, in 1866, he entertained a plan to rouse up the Czechs and Magyars. Though he may have learned from Napoleon III, still we do not find in him any trace of admiration for the demoniac figure of Napoleon I. In his youth, he went through his 'romantic' period; but, once the storms of youth were past, *déborder* became foreign to his nature. The traditional rules of conduct provided that in cases of extreme necessity one need not think twice about using any weapon at hand. If we wish to probe for the ultimate cause of all the processes which gave rise to Napoleon, to Bismarck and to the leaders of the nationalities, as well as to their methods and goals, we will become aware that, in general, these processes are rooted in modern humanity. It clearly was not at all the same thing when the old sovereign states used their machinery of power to define their interests, and when national sovereignty came into play. The sovereign nation, once it was swung into action, did not readily accept any limitation of its scope.

We cannot condemn these methods and accept their goals.
Bismarck could attain his purposes only by such methods. How
else could he have bound together the eastern and western halves
of the Prussian monarchy, closing the gaps that lay between them?
The King of Hanover acted cautiously and beyond criticism. He
took his stand squarely on law and avoided taking any part in the
conflict between the two big powers! In order to respect the
rights of Hanover, Bismarck would have had to give up any hope
of making the Prussian state a single territorial unit. But he wished
the Prussian body politic to have one compact territory, which
would enable it to prevail completely in the North German Confederation. When this was won, he turned at once to his next
goal and established the German Empire. Prussia could have
existed in it even if she did not have Hanover and Hesse. In any
case, in spite of the federal organization of the state, which was
inevitable at the time, the decisive fact remains that Bismarck did
not free himself from the old political conception of the isolated,
territorially-compact, state body. In this old classic policy,
Machiavellianism, because it arose in fact out of the struggle of
sovereign powers, was not something put in afterwards, but the
principle of its very life. Though national sovereignty merely
took the place of the princely sovereigns, it vastly intensified, as
we know, the drive of Machiavellianism, extended it widely and
made it all-inclusive.

We may correctly speak of Bismarck's being 'misunderstood'
nowadays in the sense that his work and activity have been viewed
apart from their connexion with the previous system of states
and its political conceptions. Bismarck's conduct was dictated by
a line which traced back to Frederick the Great, Richelieu,
Gustavus Adolphus and Maurice de Saxe. They all contributed
to the destruction of Western unity, to the establishment of
sovereign states, and to their mighty expansion by conquest,
treaty-breaking and violence against the weak. For a long time,
Bismarck merely put modern nationalism to his own uses. He
was, first and foremost, the managing director of a state which
played the role of a great power in the European state system of five
great powers and many smaller powers; as yet, Prussia was not
'saturated' within this state system. Once he said that Prussia
wore too heavy armour for her small body. It is an image which
corresponds to the old political thinking. Bismarck did not learn
the new metaphors of nationalism. He was concerned with the

interests of the state, with the state as a rational system of analysis and action. Hence he remained strange to the voluntarims of the period of national states and democracy. The programme and slogans of nationalism—natural living space, historical borders, assimilation and national will—which derived in part from the French Revolution and for the rest from German romanticism, were widespread among the liberals in the sixties and seventies, and were already being fully acted upon among the eastern European peoples. Bismarck did not heed any of these slogans; he disregarded this programme. Even when he annexed Alsace and Lorraine, military considerations were paramount in his mind. He belonged to the system of states as it had been, when states looked out for themselves and wished to please only themselves, when the interests of the state were all that was at stake and the interests of the people were only of secondary concern. He brought two new great powers, Prussia-Germany and Sardinia-Italy into the old European state system. As a result, he transformed the 'European concert'. The forces which later put an axe to the entire historical state structure had been in being for a long time, and Bismarck had to reckon with them. But he still hoped to be able to bring them under control.

The methods used by Bismarck therefore derived from the old policy of European governments. It saw in power the proper purpose of the state. It had extricated the states from the mediaeval bonds of universalism, and involved them in the struggle for hegemony or balance of power. Modern nationalism was a new form of this spirit of separatism. Therefore, Bismarck had been able to make it his ally; with it he brought new elements of power into the battle array. He saw that, as a result, Europe would have to make rapid progress toward ruin. But he thought that the traditional state system, in whose categories he thought and acted, was strong. It would survive the profound contradiction which he brought about when he created a Prussian-German national state in central Europe and at the same time tried to protect and preserve the pure dynastic states against the nationalities in eastern Europe. For historical judgment this question is therefore clearly crucial: was there, in fact, any chance in Bismarck's time of giving up the free competition of interests? It would have made superfluous the old methods by which affairs had been conducted until then. Could there have been established as a consequence, co-operative life of men and peoples upon

Christian principles, or at least a system corresponding to these
principles more closely than the previous system? It cannot be
maintained that Bismarck did not dare to set himself against his
time. He thrust himself very energetically athwart the liberal and
democratic movement, which certainly belonged to the advancing
forces of the time, and hindered their development. On the other
hand, the Frederician tradition in which he grew up was no
longer a vital force at that instant; it regained its power during
Bismarck's lifetime and mainly by his exertions. The choice was
up to him. Would he remain under the spell of the old diplomacy
and adopt in consequence its theory that the compact national
state was the necessary form in which the nations could achieve
their fulfilment? In that case, to be consistent, he would have had
to 'write off' the Habsburg monarchy. But he did not. Or, would
he feel himself called upon to seek new paths in order to satisfy
the nations of central and eastern European territories into a
jumble of lands like the Balkans?

A statesman who did not accept the compact national state
certainly had no lack of allies and forces at his disposal. Everywhere the majority of peoples still adhered to their hereditary
princes. Of course, a small ducal state with a Serene Highness at
its head no longer furnished an adequate area in which to function.
But numerous connexions had by then been set up between
countries. Extension of the Prussian customs union (*Zollverein*)
was possible; it was wholly justified by economic conditions, and
only the school of the old diplomacy thwarted its achievement.
Above all, however, the German Confederation could have been
further developed. After the events of 1848 and 1849, the
governments, including that of Prussia before Bismarck came
upon the scene, were ready. Moreover, the question whether the
vital rights of the nation could not be satisfied in this way as well,
still remained completely open. The Danubian monarchy of the
Habsburgs was not to be saved. It could break apart into national
states. There would be frightful struggles especially in territories
of mixed national composition. Or the Habsburg realms could be
transformed into a central European federation of nations, each
living its own life again under new constitutional arrangements.
In Vienna, as in Berlin, the decision had not yet been taken.
Despite 1848-49, the awakening of the nationalities in eastern
Europe had only begun. They took what they could use and were
as yet not out of control. Only in the eighties did radicalism

finally break through to them as a consequence of the system of 1866. There had been a time when national hatred between Englishmen and Scotsmen was elemental and fierce, yet it had been buried. To be sure, with the Irish this did not come successfully to pass. The examples of the United States and France were beyond contradiction. The nationalities were also set in motion by the doctrines of German romanticism. But after 1849 there was everywhere very great fear of Russia, and Panslavism was still just something happening within literary romanticism. There was a profound basis in the course of modern history for the endeavour of all the peoples of Europe to develop, each in its own way, toward the goal of forming its own state. They were still in the habit of calling in a king from old dynasties, from foreign lands. Personal union was found to be a satisfactory solution, and there were many other such solutions. The demand for a compact national organism came only from a few parties, and was chiefly a product of the scholars. Furthermore, if a statesman knew world conditions, he could not help but see the problems of the Continent more profoundly than could Bismarck, whose policy was limited to the Continent. He could not escape the deep contradiction which cleaved apart the entire age: When nationalism had free course, it led to a dismemberment of Europe; at the same time, the technology of communications, which in the shape of the locomotive had already outrun the small states and was a pacemaker for the nation and for democracy, was advancing. It was overcoming distance ever more quickly and thereby compelling a changeover to world communications and a world economy.

There was, therefore, a good basis in the actual conditions for federal union of the central and eastern European peoples. The new arrangement could be developed upon an existing foundation with existing forces and energies. Any other goal signified an extension of the revolutionary policy which had already shaken Europe for so long a period of time. The revolutionary forces at various times had brought to the forefront one or another artificial power-state. These forces now included as well the active portion of the urban bourgeoisie which, as Ranke said at the time, dreamed that they could 'construct out of their wits' their fatherland. Some constructed a *kleindeutsch* monarchy, other a *grossdeutsch* centralized republic. But the time when Bismarck was preparing and carrying through his work was also filled with plans tied to existing reality. Constantin Frantz was only the most active and the intellectually most important of those who told Bismarck that the security which the German people so urgently required when future world decisions would be made, could not be guaranteed by means of the isolated national state, and by the combination of alliances which Bismarck with great skill formed anew time and again. It should not be said, therefore, that the conceptions of a federative Europe were mere literature. The very *kleindeutsch* doctrine which came so conveniently to Bismarck's hand, had been elaborated in scholars' studies. And it is not correct either to say that the conception of a central European federation of national states was premature, that it would only be justified when the nations would come to fear their own likeness unto God and saw themselves placed between two rising world powers. The moment quickly passed during which, as fate would have it, serious discussion of such a federation of Europe was possible. No one talked any more of union of the nations of central and eastern Europe, or of a Europe existing upon the basis of its own strength. Only in Bismarck's time could this idea have been carried out and the self-laceration of the nations prevented. It was already obvious that the appearance of Russia in central Europe, which anyone could see by 1849, was a world event of incalculable consequences. It necessarily opened up a new world epoch, with new methods in diplomacy and a new European attitude.

Here one may well object that no serious opponent of Bismarck, able to carry through such a policy, came forward. Controversial historiography, though it has its rights like any other, should never lose from view the fact that Germany at that time had lived for many centuries in political decrepitude. The German Confederation did indeed constitute a new beginning, but it was not yet a living political organism. Metternich, on whom rests responsibility for the three decades of German history from 1815 to 1848, permitted political life in the individual states to go farther. It was certainly of great value that the German people got the habit of acting in accordance with free political forms in the legislatures of south and central German states. But 1848 was the penalty paid because only those who supported the national state solutions had set programmes. Austria's leadership in fact signified stagnation and reaction. Bismarck was the only statesman who took energetic action; he opened the valve to release the accumulated energies. An immense conflict in German life now broke out again, to be decided once and for all—on the one side the House of Habsburg, which for centuries had found its profit in maintaining things as they were; and on the other Frederician policy brought back to life! The liberals joined Bismarck's camp when he began to prove successful. The more they had previously placed their hopes upon Prussia and the Prussian monarchy, while rejecting Prussian methods, the longer was their resistance. The power of the personal factor in history was displayed with particular vigour in this regard. Yet the fact remains that the organization of Germany permitted of no delay, and that, in any event, whenever Austria would prove hesitant, Prussia would act.

Although Bismarck was therefore able to drive German history along the road to disaster, clearly he did not shoulder sole responsibility. It was borne equally by those other German forces still in existence at the time which did not set up a rival leader of equal stature. He was far superior to his liberal adversaries, like Roggenbach* and Benningsen,† who wished to give a different constitution to the national state. One looks in vain in Prussia for a statesman of rank who would have been able to carry on the policy of peaceful dualism. In the middle-sized states there were no German princes as active on the *grossdeutsch*, federalist side as the Grand Duke of Baden was in the *kleindeutsch*, liberal camp; none was so popular as Duke Ernst of Gotha, the 'sharpshooter Duke'. Even Windthorst did not have his king's support; he was only an administrative minister and, when the hour of decision drew near, had once more been dropped from the ministry of state. In any case, we must look into the actual capacity of Count Beust‡ as a statesman who, in the years of the foundation of the Reich, was Bismarck's leading opponent. Did he lose out to Bismarck because the Prussian statesman took a course of action which did not look far into the future, and so was much simpler and easier to follow? Because Bismarck opened the way for his policy, and followed it with no scruples of conscience, brushing aside violently considerations of law and justice? But it is still very doubtful whether the governing caste of the old Austrian monarchy would have permitted any statesman to carry through

* Franz, Freiherr von Roggenbach (1825–1907), German statesman, active in the government of Baden; favoured a liberal, *kleindeutsch* Reich.
† Rudolf von Benningsen (1824–1902), German political leader; leader of the National-Liberal Party.
‡ Friedrich Ferdinand, Count von Beust (1790–1886), Saxon and Austrian states-man; led opposition to Bismarck as premier of Saxony (1858–66), and Austrian foreign minister (1866–71).

fundamental reorganization. It is true, of course, that Count Julius Andrassy,* who was certainly a statesman of scope, received a free hand for a foreign policy which differed very greatly from that previously in effect. The nationalities brought forth personalities like Deák,† who wished to guide nationalism along orderly channels. But, while Bismarck gave the example and brought on the decision, it was the Magyars who none the less were the essential driving force. The Czechs, on the contrary, hesitated for a while. At that time, there were important intellectuals among them. For a long time they endeavoured to achieve peaceful reorganization of the monarchy, they kept in sight the danger threatening them from the East. But, for much too long, the answer which was given in Vienna, and in Berlin as well, was that things would not be changed under any circumstances. Archduke Franz Ferdinand‡ came much too late. But it is often true in history that when the political turn of affairs is propitious, it brings forth the statesman who is needed. Who will deny that there were still many chances of development which even the Austrian court could not reject in the long run? It was Bismarck who destroyed these prospects. It may reasonably be doubted that, in the long run, such a federal state would have been able to provide security against the overwhelming growth of Russia. But the fact remains that there were forces in central Europe which could have been spared and combined, which the rivalries and competition of the national state system used up at an enormous rate. Because of his origin and character, Bismarck was never able to take this path; in fact, as a result, he gave an intensely personal direction to the history of Germany and Europe. The situation which he faced at the start of his career was that the peoples of Europe were attacking the work of the Congress of Vienna; they wished once more to destroy it. But the decision was his that this would come about only by way of annexations and militarism, and that the nations had to adopt the capitalist system in self-preservation. Thus, very much against his will, he did most to bring about the dissolution of central and eastern Europe into purely independent national states.

* Julius, Count Andrássy (1823–1900), Hungarian statesman, as foreign minister of Austria-Hungary concluded alliance with Bismarck (1879).

† Ferencz Deák (1803–76), Hungarian leader of moderate liberals; established *Ausgleich* of 1867 with Austria.

‡ Archduke Franz Ferdinand of Habsburg (1863–1914), heir to Austrian throne, whose slaying at Sarajevo precipitated First World War; advocated collaboration of Germans, Magyars and Slavs within Habsburg monarchy.

We now know the steps by which this disaster, as we must call it today, was brought about. From the very first day of his official activity, Bismarck with fiery zeal loosened the ties with Austria, forced it out of Germany, abandoned it to the struggle of nationalities within it and created the Prussian-German state which could maintain itself only by alternating alliances with other power-states in the fashion of the old political system. The enormity of the enduring alliance with Russia against Austria was in itself a demonstration of the extent to which the new Empire was totally incorporated into the great power system, entirely abandoned to the uncertain play of forces between the powers, and remaining wholly dependent upon one man's virtuosity. The many eulogists of Bismarck among German historians have praised to the highest his ostensible moderation in making the armistice with Austria at Nikolsburg in 1866; because it prevented the collapse of Austria at that moment, the later national radicalism of all nationalities found cause to regret it. In truth there is nothing in it either to be praised or blamed. The whole system of 1866, this last and much extolled 'masterpiece' of the old style, resulted at once in the decline of the Habsburg Empire. Thus it was the cause of the isolation and downfall of the Bismarckian Empire as well. The nationalities were in fact encouraged by the success of the German movement. They took advantage of the weaknesses of the monarchy which had been defeated on the battlefield. As soon as the nationalities lay free and unprotected along the Russian border, central Europe in turn could no longer maintain its own position. The old statecraft was utterly confounded.

In the latest biography of Bismarck there is little or no mention of all these historical points which illuminate and call into question not so much Bismarck's means and methods as his goals. A biographer of Bismarck whose critical views are taken over from the arguments of the liberal movement in favour of the national state, remains a prisoner of the time; he can only draw a false picture. We achieve a different result when we look at things in the broader relationships, including the entire course of development until the present day. The leading statesman of Prussia did not recognize, or, because of personal idiosyncrasy, could not recognize, that the old diplomacy led only to the old struggle for hegemony in Germany and in Europe, and that, with the entrance of newly awakened elemental forces, this struggle would necessarily result in dismemberment of Europe. That this was already visible was publicly demonstrated by Bismarck himself in numerous expressions of anxious foreboding, but he did not break through to a new decision. Thus success was possible only in the old way, by violation of law and justice, and in the end by a final rupture with all historic relationships. All too easily the German people became habituated to going farther in this direction, far beyond what Bismarck wished, wanted or expected. To be sure, alongside the 'legitimacy of princes' there was a new 'legitimacy of peoples'. For a long time, the former had been repeatedly violated by the princes themselves, and the latter led to an enduring rule of violence. Though everything was beginning to slip into motion, the Prussian statesman believed that he could expand the power of his king and his state in the manner of the old princely revolutions and at the same time maintain the old structure of society. It is not true that the German people lost their traditions only because of Bismarck. Since the downfall of the old Empire, how much had been cut short, how many old legal safeguards had been abandoned since then, even as the result of liberal legislation—the individual became personally free, but lost his corporative protection at the same time. In our history books there is absent a great and tragic chapter on the 'death struggles of the nineteenth century'. We call it tragic because it developed with a certain necessity and led to chaos. Despite the French Revolution, it was not the French but the German people who were shattered to their very depths by this destiny. Because they lacked a genuine tradition, romanticism contrived tradition for them. Ludwig Jahn,* and the applause which he gained, were by that time warning signs of the unhistorical and destructive results this new tradition would have. It is true that historical and individualistic thought is a product of German romanticism. It is true that historical research now encompasses all times and peoples and is conducted with greater diligence than ever before, so that every historic form is imitated in every area of cultural life. Yet it is also probably true for just these reasons that the ruling spirit of the nineteenth century became and remained most profoundly unhistorical. Bismarck gave a powerful impetus to this development. His activity demonstrates the old adage that men often want the causes, but not their results. The concentration of forces, tremendous for

---

* Friedrich Ludwig Jahn (1778–1852), German teacher of gymnastics, organized nationalist movement of gymnastic groups (*Turnverein*).

the time, which he brought about, again and again compelled the amputation of old and still vigorous relationships, even when they have become part of the new constitutional life. Freedom could not be granted. Although the greatness and richness of German life until then had consisted in the multiplicity of its regions (*Stämme*) and states, the activities of the spirit began to become uniform under Bismarck. He vigorously accelerated this development, which was rooted in the modern world. Because their programme became inapplicable, the liberal parties of all shades had to remain powerless. The conception of law and justice could not be applied in practice because there was always cause to use hastily, methods not beyond reproach.

It is a fact that a state finds it difficult to re-establish itself when its moral foundations have been shattered, when law and justice, which are the foundation of states, are held in scorn, when its leaders, citing expediency, exempt themselves in their policies from those very principles without which no state and in general no human society can be maintained. Even the acceptance of Christianity in the declining Roman Empire could no longer prevent its collapse. The centuries during which European civilization ripened into world civilization were also centuries filled with endless struggle, wars without number, law-breaking and acts of violence with an incessant struggle for power, for hegemony or balance of power. It developed out of the spiritual and moral forces of the Romanic and Germanic nations, from antiquity, Christianity and Germanic life, and it could thrive because the competition of states and peoples was still an emanation of the will to remain multifarious, not to become uniform. By this will the elements of resistance to any unbounded extension of power over the conception of law and justice were strengthened again and again. Bismarck, too, was fully aware that freedom from law had to lead to slavery for all. It is therefore a most fundamental question to know how Bismarck tried to bring into consonance his Christianity and his oft-times slight respect for law. There is hardly reason any more to doubt seriously that he did not embrace modern religious indifferentism, but achieved and practised a devout Christianity. This is shown by numerous documents from his hand, not intended to prove such a point; there can be no deceit in them. But the universality of the Christian world view hardly ever came alive in him. We should not attribute it too much to the fact that he learned to know Christianity only in the pietist conventicles of the East Elbian landed estates, and was hence less concerned to overcome distress in a Christian spirit than to have an opportunity to live out his personal faith. The man whom he replaced in leadership of European affairs, Prince Metternich, was certainly farther from living Christianity, but carried within himself more of the spirit of universality. This resulted from the period of time in which Metternich worked and from the tasks of the Habsburgs. It is difficult to maintain a fundamental difference between them; both held their position in the modern state world. But Bismarck intervened in it and brought it to its downfall; he could no longer provide it with a new foundation.

By destiny and tendency Bismarck's profession became the modern political system of reason of state and embattled interests. He found joy in this activity. He considered that territorial compactness and the independence of modern great states, which recognize legal order among themselves only in the shape of alternating alliances, constituted not merely a valuable, but in fact a final achievement of civilization. In order to safeguard and to extend this system of state power, he promoted the welfare of the people, though wholly in the spirit of the old statecraft, and was convinced that only a power-state could guarantee happiness and prosperity. Since the situation in which he found himself demanded his active intervention, he was not squeamish in the choice of his means and did not seek farther afield after new, better ways. He took for granted the state world in which he lived, and believed that Prussia was called upon to achieve something valuable in this system. He considered a compact state organism in the heart of Europe to be a higher form of life than a federation of states carried to another stage of development. There were many esteemed thinkers who, though they had their doubts, still sought to justify the statesman and to encourage him in this course. Powerful intellectual currents of the time assisted in this change. They led farther and farther away from the conception of law and from Christianity. But the statesman did not wholly realize what an alliance he was accepting. The life work which he built was certainly not profoundly thought out, but one would do injustice to its master if one were to forget that the spiritual life of his time had in general lost all direction, that numerous and contradictory standpoints were represented with scholarship of equal breadth and with equal impressiveness, and that it was extremely difficult for the statesman to reach a position of fixity and validity. The creator of the second German Empire remained entirely gripped by the contradictions of his age. He made shift with the old means and the old purposes. This had never before led to enduring order; now the passions were all aroused as well. Bismarck took part in this release from control. He believed that he could utilize the new impulsion to be found in the crowd for the power of his state, and at the same time limit it by a rational system called reason of state. He did not come to a realization that in a world of such confusions there are tasks which go far beyond the state, and that it was becoming extremely necessary to bring the state back to its original purpose, to help establish the good, the right, the higher order. His position remained that the statesman's task consisted in nothing more than development of the state. Were there statesmen who saw farther than he? We cannot be sure. But he did become the first man of his time. Upon him depended essentially the further course of events. In history, however, only those forces are preserved which devote themselves to world historic goals. And the only standard by which peoples and civilizations can be measured and differentiated is whether a belief in a higher world order lives on in them.

CHAPTER FOUR

I. BISMARCK AND OURSELVES

A CONTRIBUTION TO THE DESTRUCTION OF AN HISTORICAL LEGEND

by *Alfred von Martin*

Alfred von Martin was born in 1882. After participating in the First World War, he taught mediaeval history at the Universities of Frankfurt and Munich and became professor of sociology in Göttingen in 1931. With the advent of the National-Socialist government, he resigned his position to resume his teaching in 1946 at the University of Munich. Most of his earlier works dealt with the intellectual history of the Middle Ages and of modern times. His book *Soziologie der Renaissance* (1932) was published in English translation by Kegan Paul in London and Oxford University Press in New York in 1944. It was also published in Spanish and Dutch.

His more recent works were largely dedicated to a critical examination of German nationalist historiography, among which are *Nietzsche und Burckhardt* (1940); *Die Religion Jakob Burckhardts* (1942); *Geistige Wegbereiter des deutschen Zusammenbruchs* (1947); *Der heroische Nihilismus und seine Uberwindung—Ernst Jüngers Weg durch die Krise* (1948); *Geist und Gesellschaft* (1948). Of the two following selections, the first one, 'Bismarck und Wir. Zerstörung einer politischen Legende', appeared in *Der Monat*, number 20, and was reprinted in *Neue Zürcher Zeitung*, December 13, 1951. The second one represents extracts from an essay 'Zum neuen Geschichtsbilde' published in *Geschichte vom Standpunkt der Humanität* (Pandora. Schriften für lebendige Uberlieferung, Ulm, 1946).

In the register of German sins there is a place for some of the history written in Germany—that produced by the Prussian school of historiography. From its inception it took a questionable attitude toward standards of objective criticism and hence toward scholarly method. As was to be expected, it did the most serious harm in works written for the general public. In this literature of edification, Bismarck, the great 'folk hero' of Prussia, was apotheosized most uncritically. These works, nationalist,

wholly secularist, and given over to Bismarck-worship, were put
forward by a Protestantism turned political, that is, nationalist. In
this literature, Bismarck's figure was placed beside that of Luther,
the German, in the pantheon of that North German religion
which Constantin Frantz once called 'the religion of National-
Liberalism'.

The people wish to have their 'great man'. Their historians,
too, like to say dramatically, 'Men make history', but fail to ask
what is the result of such history. The 'great men' themselves, in
rare moments of reflection, were more honest. Frederick II of
Prussia once said frankly that 'great men' were in the habit of
making their peoples 'very unhappy'. On occasions Bismarck
expressed wonder that 'the greatest butchers of men are those
most loved and admired'. When Jakob Burckhardt, in his letters
to Friedrich von Preen, comes to speak of Bismarck, he always
calls him 'the great man'. Still this does not prevent Burckhardt,
the humanist among historians in the German language, from
remarking how 'obnoxious' Bismarck's personality was to him.
He knew that the morality of all 'great men' in history was open
to doubt. Yet not once did he carry this criticism through to its
logical conclusion.

In Robert Saitschick's book,[1] we now have an impressive and
informative work of Bismarck criticism, which yet is popularly
written in the best sense of the word. It is the kind of book we
have needed. In reading it, one gains the conviction that Bismarck's story is very much a part of the history of the German
catastrophe, whose origins, therefore, go back long before Hitler.
It is a worthwhile destruction of the Bismarck legend. It corrects
the false picture of history upon which a good part of the German
nationalist ideology was based. To be sure, this ideology is kept
up to date in new guises. The most recent position of Bismarck
apologetics is that his policy was an end-product of old-fashioned
cabinet policy. It was an *étatist* policy 'from above', in opposition
to the revolutionary nationalism which forced its way up from
below and served as a prelude to the power politics of the new
twentieth century. They say that the old sorcerer, while using
this nationalism, tamed it. According to this view, Bismarck was
really sated after 1871, not just simply in the fashion of someone
who wisely realizes that what has been devoured must first be

[1] *Bismarck und das Schicksal des deutschen Volkes: Zur Psychologie und Geschichte der
deutschen Frage* (Munich, 1948).

digested, that renewed robbery should not be risked immediately, but because Bismarck had reached the goal he had set himself in his previous policy. He still wanted it to be state, not national, policy. And we should probably add, because he trusted none of those who would have to take over the inheritance he passed on, to be able to do more, under the most favourable circumstances, than maintain what he had created. A self-made man has every reason to take for granted that his practical genius will not be transmitted by inheritance.

Is such an attitude really 'conservative'? Saitschick correctly calls Bismarck the revolutionary (he was one, as Frederick William IV, the most un-Prussian of Prussian kings, had already accurately pointed out), the adherent of a Prussian 'Bonapartism' which was 'older than Bonaparte' himself (Bismarck had already thus characterized himself to Leopold von Gerlach, the conservative adjutant-general of the conservative king).

Even if statesmen, after 1789, and indeed after 1848, only continued the practice usual before 1789, that is, a policy—a policy of conquest, of course—which arose out of their lust for power, pure and simple, and their personal vanity, it was no longer the same. Since 1789 the voices of the people have also been heard on the European continent. The application of pure power politics in the era of the political collaboration of the nation would necessarily destroy 'the forces supporting the state within the people itself', as Ludwig Bamberger, the liberal critic of Bismarck, remarked. Bamberger bears witness to the necessarily anti-conservative results of Bismarck's policy. It is playing with fire to arouse the revolutionary and nationalist passions of the people for political trickery.

Cui bono? Previously it was Frederick II who found shelter and concealment behind 'service to the state'. At least ideologically he was under the influence of the Enlightenment, though, in practice, to be sure, more under Machiavelli's. Meanwhile, idolatry of the state was made fashionable in intellectual society as well by Hegel, the Prussian state philosopher. But, on the other hand, Bismarck, like Frederick II before him, admitted openly, though not publicly, that vanity was the motive force of his powerful passions. He, too, sanctioned his political activity by ideological appeals to love of fatherland, but at the same time he looked upon men with cynical contempt. He was a born tyrant who wanted nothing from men but 'subordination and discipline',[1] and indeed did not tolerate independent opinion, criticism or control by parliament. As a matter of fact he permitted only creatures around himself just as he could govern only with the assistance of a Press which he had made tractable by bribery. The Prussian Crown Prince and Princess, the future Emperor Frederick III and his wife, Victoria, were wholly justified when they called him an 'evil' man, because he was 'without principle' and was driven by a demoniacal will-to-power. Later, Bebel spoke of the pact which Bismarck made with 'the devil' for the sake of contemptible political 'advantage'. On the eve of the war of 1866, August Reichensperger* meditated upon the recurring importance of arrogance in history, 'from the fall of the Angel until our own day'. In fact, Bismarck himself admitted to the Crown Prince at a later date, in November 1870, that he had already fixed upon his policy of war when he took office in 1862, but made no mention of it even to the king, until the 'proper moment', of course. Thus he hoodwinked William I, though, to be sure, the king's sense of his Prussian political and military 'honour' was always available for the '*suum cuique rapere*' (to rob each of his own), as Ludwig von Gerlach† realistically amplified the ideological device—*suum cuique* (to each his own)—of the Prussian kings. According to the sound judgment of the Crown Prince, Bismarck's entire policy was a 'frivolous game with the most sacred things'. He embodied Machiavelli's *virtù*, which included *sceleratezza*; Bismarck himself felt that a Teutonic devil dwelled within him: the Germans, as a matter of fact, had not worshipped the sun, but the thunder and the lightning.

But the problem of historical guilt, properly speaking, is less concerned with individual motivations, however fascinating for the biographer, than with the objective results and consequences of political activity. It is significant, therefore, that the thoughtful, even among his faithful followers, like the historian Heinrich von Sybel, felt that Bismarck's work was very far from being a fulfilment of their wishes. Scarcely was his work ('performance', one might better say) completed in 1871 than there was a feeling of emptiness. 'Now what?' they thought. Here we can already see the psychological pattern for the development out of psychic

---

[1] Sidney Whitman, *Errinerungen an Bismarck*, p. 238.

* August Reichensperger (1808–95), Prussian art historian and political leader, founder of the Centre Party in the German Reichstag.

† Ernst Ludwig von Gerlach (1795–1877), German publicist and statesman, one of the founders of the Conservative Party in Prussia.

horror vacui, of a universally dangerous pan-Germanism. Bismarck himself in his old age caused bitter disappointment, indeed discouragement, for instance to young Count Harry Kessler, because he lacked awareness of any ultimate meaning of the universe.

Saitschick, for whom these psychological relationships do not arise, discusses in pragmatic terms, first, the seed which Bismarck sowed, and, then, the harvest which inevitably grew. In this way he tries to prove that Bismarck's guilt was our 'destiny'. We question, in the first place, whether Bismarck was 'destiny', in the sense that, had he not been there, 'everything would have turned out differently'. Then we doubt that we should thus thrust all our guilt upon this certainly portentous historical figure so that we ourselves appear blameless.

Viewed from without, the fateful moment of history was the year 1862. King William I was determined to abdicate on the issue of control of the army, but yielded to the persuasive power of Bismarck's energy, as he was to do so often thereafter. Had Frederick III taken over the government at that time, there would have been no 'age of Bismarck'. For, by then, at the time of the constitutional conflict, the Crown Prince already saw so clearly, as he wrote in 1863, the 'frightfully logical' road to 'disaster' in Bismarck's policy of force, which openly trampled all law and justice, that he did not shrink from a conflict with his father.

Would the policy of 'Blood and Iron' have been avoided by a government of Frederick III? Or, in the sad, final analysis, even if there had been no Bismarck, could things have turned out no differently than they did? Neither the German Confederation nor the supra-national atmosphere would have endured. The restoration system of 1815 was only a provisional interruption of the age of the revolution which continued to go forward, at least covertly, from 1789. Bismarck was only the man who, in Jakob Burckhardt's fine formulation, said '*Ipse faciam*' (I myself will do it). Certainly by setting the stone into motion he defined its path and chose the moment when it began to move. But, in any case, the stone was loose and it had to start rolling.

Saitschick rightly stresses that Bismarck's establishment of the Empire was 'artificial' creation, a reversal, by means of true Prussian organization of the process of organic growth. But this course of events cannot simply be charged to the person of the organizer. So individualistic—that is, one-sided and unsociological —a method of historical analysis does not take into account that, however much one may deplore it, the development, in one way or another, from the organic and the federative, to the technically organized and centralized state of affairs, belongs to the fundamental tendencies of modern times. Finally, we must still ask just how much even so 'great' a man can do if the people do not join him sooner or later. Thus the National-Liberals, the predestined Bismarckian party, so to say, were those who accepted Bismarck's principle (which also had the historiographical sanction of Ranke) of the primacy of foreign policy over domestic policy, at least in those circumstances where the geopolitical situation of a country leaves it open to unremitting pressure from without. It was the National-Liberals who betrayed freedom to 'unity', that is, to power. There had long existed as a popular current a liberal and centralist nationalism, which sang 'My fatherland must be greater!' and therefore created danger of 'that dismemberment of the European community' which Saitschick sees as coming into existence for the first time only in Bismarck's era. Against Erich Eyck's liberal critique of Bismarck, Franz Schnabel has correctly emphasized how strong were the nationalist aspirations cherished even by the pre-Bismarckian German democratic movement. Heine already anticipated an unparalleled outburst of political radicalism as a result of the revolutionary development in Germany, first in religion, then in philosophy.

Fixing our attention upon a 'great man', however grave the burden of his individual responsibility, diverts us too easily from the guilt manifestly shared by those who collectively went along with him. In the final analysis, a people always has the government it deserves. We should not, therefore, in all too simple fashion, replace previous customary glorification of the 'great' man by accusations exclusively against the 'evil' man. We are not divested of guilt because we have been influenced. For influence to work, someone must be open to it. Behind the endeavour to thrust all guilt upon Bismarck, and then upon Hitler, the old lack of civic consciousness and sense of responsibility, which was inculcated by the authoritarian state, none the less lies always concealed. We must ask ourselves how the German people came to give first Bismarck and then Hitler their opportunities. Indeed, how did they come to raise Bismarck and Hitler to idols? Because they have tended to worship force, because they consider every kind of inconsiderateness, especially in the military field and in domestic and foreign policy, to be proof of increased strength, so

that the borderline of brutality becomes fluid; in short, because
they are always impressed by the cavalryman's boot and a fist
banged upon the table. The German people saw their ideal of
power embodied in Bismarck. He was their great man. We
ought to have a history of his fame, a history of the *Bismarck
myth*, a critical history in which we would see ourselves depicted,
as a mirror to hold up to ourselves, a mirror of the path of error
by which we attained to ideals of such falsity. This is what we
miss in Saitschick's book; he disregards this side of the problem,
in the final analysis the most important one. The examination of
Bismarck ought to have led directly into necessary German self-
criticism.

Is it not highly suggestive that Bismarck himself felt that he
was possessed of a 'Teutonic' devil? Bamberger called Bismarck
'the *barbare de génie*'. Straight through the soul and conscience of
the Germans runs the uncertain frontier between the Christian
West and barbarism, said Quariglia, the Italian anti-fascist, during
the last war. What is worst is that so many among us have always
been proud of our participation in barbarism, even before Hegel,
then particularly after Nietzsche, and all the way down to Ernst
Jünger. Barbarian or Christian? We ought to put that query to
Bismarck, we must address it above all to every German. Unfortunately, Heinrich Heine was not far wrong when he expressed
the opinion that Christianity had only thinly and temporarily
tamed the barbarian instincts of the Germans. We must add as
well the Prussian-German faculty for having simultaneously a
private Christianity and a deliberately heathenish public policy
which, as we saw, could call up old Thor or Donar. Ernst
Troeltsch recounts that an ingenuous, but very serious Scottish
pastor once declared to him, 'I could not be a pastor in Germany.
It just is not a Christian country.' We should ask whether
Bismarck's unscrupulous Machiavellianism would not have met
more vigorous resistance if this had not been so.

Yet the glorification of war by Treitschke had been prepared
by Hegel, and before him by the historian Luden. So we should
not marvel that men of intellect, indeed jurists such as Rudolf von
Ihering,[*] swarmed about the man of success and fell on their
knees before him. The Prussian-German opposition to an international court of arbitration, after the period of Kant, the

---

[*] Rudolf von Ihering (1818–92), German jurist, famous for his *Geist des römischen
Rechts* and *Der Zweck im Recht*.

disqualification of desire for peace as weakness, corresponded to the fundamental defects of the German national character: the calamitous romanticism of force, and the tendency toward extreme solutions. Frederick William IV called German logical consistency the most wretched of all virtues; and Frederick III, while still a young man, said to his teacher, Ernst Curtius, that Prussian statesmen lacked the ability to give in.

Was there 'another' Germany, better and wiser, besides Bismarck's Germany? There were, in any event, individual Germans who did not share his ideas and who foresaw the oncoming time of troubles, the era of destructive wars and the inevitable catastrophe. Paul de Lagarde* and Constantin Frantz are brought forward from time to time by Saitschick among Bismarck's contemporaries. Ludwig von Gerlach deserves no less a place. In general, the enemies of Bismarck ought to be portrayed together by someone—it would be a small German hall of fame. Yet they were never anything but solitary individuals, and their voices died away, almost unheard. To be sure, official policy and semi-official historiography deliberately did their best to bury them in silence. Thus they remained voices in the wilderness. Their warnings were in vain. For behind these Germans, among whom Crown Prince Frederick stood not among the last, there was no Germany they could represent. The hope of Germany rests, in spite of all, upon the possibility that such Germans may become representative of Germany. But no insight holds hope unless it makes us search into our own hearts.

II. HISTORIANS AND HISTORY

by Alfred von Martin

I

Ranke's formula that the historian only wishes to know 'how it essentially was' (*wie es eigentlich gewesen ist*) is in fact the most unfortunate definition of historical purpose conceivable. It has become celebrated due to its ring of *naïveté*, which was, of course deliberate and therefore dubious. It makes everything vanish

* Paul de Lagarde (1827–91), German Orientalist and publicist.

into a haze. Our principal question must be: To what kind of 'it' does Ranke's formula refer? Is there a reality which can be simply 'reproduced' as such, quasi-photographically? Does not science always mean 'working up' reality in one way or another? At least, does not history, a scientific study with very little scientific rigour, make a choice, determined by its own approach, of what is 'interesting'? Or does the particular vogue won by Ranke's much-quoted remark merely give unintentional expression to a belief that history does not possess its own approach? One could also ask, sceptically, whether man can ever know 'how it essentially was'. But we are less concerned with this question than with realizing that the historian must wish to know more in terms of quality. Ranke's formula, unfortunate but repeatedly used to a noteworthy degree, gives the impression of an intellectual humility which must be characterized as inadequate. Our goal cannot be just to satisfy legitimate curiosity—quite apart from the sceptical question whether the satisfaction derived will not always be a mere illusion. It does not make clear what belongs to history or why we pursue historical studies. Jakob Burckhardt, once a student in Ranke's seminar, who would have become his successor had he not preferred to remain in the humanistic air of his native Basel, was fundamentally critical of the 'value' of preoccupation with external facts, in particular political and military events. For he saw in them too much 'rubbish' and too little 'sense'.

Certainly it is not worth knowing anything that merely 'was'. It is worth knowing either what still lives, or what deserves to be kept alive or brought back to life. The past is only 'important', therefore, to the degree that it is still not '*passée*'—to the extent that we know a direct connexion exists, or that we are still obligated to the past. In keeping with a well-known remark of Goethe's, the 'fruitful' is inseparable from the 'true'. But the 'true' must always be differentiated from mere 'reality'. The fruitful is only whatever arouses us to seek truth, and, where men are concerned, justice. The history of the beautiful belongs, obviously, to such history worth knowing in a humanistic sense. One cannot engage in the study of art 'history', one cannot understand the European art tradition, from a standpoint like Picasso's 'What pleases *me*, is beautiful.' The supreme history is history of the sacred. And, no less instructive than positive history, is negative history—the history of the fall of the spirit from the sacred and true, from the just and right.

II

If history is the history of men, it must be understood in the spirit of humanity, which is not the false spirit of national isolation or arrogance, but a universal, supra-national spirit which basically gives a place to the particular or individual (including the nation as individual) within the general. For the general represents value of a higher order. The idea of 'world history' should therefore be understood as a value conception, implying and giving meaning. A patriotism which feels itself called upon to over-estimate and exaggerate 'one's own', and to deprecate and abase 'someone else's', is self-evidently false, for it lacks the spirit of truth and justice, without which no good can come, not even for the fatherland. Truth is always a general truth. It is, therefore, supra-national.

All inward things only prove their soundness by their effect in the world outside. This external manifestation of the spirit must rest firmly upon the classic foundations of explicit geography. For us it is Europe. But more precisely, for culture history, it is the Occident, the West, including, of course, the entire American continent. Only from this vantage point does concern for 'other' cultures, principally the Asiatic, really become fruitful for us. Only then does it take on a value essentially above interest in the 'exotic'. Only then can we learn from what is most strange, but in no sense inferior. To learn this can only be helpful in curing presumptuous self-satisfaction. It may move us to look within ourselves and to see what we most truly are.

To be a world citizen was once part of culture in Germany more then elsewhere. We are Germans by nature. To wish to be what one is already by nature is silly. When German historical study sought to be only 'German', it became, in fact, fundamentally un-European and '*borussisch*' (Prussian nativistic). What we need is a historical conception which rejects nationalism in favour of the best German traditions and strives for honest, unbiased understanding. Such understanding means thinking as Christians, at least in the sense of being aware of an obligation to the tradition of Christian civilization, and as humanists, so that in our judgment of the historical we are ready to accept those general human norms which are themselves subject to divine norms.

In political history, too, the values of religion and culture must resume their leading role. In political history, above all, it is necessary to look out from the standpoint of all mankind.

III

Bismarck, of course, was so undoctrinaire, so unphilosophical, that it was his principle not to act on principle. Such a policy was the very contrary not only of 'liberalism' but also of 'conservatism'. The war of Prussia against the German Confederation in 1866, in Bluntschli's* judgment, was 'the German revolution in the form of war, directed from above instead of from below'. Treitschke, too, called the events between 1864 and 1866 'the German revolution'. Only by superior statecraft did Bismarck avert a general political and military conflagration. None the less, Nietzsche was right when he expressed the opinion on Bismarck's handiwork that 'the so-called national state' was anything but a weapon against 'the Revolution', since it was much more 'just an increase in the general insecurity and state of danger'. In point of fact, Bismarck's policy, by its underlying conception, opened the door wide for anything and everything. His collaborator in the *Kulturkampf*, under-secretary of justice Friedberg, expressed this conception in the formula that 'reasons of morality must stand back behind what seems expedient and necessary in present-day conditions'. As Nietzsche recognized, there were two things a state thinking in this way could not endure in the long run—a religion which took seriously the duty of its moral office of 'judge', and independent intellectuals aware of their obligation to serve only 'truth'. Nietzsche had said that 'the German spirit' had been bartered away for the 'German Reich'. Bismarck was applauded, however, by German historians who became his adorers. They carried a full measure of responsibility for the 'miseducation', the moral confusion and uprootedness of German public opinion, which later applauded quite 'other' things as well.

The revolution from above considered itself to be the opposite of the revolution from below, the spirit of which spread through Europe from 1789. A semi-official Bismarckian historiography did its part to strengthen public opinion in this attitude. Only Jakob

* Johann Kaspar Bluntschli (1808–81), Swiss-German jurist and political theorist.

Burckhardt saw clearly that since Napoleon I only two forms of one and the same revolution were involved. How correct this view was became obvious when the typical 'mass man' established his dictatorship.

IV

Whether it is a national revolution or a revolutionary national-ism which seizes power, whether it is a tyrannical demagogue or a despotic statesman who establishes control, the ideology of *salus publica* is always put forward, with the proviso, spoken or silent, 'as I understand it'. This elastic ideology must always provide the 'justification' when a power wishes to destroy the limitations of law and justice, morality and religion. In his political activity, in the lust for power which he obviously identified with the 'general' welfare, Bismarck was not in the least troubled by his Christianity, which he reserved strictly to private uses, or, in general, by 'principles'. Historians followed suit. Even a historian like Meinecke was in the close grip of Bis-marckianism, and could free himself from it only gradually and too slowly. Thus, he failed to recognize the ideological character of the favoured appeal to *salus publica*, which means that he failed to recognize the daemon in 'reason of state'. He considers ideology to be an authentic idea, though 'reason of state' specifi-cally means emancipation of the idea of power from any but con-siderations of political cleverness. He therefore goes so far as to accept the existence of two 'moralities': a special 'state morality' and general morality.

This expresses a pride, as yet not overcome, in 'progress' from ideas still strongly rooted in 'cosmopolitanism', to ideas increas-ingly and finally solely concerned with the 'national state'. But there exists no *salus publica* apart from *justitia*, which is always supra-national and alone can be the *fundamentum regnorum*. And, in the cosmopolitan age from Augustine to Kant, an essential part of *justitia* was the ideal of peace, until, in the guise of nationalist and imperialist 'progress', it was replaced by militarism, in turn exalted as an ideal.

If history is to educate, it must use value judgments in its methodology, that is, it must be considered as the struggle for the realization of values. What must be overcome is the absolutiza-tion of the factual, which dates from Hegel. We must take our point of departure in political history as elsewhere from what stands above history, the eternal.

In the final analysis, all history is 'the history of ideas', over values. The battle is waged for ideas and values, or even, and overwhelmingly, against them. Only a 'doctrine of ideas' which has fallen away from Plato's lofty wisdom can try to derive the content of this idea out of history—and then can maintain that all times are 'equally close to God'. Twelve years of training our sight, from 1933 to 1945, may have done in their own way what was needed to make us truly see that there are also times 'closer' to the devil than to God. To be sure, only when we again reverently believe in a meaningful 'order' ruling the world, and therefore world history too, will we again be able to recognize the negation of 'order', the opposition to order, the diabolic opposition to the good and the godly, for what it is. Whoever, in the years of the terror régime, found things in order, even if only on the whole, and now complains about the mistakes which the 'Westerners' cannot help but make on occasion, only reveals that he has understood nothing, that he has not grasped the fundamental difference between the principled inhumanity of the neo-Prussian and Eastern kind, and the human shortcomings to which everyone is prone.

But the 'world' ran after the 'great man'. Treitschke said, in May 1866, that Bismarck 'despised' ideas and had only a 'very slight understanding' of 'moral forces'. But only a few weeks later, the same Treitschke had swung completely about and began to demand, not that 'politics should become more moral', but that 'morality should become more political'. We have since learned, to our horror, where this road leads. One who had occasion to know Hitler well, General Jodl, said of him, 'Moral or legal arguments he called just stupid prattle.'

But is the absurdity of this road now at least recognized? Has appalling experience at least brought us to understand that 'will to power' is not the key to understanding the work, that it is not the centre of history? Among the Hitler generals, after all, Jodl was far from the worst, and yet, for him, too, Hitler was 'the great man'. Jodl, for all that, was critical of Hitler. Afterwards, he called him a 'great man . . . even if an infernal man'. Always a 'great man'. And then he was 'the supreme war commander', too. Once he decided, there then existed for Jodl only the absolute 'duty' of obedience. Then Jodl's own judgment, as well as concern for the general laws of humanity, had to be silent. Any-one refusing to obey, for any reason, would 'have been purged with full justice'—this was Jodl's convinced, and obviously honest belief, even when he stood before the Nuremberg tribunal. Even there he called the conspiracy of July 20, 1944, a 'breach of loyalty'. How abysmal this confusion of all ethical notions—to declare that one owes 'loyalty' to the criminal as long as he is chief of state, no matter if he has committed the greatest of possible sins against God, mankind and his own people! What a confusion of ethical conceptions, furthermore, to mistake Ger-man 'loyalty' for Prussian cadaver obedience!

Compromises could not help. Treitschke's 'National-Liberal' endeavour to synthesize 'Potsdam' and 'Weimar' was the en-deavour to reconcile the spiritually disparate. Erich Marcks, the biographer of Bismarck, recently sought to establish a bond between Bismarck and Goethe. But when Baldur von Schirach, the Nazi commissioner in charge of education of the German youth, wished to link Hitler and Goethe, then it became clear that some juxtapositions are impossible.

What is true and what false, what is good and what evil, what is the will of God and what the temptation of Satan, we must know this before we study history. For history can merely reveal to us what happens to the true and good in the roaring whirlpools of reality, in which only a dim copy of pure being can be mirrored. Its primal image always sits enthroned, high over us, like the stars in the firmament. These constellations are the compass to guide and lead us if we do not wish to journey into error.

CHAPTER FIVE

MILITARISM IN MODERN HISTORY

by Hans Herzfeld

Hans Herzfeld was born in 1892 and taught modern history at the University of Halle from 1923 until 1938 when he was dismissed by the National-Socialist government. He was not able to resume his teaching activities until 1946 when he became associate professor of history at the University of Freiburg. From there he was appointed in 1950 as professor of history to the Freie Universität in Berlin.

Among his recent publications were a two-volume biography of Johannes von Miquel (Detmold, 1938–39), the edition of *Neue Briefe* by Ranke (Hamburg, 1949) and a text-book on modern world history, *Die Moderne Welt, 1789–1945* (Braunschweig, 1950). An essay of his, 'Das Problem des deutschen Heeres, 1919–45', appeared as number 6 of the series *Geschichte und Politik* (Schloss Lauppheim: Ulrich Steiner Verlag, 1952). The following article was first published in *Schola*, Monatsschrift für Erziehung und Bildung, in September 1946. It is reproduced here in a shortened version.

One of the tasks we now face, after the catastrophe of the second world war in a single generation, is to determine the content and the scope of the concept of militarism, which seems to sum up the forces driving toward war. We must find out the characteristics of militarism, the energies involved in it, how it began and how it evolved. . . .

The non-German world has overwhelmingly considered Germany, and Prussia in particular, to be the native land of modern militarism. This militarism reached full growth in the army of imperial Germany prior to 1914, even before the advent of National-Socialism. The German people must therefore practise self-criticism. They must ask how it became possible to subject every phase of life to total militarization during the decade of National-Socialist rule. . . .

According to Alfred Vagts, the expression 'militarism' was coined in the controversy over the Second Empire in France. Soon after 1871 it came into use in Germany as well. It rests for the most part, however, on older ideas. We must look for its historical antecedents to the century of revolution in England, the period of Cromwell and the Glorious Revolution of 1688. The development of the modern English state, with its fundamental supremacy of civilian over military authority, begins with 1688. The Bill of Rights of 1689 made the existence and strength of the standing army dependent upon parliamentary approval. Simultaneously, military discipline was made dependent upon passage of an annual Mutiny Act. Modern liberalism and democracy were then able to go forward in systematically subordinating the military power to civilian political authority. This evolution was facilitated because the two great Anglo-Saxon states until very recently did not need to maintain true mass armies, thanks to their favourable geographic situation.

In contrast, the continental European states had to work in a more difficult geographical situation. The system of universal military service was introduced in all great powers on the European continent. It began with the French Revolution and became general throughout Europe. Other states were impressed by the success of the Prussian army upon the basis of universal conscription. The wars of liberation against Napoleon and the wars for the foundation of the Reich gave unparalleled prestige, particularly in Germany, to this conscript army. Thus, until 1914, men thought of it not only as a measure of dire necessity, but also as a part of the education of the nation. They believed that universal military service was morally better than a mercenary army as a method of defending the state against foreign threats. They also considered it a justified technique in power politics. This attitude was widely adopted in the other great European nations which introduced universal military service after 1871. To be sure, in France a Jean Jaurès* fought passionately against the dangers inherent in such powerful expansion of the military forces. But he, too, held firm to the doctrine that it was each man's duty, in a Europe armed to the teeth, to protect the soil of the fatherland as a soldier, while enjoying equality of rights as a citizen. He proposed to call everyone capable of service to duty in a militia-like *Nouvelle Armée*. He believed it would be stronger than the traditional standing armies.

It was already clear before 1914 that the armaments race between

* Jean Jaurès (1859–1914), famous French Socialist leader assassinated in 1914 by a nationalist fanatic.

the great powers was driving them all constantly to enlarge
their mass armies, to improve their training and to expand their
equipment. There had been a dubiously optimistic belief that the
way to prevent war was to prepare for possible war, and that the
very increase in the danger of a war served to avert it. It was
supposed that the dangers of a war would be calculated in advance,
and the questions awaiting decision would be settled by continued diplomatic negotiation. It later became clear, however,
that any of the great powers which came to fear that its comparative strength would decline, would feel tempted, if not
compelled, to employ its apparatus of power.

One of the gravest questions in the history of the origins of
both the First and the Second World Wars is the extent to which
this idea of preventive war served to bring on the catastrophes of
1914 and 1939. As for 1939, we have palpable evidence of the
influence upon Hitler of his fear that in the long run he would
lose the temporary advantage he had won by speeding up German
armament. Non-German historians are still for the most part convinced that similar motives played a role in German policy before
1914 as well. . . .

This should make clear the essential difference between
militarism and military organization as such. It comes about when
the armed forces begin to determine policy from within themselves, when they discard the doctrine that war should be the
continuation of politics by other means, when military organization becomes its own end, so that, by its own authority, and in
response to its own technical requirements, it determines what
the state shall do. In recent years Gerhard Ritter has stated the
distinction between the type of war which is intended to re-establish in the end a new, better and juster peace among the nations,
and the war in which there is no longer any limit upon the use of
power, in which blind shock action rules.

When this happens, war ceases to be a step taken only in dire
necessity, an abnormal situation, and it becomes a normal
phenomenon in the life of the nations. At the very least, war and
the threat of war come to be considered as an inevitable and
always permissible method of exerting political pressure on behalf
of the political aspirations of one's own state against other states,
whenever circumstances are favourable. The danger arises of
international anarchy, uncontrolled by any principle of law and
justice.

The emancipation of the human spirit from religious belief, its increasing concern with rationality and technological advance— these turned loose forces unknown to any earlier times. Ever since the Renaissance, war and military technology, like politics, have been made increasingly rational and systematic. The pursuit of arms, which had once been part of the task of every free man, became the special duty of the military profession. Modern militarism is not just the interference of the military on its own authority in the field of political decisions, it is also the greatest possible utilization of the resources of military organization.

War then ceases to be merely a question of self-defence. The concept of just war is invalidated. Instead, war is justified by the completely naturalistic doctrine that the victory of the stronger over the weaker is inevitable. By means of the accumulation of raw materials, systematic expansion of the arms industry and feverish promotion of invention, war spreads over all economic and social life, and military training of the people becomes an end in itself. Historically, skill in combat has been held in high esteem. The new rational and technological militarism allied with this tradition and thus was able, in an overwhelmingly civilian age, to heighten the prestige of the professional caste of the soldiers.

We can now determine historically how far militarism in this restricted sense was a part of recent German history and to what degree it was a cause of the catastrophe we have witnessed.

In a recent essay, Friedrich Meinecke stressed that a prototype of rationalized, systematized, technological and utilitarian militarism may be found in the Prussian military state as it evolved since the reigns of Frederick William I and Frederick II in the eighteenth century. It was the misfortune of German history that Prussia, as the political leader of modern Germany, could and did rise to equality with the older great states of Europe only by harsh concentration of its energies upon warfare.

Military thinking and pride in successes won in hard battle thus became the special characteristics of historic Prussianism, particularly in the officer corps, which was the leading caste in the Prussian state. The lesser nobility of North-east Germany who comprised that caste, being not exactly blessed with wordly goods, were dependent upon service to the state, which meant, under these typically soldierly kings, a close and permanent alliance with the Prussian crown.

As a result, the activity of the state in old Prussia was sub-ordinated to military objectives and assignments. Three-quarters of government expenditures were devoted to the military, so that inevitably the military became dominant over the bourgeois and civilian groups. The king of Prussia felt himself to be the first officer of the country, and the officer nobility were the uncontested and legally recognized privileged leading group in the population. The sons of the peasants called up as recruits were trained in a rigid drill of barbaric severity. To be sure, such drill, which made the individual into an automaton without any will of his own, was known outside Prussia in the eighteenth century. But in Prussia the civilian administration and officialdom had to work so predominantly in the service of the army that they themselves took on to a large extent the coloration of the military. Even in the changed conditions of the nineteenth century, the reserve officer corps continued to be deeply impregnated with the conceptions of the professional officers and carried them over into the ranks of the upper strata of civilian society. Prussia in the cen-tury before the battle of Jena was distinctly a soldier's state in which all other tasks and activities in the life of the people were in danger of being overshadowed and forced into the background.

The reform legislation in Prussia in the decade after 1807, called forth by Napoleon's victory at Jena and Auerstedt as well as by the stimulus of the great French Revolution, made an important start in shifting the balance between the military and civilian forces in Prussian life. It was an effort to weaken the strongly entrenched military system in favour of a liberal and civilian system. In this reform period, in an endeavour to weaken the traditional influence of the hereditary nobility, the promotion of officers was put on the basis of education and training. One-year voluntary service was instituted for the purpose of making civilian education and property more important within the army. The original purpose of the Landwehr was not only to strengthen the army by establishing universal military service, but also to break down the rigidity of the professional army and to implant a civilian and liberal spirit in it.

It was a portent of the future that these beginnings of an evolution toward a victory of the liberal bourgeoisie in Prussia did not come to fruition, and that the army always managed to maintain its special position. After 1815 crown and army returned to their harsh opposition to the current of modern liberalism. It was a disaster for the whole future course of German history that the Revolution of 1848 ended in the violent defeat of the people by the monarchy and the army.

After that, the monarchy, and with it the professional officer corps savagely protecting its character as the citadel of the nobility, opposed the new tendencies with increased vigour. The reform of the army in the 1860's was personally initiated by William I, a soldier in the traditional sense. Universal military service was adopted, but its logical consequences were rejected and the traditional predominance of the professional officer was preserved. In contrast to Boyen's reforms, the reforms of the sixties sought to assimilate the corps of reserve and Landwehr officers, who were allowed to share the traditional social prestige of the officer. The special position created for the Landwehr in 1814 was abolished and it was merged to the greatest possible extent with the regular army. It was also of decisive importance for the continuance of the army as a separate force in the political and civilian life of united Germany after 1871 that during the conflict over the army in the 1860's, control over the officer corps by the crown was maintained intact, keeping them firmly bound to each other. The military cabinet, having been placed under the war ministry in the reforms after 1806, was now made subordinate only to the crown; thus, unlike the war ministry, it ceased to have any formal responsibility to parliament in Prussia or the Empire. The monarchy thereby kept exclusive control over appointment and promotion of officers, an especially effective foundation for the monarch's position as supreme war lord. In this way the Prussian nobility, in close conservative alliance with the monarchy, was able to maintain its traditional position as the heart of the officer corps, for the most part, until the world war of 1914 and until the overthrow of the Hohenzollern monarchy.

Bismarck's first great domestic political success was shielding the monarch's power of military command in his capacity as supreme war lord, against all attacks of the liberal opposition in the conflict over the army between 1862 and 1866. After 1871 he stubbornly defended this power against all the attacks of the Reichstag elected by universal suffrage. In its overwhelming majority, however, the nation was ready after 1866 and 1870-71 to accept the maintenance of the traditional fundamental character of the Prussian military state. The brilliant victories of those

8

years and the fulfilment of all their dreams of unity were accomplished not only by Bismarck's wholly personal achievement, but principally by the stern energy and the striking power of this apparatus of military might. The struggle over liberal reorganization of Prussia in the nineteenth century therefore ended with a far-reaching success of the military tradition. This victory was not destroyed by the grant to the Reichstag of the right to pass upon the budget. Though this gave the Reichstag some control over army appropriations, and thus influence on its size and equipment, the parliament could not control the internal organization of the army.

Before his fall Bismarck himself came to know the serious burden which this army could be for the politically responsible leader of the state. He came to know the danger of military intervention in politics. On the question of political influence over military operations, and, contrariwise, on the question of military influence upon peace negotiations he already faced a sharp struggle during the war of 1866 and even more strongly in 1870–71. But this tension probably was no greater than in any other states when a divergence inevitably appeared in the demands and the attitudes of the political and military leaders, unless they were the same person, like Frederick the Great or Napoleon. Thanks to Moltke's strategic achievement, in the period of the establishment of the Empire the Great General Staff rose to a position like that of the military cabinet, immediately subordinate only to the monarch. It was not under the control of the political leaders of the Empire. Even during peace time the planning and preparation of war were concentrated in its hands. The Great General Staff developed alongside but apart from the war ministry, which had to reply to questions in parliament. It became the strongest and purest expression of specifically military organization in Germany during the second Empire.

Helmuth von Moltke,* the creator of this Great General Staff, refused to interfere in politics. He endeavoured at least to confine himself to the performance of his tasks as a military expert, though he did come into temporary conflict with Bismarck on the question of the possibility and admissibility of preventive war, as in 1867 and 1875. His personal modesty and self-criticism were not shared by his successors. Moltke's deputy and successor in

---

* Helmuth Karl Bernhard, Count von Moltke (1800–91), German field marshal, commander of the Prussian forces in the wars of 1866 and 1870–71.

the leadership of the Great General Staff, Count Alfred Waldersee, repeatedly endeavoured during the long European crisis of 1886–88 to compel Bismarck to launch a preventive war against Russia or France, if necessary against both simultaneously, before the alliance of these two neighbours of the Reich became a fact. Bismarck had to call upon his unequalled prestige, and upon all his energy and stubbornness, in order to maintain against Waldersee his fundamental principle that responsible statesmen should not anticipate God's action in history. Preventive war, he believed, would be an impermissible gamble for the new Empire still engaged in cautious consolidation. Waldersee made every effort to draw the heir to the throne, the later William II, to his side. He used all the arts of political intrigue to undermine the position of the founder of the Empire. He endeavoured, in very characteristic fashion, to transform the military attachés into a kind of special diplomatic corps; the military attaché, because of his personally influential position as aide-de-camp to the monarch, could reach his ear at any time, even by-passing the imperial chancellor. Under William II the military attaché retained the right to direct correspondence with the ruler, even after Caprivi* placed his official reports under the control of the ambassador.

It is characteristic of the politically dangerous strength such militaristic elements could attain because of the army's historic prestige, that the very circles which ever since the crisis of the sixties owed their whole position of influence to Bismarck, were among those who contributed basically to his overthrow. Many generals, even some who did not at all belong to the most narrowly conservative of the Prussian officer corps, were convinced during the crisis that preceded Bismarck's overthrow that the warriors were definitely the leading class in world history, so that Bismarck, a civilian, should be succeeded as imperial chancellor by a general, a professional soldier. The ease with which William II, a youthfully inexperienced monarch of dubious strength of character, was able to dismiss the founder of the Empire, impressed both contemporaries and later generations. It is probably the strongest proof of the profoundly militaristic way in which the Empire was established. . . .

Germany's struggle for existence in the years 1914–18 led to

* Georg Leo, Count von Caprivi (1831–99), German general and statesman, succeeded Bismarck as imperial chancellor (1890–94).

the expression of all the possibilities, latent during peace time, for the development of military organization to the full, to the increasing exclusion of other elements. Militarism found its classic exponent at the height of the struggle, in the energetic personality of Ludendorff. Such military personalities as Ludendorff, undoubtedly stronger than the political leaders brought forth by the same times, exerted ever greater pressure upon political decisions. The civilians themselves were more inclined to give way to the military approach than was permitted in the politically more consolidated western European states.

The fact of National-Socialism is sufficient proof that militarism is not necessarily bound up with the particular conservative and monarchist form of the state under which Germany lived during the Second Reich. Non-German states also had to take into account the appearance of militarist influences in politics, thanks to the rise of nationalism and the doctrine of power politics. Even in England Lord Fisher* brought forward for consideration, in his Copenhagen proposal, the idea of preventive war, but it was always rejected by king and cabinet. Sir Henry Wilson† tried as strongly to apply military ideas to political thinking in the English army as did Count Waldersee in the German. The proposal of the French general Joffre to take up for consideration immediately upon the outbreak of war the question of marching at once into Belgium was of the same order, but in France the responsible government rejected it for political reasons. During the general mobilization in Tsarist Russia in August 1914, the statesmen were disastrously burdened by the pressure of the military experts who desired to speed their own deployment to the greatest possible degree in the face of a German mobilization of greater rapidity.

The crucial fact was that in the parliamentary states of the West, England and France, the political leaders for the most part maintained their supremacy over the military men during the preparation of the war as well as during its conduct. There was friction and even severe strain between them during the war. Strong and stubborn military leaders like Joffre, Foch and Haig often advocated the soldier's viewpoint before their governments with great vigour. The preparation for the Dardanelles expedition of

* John Arbuthnot Fisher, first Baron Fisher (1841–1920), British admiral, first sea lord (1903–09, 1914–15).
† Sir Henry Wilson Hughes (1864–1922), British general, chief of the Imperial General Staff (1918–22).

1915 and the Flanders battle of 1917 are instances of the severe struggles which could develop over this problem even within the framework of the liberal democracy of the West. The historically decisive fact, none the less, was that the political leaders in the final analysis passed judgment on all the great military operations. The soldiers, who gave advice and carried out their orders, were their subordinates. Thus the primacy of politics was basically maintained even in the conduct of war.

The weakness of political leadership in the face of the military probably explains the relation of Imperial Chancellor von Bethmann-Hollweg to the military. In his memoirs, Bethmann-Hollweg, who was in general so critical of the military, stressed that, with regard to military operations, he had been compelled, as a civilian and a layman, to bow before the judgment of the military expert, and that he therefore avoided interfering with the conduct of such operations. But that meant giving up full control over the course of events once war broke out. He voluntarily abandoned the primacy of politics in war time. For it is in the nature of things that the great military decisions about operations cannot be separated, in a pure state, from problems of the political conduct of war. To make military leadership the task of a special expert is to erect a cult of the specialist which drives a wide cleavage between the statesman and the military commander. This is inalterably opposed to the political conceptions of western Europe. There all the essential decisions in politics and the conduct of war are brought together into the hands of the political leader, the statesman, who has the benefit of the expert advice of the military man.

This supremacy of the military brought tragedy to Germany at the very beginning of the First World War. At that time the invasion of Belgium was begun with the passive approval and cover of the imperial chancellor. Yet this decision arose from purely military considerations, though there were already evident political objections to it which later events confirmed. The more hopeless the situation of Germany became during the course of the war, the greater became the effort to find a strictly military solution. But the war had been lost politically at the start, and its loss was sealed at the very latest by the entry of the United States in 1917.

From 1917 onward, therefore, Ludendorff was to reject with increasing vigour the interference of political forces and to make the conduct of war a purely military matter. Bethmann-Hollweg, who had permitted the invasion of Belgium in 1914, was quite aware of the disastrous effect which renewal of unrestricted submarine warfare would have in Washington. He therefore resisted a decision in its favour as long as he could. He finally gave in when the military leaders told him that unless this extreme method of warfare were adopted, the war would be lost for Germany. The supreme army command determined the form which the total mobilization of economic and social life would take, as in the case of the auxiliary service law of 1916. But it was already a question whether, in the face of a world of more powerful enemies, increased mobilization of the people's energies did not do more harm than good, whether there remained any political justification for such mobilization. In the course of constant pressure upon the political leaders, who kept submitting, the supreme army command also maintained its supremacy in deciding how far the people in the occupied countries, particularly Belgium, would have to contribute to the German war effort. Even during the First World War, the supreme army command compelled the government to violate the rules of existing international law. After the war, this had serious consequences for the relationship between the Germans and their neighbours.

The supreme army command played the decisive role in overthrowing Bethmann-Hollweg. His successors, Michaelis and Hertling,* were so dependent upon the supreme army command that one can scarcely speak of their individual responsibility. The Reichstag struggled against this situation on various occasions, such as the crisis over the peace resolution in 1917, but could not achieve any permanent gains. The supreme army command, by its annexationist aspirations, which were Utopian in their exaggeration and contradictory to the real situation of Germany, made the position of the imperial government more difficult, even though the question whether it was not already too late to end the war by means of negotiation must remain open. Finally, in 1918, during the discussion of a special peace with Russia, the supreme army command urged demands which on the whole anticipated Adolf Hitler's Russian policy. Despite the qualms of

---

* Georg Michaelis (1857-1936), German imperial chancellor (1917), followed Theobald von Bethmann-Hollweg (1856-1921) in office. Michaelis was followed by Georg, Count von Hertling (1843-1919) who was chancellor from November 1917 to September 1918, and Prince Max (Maximilian) of Baden (1867-1929), who was chancellor from October to November 1918.

Secretary of State von Kühlmann,* most of these far-reaching demands were carried out. The supreme army command therefore bears a large part of the historic resonsibility for the constant difficulties created for German-Russian relations by the Brest-Litovsk peace.

Despite all the real differences between Germany's policy and conduct of war during the First and Second World Wars, in one respect the first war certainly represented a prelude to the catastrophe of the second war. During the First World War, the military stood forth as the saviour of the nation in its distress, though the war against a world-wide coalition had to end inevitably in collapse. The army command itself confessed this when, in October 1918, it demanded that the government of Prince Max of Baden swiftly conclude an armistice in order to end the war, which was already lost. To be sure, this was different from what was done by National-Socialism in 1945.

We need merely outline briefly our conclusions as to the history of the last decade. The Weimar Republic made an honest but tragically unsuccessful effort to overcome the obstacles in its way. Then, after 1933, National-Socialism under the personal dictatorship of Adolf Hitler made the politically impossible endeavour to repeat, with redoubled energy and redoubled blindness, the experiment of the First World War, a war which it fundamentally misunderstood. It renewed, with harsh cruelty and ruthlessness, the endeavour to mobilize the entire German nation, which had failed at the height of the First World War. It put all the material resources of Germany to use in this task. It tried to use all the spiritual resources of the nation to similar duty, and in the end it slaughtered all those who resisted.

In foreign politics the National-Socialist régime became the embodiment of militarism in the strictest sense, because it viewed Germany's whole position in the world from the viewpoint of allegedly militarist thought. It began the war in 1939 as a preventive war, in order to safeguard its advantage in the armaments race. Dazzled by initial success, Hitler extended the scope of the struggle until it became unlimited. He attacked one country after another, arguing that only thus could he prevent them from joining the world coalition of his foes. When, with this selfsame argument, he began the assault upon Russia and then, despite the

* Richard von Kühlmann (1873–), German diplomat, foreign secretary (1917–18), represented Germany at the Brest-Litovsk negotiations.

warning of the First World War, again made the intervention of the United States inevitable, he sealed his own doom.

Hitler endeavoured in vain to save himself by increased savagery in his conduct of war, and by multiplied demands, enforced with barbaric cruelty, upon the occupied territories. He tried to conceal the increasing hopelessness of his desperate gamble by the conception of total war. This last and grotesquely exaggerated consequence of the idea of militarism was only possible in the modern world, with its ideological uncertainty, its religious vacuity, its limitless dynamism and the total lack of purpose in its technical organization. It made manifest the full invalidity of the naturalistic will-to-power, which the Hitler régime raised to an absolute.

Hitler could carry through this gamble to its bitter end, only because, by the demoniacal quality of his unbridled will-to-power, he was able to draw into his service all the forces of historical tradition which lived on in the German people, all their energy and their capacity for accomplishment. The nation was driven farther than it wished to go, beyond its strength, until no way out remained.

The German army, originated by Prussia and utilized by National-Socialism as the principal instrument in its great gamble, was buried beyond hope in the final collapse. The relationship between the army and the National-Socialist party during the Hitler régime was quite characteristic. Much of the strength and special political character of modern militarism is due to specially trained professional leadership. This was particularly evident in the Reichswehr of Seeckt, who fled from politics in order to maintain its soldierly tradition undisturbed. It thereby shared an essential part of the responsibility for the downfall of the Weimar democracy. But, in the resulting estrangement from the modern state, it also lost the chance effectively to resist the seizure of power by National-Socialism and its subsequent rule. After 1933 the Reichswehr at first sought to maintain its own character and tradition in the face of the National-Socialist system, an untamed mass movement so alien to its own ways. As we now know, a portion of the Reichswehr leadership realized, from the standpoint of the military specialist, that catastrophe was approaching. On July 20, 1944, they finally sought to stop the tide of events, but in vain.

Modern militarism has been, in general, overwhelmingly an

affair of the military man alone. The situation during the decade of National-Socialist rule was characterized, on the contrary, by the enforcement of a dilettante's control over the army. Hitler compelled the army to obey blindly, by means of all kinds of corruption as well as by violence. His dilettantist militarism became the lord and god of politics. Only this explains the events of the last decade. Militarism, falling into the hands of those who were unable to judge the meaning of their own activity, drove mankind to the precipice. Now mankind faces for the future, as a question of its existence or destruction, the problem of the abolition of militarism.

CHAPTER SIX

GERMANY AND THE EPOCH OF
WORLD WARS

by Ludwig Dehio

Ludwig Dehio was born in 1888 and has been for many years one of the leading archivists and mediaevalists in Germany. After the First World War he published a great number of articles using newly discovered sources for the elucidation of Prussian-German history in the nineteenth century. At that time he was director of the Brandenburg-Prussian archives in Berlin-Dahlem. He is now director of the archives in Marburg and professor at the university there. When the *Historische Zeitschrift* was revived in 1949, he became one of its two editors.

The following study was delivered originally as a paper at the second meeting of the German Historians after the Second World War, which was held in Marburg in September 1951. It was printed in the *Historische Zeitschrift*, CLXXIII (February 1952), pp. 77–94. It forms the continuation of his book *Gleichgewicht oder Hegemonie* (Krefeld, 1948), in which he supplied the background in the field of foreign policy for his interpretation of German hegemonial struggles.

After years of political passivity, Germany is now coming back into a position of self-responsibility. More than ever she now needs to understand clearly the period of the two world wars— the period that preceded her exclusion from self-responsibility. In discussing this problem here, we can only state our views with aphoristic brevity. We shall merely mark a number of points which, linked together, may indicate a rough profile of events.

First, let us state our guiding idea. It is adapted, I think, to serving as the central point in this discussion, or indeed in any discussion that strives to rise to a third position above current accusations and defences—to a historical picture standing by its own strength. I have in mind the idea of struggle for hegemony. For, each of the two world wars, like two consecutive acts in the same tragedy, displays in the most exacerbated form possible the familiar generic traits of those great European wars associated with the names of Charles V and Philip II, Louis XIV and Napoleon I.

I shall make no effort to support this thesis by comparison and analysis of everything which happened in the whole broad field of relations between the great powers of Europe. But I will try to make use of such comparative analysis in considering the history of Germany, especially in our period and in domestic policy. Here we may profitably use another idea—the idea of the demoniac character (*Dämonie*) of power. It is not difficult to show its close connexion with our initial conception. It impressed itself very strongly upon our minds mainly during the Second World War, the most recent struggle for European hegemony. By attaching preponderant importance to my central idea, I am compelled to reject other explanations at least in part. This is particularly true of those interpretations which view German history in our period as a thing apart, like a tree rising straight from roots in German soil. They fail to keep in mind how tangled the history of Germany is with that of other lands. But neither can I accept explanations which, taking a broader view of events, stress analogies with typical processes of our time. To be sure, there is truth to both explanations, but both require amplification. This is especially true of the one which views Germany as an isolated phenomenon. This attitude, more common outside of Germany, tends to place too much stress upon special German characteristics. We may easily balance out the error in this explanation by keeping the other in mind. If you take my position, that Germany was *the* hegemonic power of our time, then you avoid both errors. For on the one hand, Germany, in her very function as a hegemonic power, presents herself to us with characteristics utterly unlike those of her fellow-members in the family of nations. But on the other hand, it seems certain to us that Germany did not always have her own distinct personality! Consideration of events from a broader historical view warns us to pass judgment cautiously. When we look back over the history of the old hegemonic powers we do gain caution, for then we become aware that many of the characteristics of modern Germany which, when we see them only in terms of the twentieth century, impress us as being uniquely German, were anticipated by the earlier hegemonic powers, to say the very least. Thus, when these modern German characteristics are considered in terms of the earlier centuries, they appear typical. Of course, this comparative investigation of

the past makes us aware of the precise degree of unique significance, within the whole series of hegemonic wars which should be
attached to the two such wars fought by Germany. In the last
analysis, when we make comparisons with past or contemporary
phenomena, as the case may be, this is the conclusion which
emerges with ever greater distinctness and certainty.

The victim of the demoniac character of power, however, is
flung about in a turbulent storm by overpowering will-to-rule
and amoral joy of battle. Inevitably, such demoniac character
bursts out vigorously in that most comprehensive and violent of
all struggles on earth, the struggle for hegemony. Then, since the
hegemonic power towers above these struggles in lonely pre-
eminence, before it are placed demonic temptations of a specific
kind.

We need concern ourselves no more now with these introductory considerations. We shall try to characterize briefly Germany's forcible entry into the battle for hegemony. The conflicts
which develop between the strongest power on the old continent
—we do not have in mind the Eastern or peripheral areas—and
the sea power, constitute, in our view, the central factor in all
struggles for European hegemony. But there was never any
question of such a conflict in the history of Prussia-Germany
before it built its navy. It displayed the most distinctive characteristics of the purely continental type of power, though of course
enhanced by a vehemence and youthful vigour unequalled at the
time. This was the result of the westward expansion of Prussia,
which profoundly reinvigorated the nation. From her Eastern
periphery, where there was a dearth of history and culture, the
nation received a rapturous vehemence which aroused and
moulded a new vitality, biologically, intellectually and economic-
ally, but above all politically. At work here was that trinity of
bold leadership, systematic armament and disciplined manpower,
which was to place an indelible mark upon the thinking of Germany after her new start. The tradition of the Prussian power-
state (*Machtstaat*) has been unparalleled in Western history in its
power of suggestion: it was a lesson in the triumphant power of
will that could advance in mighty leaps from the smallest beginnings to the circle of the greatest of the powers.

German history was chiefly continental until the turn of this
century. It then suddenly entered the arena of supreme and world-
wide decisions, in which no matter how great the struggle upon

the Continent, events on the sea are more important than even the most spectacular land battles. We wish now to pose a question: How was the First World War, not caused, but made possible? This is our answer. As a world war, beyond question it was made possible by the vigorous efforts of rejuvenated Germany to expand. As yet, such efforts on the part of Russia alone could not then have brought it about. It took on, none the less, the classic form of a struggle for European hegemony because of England's reaction.

Just as Prussia had once broken into the ranks of the European great powers, we Germans hoped to break out of the narrow confines of Europe and join the ranks of the world powers. We tried to do it by the authentic Prussian method, that is, by systematically increasing our armed power, in this case, by expanding our naval fleet. It was not possible unless England were expelled from her position as guarantor of the existing balance of power in Europe as well as from her position as ruler of the seas throughout the world. What was the inevitable consequence of our endeavours? We went down the road to world war. We, and only we, threatened the vital nerve centres of English global power. In that characteristic, our imperialism was unique, although the other imperialisms had a wider area of conflict with English imperialism than ours.

We then turned our fickle glance upon the wide world. Instead of keeping firmly in view the acquisition of specific territories, we speculated upon a broad modification of the *status quo* at the expense of our rival. Meanwhile, England sought to maintain herself by defending just that old European balance of power which seemed almost antiquated to us as the result of the semi-hegemonic position of the Bismarckian Empire upon the Continent. By her encirclement policy, England gradually forced us into the isolated position of a potential aspirant for European hegemony in the full sense. At the same time, our imperialism, entering into competition with the English rulers of the world seas, still endeavoured to become one of a group of world powers. Thus, each of the rivals combatted the other's hegemonic position by an appeal to the balance of power, but each understood something quite different by hegemony and balance of power!

Under the pressure of encirclement, we learned, even before 1914, to wonder whether things would turn out as well as we optimistically expected at the turn of the century. Then we seemed to think that England, held in check by our naval armament, would let herself be peacefully manœuvered out of her key positions. But the decisive fact was this—in our youthful exuberance, we failed to carry our ideas to their logical conclusion: Plehn could write in 1913 in his book, *Deutsche Weltpolitik und kein Krieg* (German World Policy and No War): 'Almost everyone in the nation believes that we can conquer freedom for our world political activity only by a major European war.'

In this way, the major European war, which was expanded into a world war, came to pass. Only then did the transformation of our situation, so far just an impending danger, become frightful reality. Only then did we accept the tasks of a European hegemonic power. Although, in destroying the old balance of power, the strongest state on the Continent could not help but seize hegemony in Europe for itself, we would have preferred to keep this logical consequence from ourselves and from others. It was only then, under the impact of the new situation, that we added to our essential character certain wholly new traits which cannot simply be attributed to an earlier period, though they do presuppose our previous history, in the way an upper story of a house presupposes the lower stories.

We will understand the course of events more easily if we stand aside for a moment and try to consider the typical fate of earlier hegemonic powers. What a lonely role of tragic grandeur they played! By their efforts, deliberate or otherwise, to establish their own predominance, they set into motion all the momentous happenings of the European great wars. These efforts inevitably took sharper forms of expression as the great hostile coalitions of the imperilled states were firmly established under the leadership of the peripheral insular power. In any case, in the final stage the hegemonic power battled by itself, one against many. But she dared to wage such battle. She swelled with pride, thinking that this was the supreme moment of her destiny, that she held a lead over all her neighbours. Neither danger nor thought of danger restrained her. Instead they worked upon her exuberant sense of power and formed an incentive not to fail in her hour of greatness. She was drawn on by the expectation that the reward for her exertions would be a new stage of self-fulfilment and accomplishment, and that she would tower over the host of her foes, who just tried to keep the position they already had. But then when the hegemonic power, in its onward movement, came into conflict with the islanders and faced the resistance of a great coalition, she felt the ground she had won in the course of her continental past give way beneath her, and at the same time, her traditional reason of state failed. At this point she added to her primary trait of character—the habit of force: a secondary trait—her own characteristic illusion in the employment of force. The merging of these two characteristics resulted in that demoniac character to which, as we have noted, the hegemonic power regularly falls victim. It is not as if the intensity of the struggle did not loose powerful demoniacal forces among other powers as well, varying according to their different traditions and situations. But in them, demoniacal character should be seen as a reaction to that of the hegemonic power. In any case, it lacked the two characteristic causes for maximum intensification which we have mentioned. This is evident in the case of the islanders. Their reason of state gave them a strong foundation in wars over hegemony, and their strength, carefully employed in conformity with their wise traditions, grew with the duration of the conflict. Their adversary across the Channel always appeared with the characteristic traits of a newcomer. She did not inherit the experience of forbears and did not pass on her own to succeeding generations. In spite of well-planned military preparations, her gigantic strength was sapped by hasty improvisations, and she was unable to lay down political plans. She aspired to make her achievement permanent by all-encompassing final victory. But when that opportunity slipped away she saw her work ruined, still incomplete. Thus, amidst the variations of the centuries, one identical pattern of events was repeated, though with growing distinctness: at the onset of the struggle, the hegemonic power reaches the culmination of her previous history and, by initial successes, gives triumphant expression to her nature in the most magnificent and clear-cut fashion. But the more the struggle becomes one of endless attrition, the more euphoristic intensification is transformed into demoniac over-intensification. Finally, the rulers, like gamblers unsure of the game they are playing, risk fundamental material and moral values. Until the last moment their hopes flare up, only to lure them on to ultimate disaster.

This typical course of events, characteristically exaggerated and altered by the hegemonic people of the moment in its own fashion, characterized German developments, too, during the First World War. In this case, the difference was that the central powers

essentially unready, threatened and threatening on all sides, played
out its role to the end, much more swiftly and destructively than
had been done before, upon the terrain of a continent shrinking
and already sinking, and in the midst of the explosive atmosphere
of an advanced civilization. She raced across every height and
through every depth in the course not of decades, but of years.
In the conflict with a world of enemies filled with hatred and
slander we experienced an intensification of our character which in
1914 brought us a feeling of bliss. But in this sudden spiritual isolation brought about by our political isolation, there was already
present the seed of over-intensification of our character. This
development, foreseen only by a clear-headed few, was rapidly
brought closer by the foolhardy passions of the many. Over-intensification shattered the psychic balance of the nation. Hemmed in
by hatred, it responded with hatred. Then for the first time came
the spread of extremist and monomaniac ideas which, under the
conditions of a quieter development, would probably only have
been able to maintain themselves on the fringes of society.

The most clear-sighted, consulting the oracle of our domestic
reason of state, endeavoured with great vigour to break out of this
vicious circle. But the obscure replies of the oracle could only
increase the confusion. The Seven Years War* had not been a
hegemonic war. The strategy of attrition on land lost meaning
when our adversary, by his attrition policy on the sea, began to
win the upper hand. Despite a noble moderation, those who called
for amicable negotiation of a peace settlement were unable to
estimate exactly the capacities of the insular foe. Meanwhile,
sinister ideas made their way among us like the words of Max
Weber,† 'Let them hate, as long as they fear', or the threat by
Otto Hintze,‡ 'At the very worst, we will let ourselves be buried
beneath the ruins of European civilization.'

Such things pointed to the future. On the whole, however,
we may say that the development of the demoniacal character of
German hegemonic aspirations reached only the first stage during
the First World War. It did not as yet wreck the structure of existing society and morality, or of the historic state and its traditions,
although it was already undermining that structure. In any case,

---

* The war of 1756–63 waged by Frederick II of Prussia against a coalition. He
escaped defeat only by perseverance and the unexpected disintegration of the
coalition.
† Max Weber (1864–1920) was a famous German sociologist.
‡ Otto Hintze (1861–1940) was a Prussian historian.

the forces of civilization were eroding the foundations of the structure. These demoniacal forces were still loyal, unrevolutionary; to that degree, they called to mind the struggle of the Spanish and French monarchs, rather than those of the French Revolution and Napoleon.

That changed completely in the first years of peace, when the demoniac character of German hegemonic aspirations became more evident. How could such an unanticipated development occur? In our discussion of this problem we will consider both what happened to Germany and what happened in Germany.

The termination of earlier hegemonic wars established peace for generations. This had still been successfully achieved in 1815 when a peace was made which at one and the same time imposed its terms on the vanquished and won them by reconciliation. But how could the victor of 1919 actually establish such an enduring peace according to the old prescriptions? The very foundation of the old system of peace treaties, the European system, was gravely damaged. On the one hand, Russia was not only forced out of it but was also transformed into a graver danger than ever for the West. On the other hand, America was drawn in, after Europe for the first time had proved unable by its own efforts to bring the hegemonic threat under control. How was it possible, in so confused a situation, to create something durable? It was probably possible only in the Western area. Even then it could never be achieved without America, the militarily decisive power in the West. Likewise, it required a new creative idea, which Wilson brought over. What he proposed was not renewal of the European system with its hegemonic wars, not establishment of a world system with corresponding dangers, but rather total abolition of foreign policy in the old sense as such, that is, total abolition of a plurality of sovereign states, each ready to wage war. Hence, he proposed peaceful unification of the peoples into a global commonwealth under Anglo-Saxon leadership. What a marvellous change in the world he heralded! Or was it destined to remain in the realm of wonderful fantasies? Until then the insular system, represented by England, had traditionally opposed the newly-risen power on the Continent. The insular system was now represented by America, a new power, which held ideas which appeared to most European statesmen at the time to be arrogantly simple minded, but which seemed like an evangel to the masses. To the Germans these ideas stood for release from the narrow limitations of their situation, to be brought about by the peaceful disarmament of the old system, with its stranglehold. It therefore appeared to be a miraculous solution of the German problem.

But the danger to the shattered psychic balance of our nation was all the greater, for the miracle remained a dream. On the heels of the catastrophe of war came the disaster of peace. Old Europe thereby won out over the newcomer, America. The outworn European system was put into operation again. The wave on which men rode did not carry them forward, but backwards. This was one of the most important explanations of the evils to come. Within the narrow framework of the old system, the great German problem could be solved neither by firmness nor by mildness. For where were powers to be found on our continent which offered a natural counterweight to the vanquished hegemonic power, such as had been found at the great peace settlements? Instead, in order to shackle Germany artificially, there were imposed conditions of all the greater severity, placing traditional terms of peace in the shade. But a rapid change ensued in the political and psychological situation. The front of the Western victors quickly fell to pieces. World public opinion shamefacedly turned its back on those hard conditions which it had just demanded. It began to condemn France, which found herself in isolation. Having been cheated out of the Anglo-Saxon guaranty by the withdrawal of America, France sought to employ instead the measures of violence provided in the treaty. France feared German *revanche* as instinctively as Bismarck had feared French *revanche* after 1871.

As for the peace treaty, it was a mass of contradictions put together out of idealistic principles and realistic paragraphs. It did not conciliate the defeated nations by the opportunities it opened, or at least did not close, to them. Nor was it effectively imposed upon them by united action of the victors to enforce it. If Germany retained any defensive will whatsoever, how could such a treaty have any but a provocative effect? The very least that the victors were necessarily doing, in going back to the outdated European system, was to call up the danger that the conquered nation would return to the outdated spirit of struggle for hegemony.

Admittedly, whether Germany did so now depended upon the way in which all external influences combined with the entire inner life of our nation. If we recall to our imaginations the situation of the older hegemonic powers, in discouragement after their defeats, we shall find that they remained relatively tranquil for a long time, partly as a result of exhaustion after decades of war, partly as a result of utilization and further development of the considerable opportunities still available to them. It is true that resentment and dreams of revenge remained. But in a society which goes on with its life after defeat, there are no energies for a serious resumption of the great struggle, and there is no compelling necessity to make leaps into the dark. But this was not true of Germany after 1918. In her case the delusion inherent in the demoniac aspirations for hegemony and her sense of strength both retained their effectiveness! Resentment and dreams of revenge, therefore, found ample nourishment in Germany. But to them was added the essential stimulus—misery, and the resulting progressive dissolution of inherited social conditions.

As had happened after 1815 in France, self-deception prevented any sober recognition of the true causes for collapse. Despite much frothy criticism of details, no one made a critical analysis of what were on the whole our limited possibilities in the realm of power politics. This was as true during the post-war years as during the war itself, or during the preceding period of encirclement. We did not wish to lose our illusions, to let the great memory of the high, heroic point of our history grow dim, to be robbed of our hopes for re-establishing our position. People felt that the catastrophe could not have happened by normal processes. The defeat was blamed on the blandishments and deceit of our foes and on errors and betrayal in our own camp. Neither then or before was there any evaluation before public opinion of the illuminating parallelism with earlier hegemonic wars. There was no evaluation of the role of sea power and the characteristic resources of the islanders. And in general there was no understanding of what the entry of America meant. But this was not surprising. Before long the Americans themselves had come to look upon their entry into the war only as something beyond the normal range of their activities which had been prompted by the hunt for profits. Only a few recognized that an authentic reason of state stood sponsor to this development, that is, the American interest to shatter the hegemonic unification of Europe as a possible threat to overseas areas as well. And so, paradoxically, whenever we thought back to the war, the chief result was that we became more, not less, self-confident. We became increasingly aware of the might of our nation, which, almost as much to our own surprise as to the world's, had been kept intact. Under clear-headed leadership, what could not have been achieved? We puzzled over the defeat in order to prove to ourselves that it need not have happened, not that it had very good reasons for happening. We wanted to prove that it came about because of avoidable errors rather than as the result of exaggeration of our general conception.

Meanwhile, the post-war years proved that, in spite of all that had happened, our national strength still greatly exceeded that of the other nations of old Europe. When we looked into the past, we could not help discovering that French power had been far more gravely damaged at the beginning of the nineteenth century, or Spanish might at the beginning of the seventeenth, than ours had been at the beginning of the twentieth century. Even though this meant that, despite the magnitude of our disaster, we still had opportunities for action, yet the rapidity with which we got back on our feet, ready for a new hegemonic struggle, cannot be understood except in terms of the stimulus of economic misery.

Of course, as a result of the profound exhaustion inevitable in the beginning, the intense combativity of the masses slackened. But it continued in illegal small groups. They employed it for purposes of infiltration and counter-attack. These groups found reserves of strength in our people, with its tradition of soldiery, who did not forget the heroic tragedy of the war. This had happened earlier in France after 1815. On both occasions the disillusioned heroism of the uprooted and the 'outlawed' was transformed into turbulent hatred, not only of foreign enemies but also of domestic foes. For if it has been said that France after 1815 was visibly split into two nations under two flags, the victors and the vanquished of Waterloo, something of the kind can be maintained about Germany, too, after 1919. The difference was that in our case, national activism, in keeping with the different rhythm of our history, took on the characteristics of the French Restoration and not of the French Revolution. But this caused it no embarrassment in adopting revolutionary methods, or in general any methods whatsoever. Idealism and criminality were joined together, and the nihilists who grasped at power prepared to destroy without compunction the ethical system of the West.

None the less, this pattern of ideas was carried to its final logical consequences only among small groups of stormtroopers. But in view of the chaotic changeability of the masses, to what extent could small groups of fanatics achieve their aims? The pendulum of public opinion began its mighty return swing. The origins of the German Republic were quite different from those of the French Third Republic and the young Russian Republic. It arose upon the basis of the momentary exhaustion of all energies, not from the flowing in of new ones; by yielding to foreign attack and not by resisting it. This gave her a family resemblance to the Bourbon Restoration of 1815, for it too lacked the nimbus of modern nationalism. Yet where the restored Bourbon régime could at least to some degree hearken back to a great past history, the German Republic could not at all. And while the rule of the restored Bourbons was backed by thoughtful moderation on the part of the victors, the rule of the German Republic was burdened by the cruelties of Versailles, which put the blemish of her birth into bold relief. Soon a third factor of great danger—social dissolution as the result of many-sided economic misery—was added to the two factors already cited. The loss of social class status was linked to the loss of national status. National activism, competing with communism, profited by the influx of the desperate. It speculated on the collapse of the entire Western order established in 1919. The strongly appealing tradition of power which came down from Prussia-Germany, but out of the context of its sociological nurturing soil, was taken over by national activism. It adopted as well the new fascist dynamism, with its rough-hewn revolutionary violence. This dynamism was reinforced by a torrid stream of popular passions from the folk *irredenta* beyond the borders; this could never have happened under the authoritarian Prussian-German state.

If heavy industry and the large landed estates had been split up into smaller units, would the final disaster have perhaps been averted, as present-day critics of the Germany of that time so often believe? In any case, there would have been a corresponding increase in the number of the *déclassés*, while economic conditions would have become even more confused. Compared with propertylessness, which makes men feel that they can only gain, that they have nothing to lose, ownership of property still works chiefly as a sedative. Furthermore, the nationalist spirit had long since ceased to be a privilege of property. Nationalism can inflame a disorganized society more dangerously than a firmly organized one; it is likely to bring the middle and lower strata into its grasp at the very time when it is already losing its grip on the upper stratum. The abolition of monarchy, which reduced the size of the middle group, had been an earlier two-edged measure. The advent of the new Caesarism in Italy, which, oscillating between restoration and revolution, sought to fill the vacuum with a new authority, whipped up spirits among us even more. But the hour of the new Caesarism had not yet rung in Germany. Still our activists could console themselves with the thought that in the long run there were greater opportunities for their activity in Germany than in any other nation. Everyone in Germany, particularly the former soldiers, inevitably longed to see wiped away the catastrophe, which was of a magnitude such as only our hegemonic people, and no other, had experienced.

Admittedly, revenge could no longer be sought upon the sea. But the catastrophe itself had left open promising prospects near at hand upon the mainland, due to the balkanization of the neighbouring countries, the isolation of France and most of all the bolshevization of enigmatic Russia. Russia could be of service to German rehabilitation as a friend (Seeckt, Brockdorff-Rantzau), or as a foe (Ludendorff).

This programme of recovery was upheld almost without distinction of party: together with the restoration of the Eastern frontiers to a healthy state, the incorporation (*Anschluss*) of Austria; not merely re-establishment of what had been before, but *grossdeutsch* continental expansion instead of *kleindeutsch* maritime expansion, which had failed; complete unification of the nation, such as had been dreamed of in 1813 and 1848, when Germany was young; a powerful increase in strength as an answer to a mortal threat; the striving for an order of greatness such as no other people in Europe could achieve, least of all senile France; therefore, the achievement of a firm continental basis such as William II should have assured himself in one way or another before undertaking a world policy, according to the judgment of critics of the time.

But how was this irredentist programme to be realized? With England's help against France? With the help of the East against the West? Or by playing East and West against each other? It could scarcely be achieved except by complete destruction of the 1919 system.

The most numerous and vital people in Europe could be

shackled only for a time within the narrow framework of the moribund system. They could not be permanently satisfied within it.

Despite all, the rays of the Locarno sun were still to shine upon Europe! But Europe was indebted less to her own insight and strength than to the return of America. The coming and going of the United States already exerted the most powerful influence upon the ebb and flow of European events. These years of happy interlude seemed indeed to stand as if in refutation of the years after America had quit Europe in 1919. Then there had been a half-decade of disorganization; now there was the most promising basis for organization, even though the return of the United States was more economic than political in character. American loans constituted the golden foundation which explains Stresemann's successes. But their effect was strictly limited. The demonic forces in Germany retreated only a short way. They gave no thanks to the liberator of the Rhineland. He likewise was careful not to make a choice in favour of the irredentist programme. What he sought was rather to have freedom of movement between East and West. The fine plans for a European union all remained in the land of dreams. The peoples of Europe had been educated by their modern system, which was restored in 1919, in mistrust and violence toward each other. It seemed that they knew how to establish their own solidarity only in a single case. That was when they united to resist the hegemonic exertions of a member of their own circle.

And soon this came to pass. For the French it was frightening confirmation of their forecasts, but was not expected by most of the Anglo-Saxons. In the very days of Locarno, T. E. Lawrence, an observer who knew the world so well, ventured the prediction that it was now probably Russia's turn, after Spain, France and Germany, to attempt to 'dominate' the world from its base on the Continent. He could not foresee that Germany would develop the strength and the will to advance again to the centre of the world stage, playing its old role of a European hegemonic power, before Russia undertook to play the new role of a world hegemonic power upon the same stage.

Characteristically, the great turn of events in Germany was brought to an end by a new turn of events in America. During the world economic crisis, America withdrew for the second time across the ocean, and thereby left the entire Western world in the grip of deeper disorganization than the first time. This was the signal which started Germany on her impatient drive for revenge. In the midst of the confusion Germany saw the road open before her, as if an earthquake had smoothed away all hindrances. The first German war for hegemony arose out of a period of great prosperity. The second arose out of a period of misery and fear. The first war was only a confused initial encounter, the second was a well-directed counter-attack from the deep rear. The arcanum of the fascist stormtroopers—like that of the communists—was a stupendous gamble upon the break-up of the Western bourgeois world. This gamble now stood the test in international as well as national politics. In international politics those charged with standing watch over Germany, big and small powers of the blighted system, turned out to be cowardly or light-hearted, perplexed or short-sighted. France, eager for peace, seemed to be crippled in the face of the genuine danger which had long filled her imagination, but which by her earlier policy of violence she had brought on more quickly. At the same time she was hindered by her fatal experiment in the Ruhr and by the attitude of her English friend. Should she make use of the weapon in her hands to exorcize the evil by the forceful methods provided in the oft-criticized treaty? Measures of interference with nations in agitation are incalculable in their results. Would a healthy situation really have been created by Churchill's proposal that the unilateral disarmament of Germany be maintained as a measure of precaution? Even to raise the question is to indicate a doubt that an affirmative answer can be made.

On the national field, the gamble on a turn for the worse really came into action for the first time. Ten years before, the phenomenon of social dissolution had already begun to strengthen activism. Now it drove millions from all strata of society into its arms. If the international guarantees and alliances of the democratic world failed, only the return to the old, tried methods of national success could bring salvation: a policy of authority within the country and of power in foreign relations. The miracle of the transformation of fear into confidence, of social antagonism into social harmony, took place under this magical sign. The question as to which form this rehabilitation would take, Caesarism or legitimism, still hung fire, however. Outside of Germany, Caesarism had long since been put to the test as a type of government; it represented a third force in the midst of the crisis which permitted one last concentration of the nation in the face of impatient communism and the confused bourgeoisie. It must now be clearly noted that, just as before 1914, Germany, on engaging in the typically imperialist movement, added to it her own characteristic traits and transformed it into a movement for hegemony, so the Caesarist movement was similarly transformed with deliberate consistency. The dictator of Germany, whom the imperialists had already yearned for as a charismatic leader, rose to incomparably larger stature than men in like position in the other lands of old Europe, though not in Russia. He employed methods of uniquely frightful intensity, even though they may have been originated elsewhere in the West. The 'movement' organized by hegemonic demonism conquered all commanding heights. But it was not sobered by the 'seizure of power', as so many of those who extolled it had expected. On the contrary, it made demonism still more intense, and forced it violently through the entire bloodstream of the feverish nation. The demonism was concentrated in Hitler, and he was the first really to make it wide spread. He was the bodily daemon of the extreme hegemonic struggle, such a demoniac figure as, by human standards indeed was to make possible the final flaring up of that struggle. It is still beyond our belief that Germany, lacking such a satanic genius, could have once more lifted herself to such dizzying heights. Hitler felt himself carried along by the dark and mysterious wave of the crisis, by the expanding forces of civilization which threatened to blast apart the antiquated world of small states. At all times, too, he was inflamed by the world-wide aspirations of the admired rival, Bolshevism. Relying, Jacobin-like, on his totalitarian power within the country, he thought that nothing was beyond his doing outside of Germany either. Like a somnam-bulist, he climbed paths that no one else could discover, between the precipices. He used the controversy between East and West to cover his tracks, till he disclosed himself to both East and West as a third force endangering them, and thus united them against himself. The same abyss then opened up beneath him which had engulfed the French Emperor and the German Kaiser. The events of earlier hegemonic wars were repeated, at a higher level. Triumphs on the old continent were followed, as before, by collapse when Germany was confronted by moral and material resources of the islanders which she did not understand. This time these resources were able to sustain the Russian sword in battle, as ideological conflicts were put aside in the struggle for existence. Thus the demoniacal character of European hegemonic struggle made its final demands for sacrifice in 1945. Germany suffered a catastrophe which was as total and frightful as its expansion and employment of power had been to the last moment. For the nihilist daemon, anticipating disaster, continued until the end to hurl all whom he could into the abyss.

We have made a rapid survey of what happened, but must not permit ourselves to be satisfied. We must go on to the end of the train of ideas laid down in our introductory remarks, and expound them to the full.

We saw how Germany, by its vitality, was driven beyond the typical, first in the period of imperialism and then in the period of Caesarism, and both times met her characteristic fate as a hegemonic power. We perceived in the course of our analysis how the role which she played, apparently unique with her when examined in terms of the present, turned out to have typical characteristics when looked at in terms of the past. Now we must discuss what special significance there was in the two links of Germany's hegemonic wars in the continuous chain of European hegemonic wars. The answer may be stated in a sentence: The German struggle is the last of the series. We think it will not be renewed upon the basis of the territory of old Europe. For those who accept this prediction, the special significance of the world wars stands out with compelling logic and utterly precise meaning, even when they are examined more broadly in terms of the recent history of Europe. Even though they surely are individual variants of the previous wars, it is impossible simply to classify them as such and no more. But they also worked as the catalyst of a new alignment of forces in the world. Though this situation has been in the making since the eighteenth century, it is new for all that. Indeed the rivalry between the Russians and the Anglo-Saxons in the struggle for world hegemony could only become reality in 1945, after the final struggle for European hegemony had been decided. The hegemonic unification of Europe threatened the world powers themselves, and compelled them to place their antagonism in the background in order together to overcome Germany. Japan, for similar reasons, had to be defeated too. Once this had been done, the modern history of Europe came to a close in the form which it had possessed till then. The old continent ceased to be the central point where global history was decided. The road was open for a new world history.

The significance of the German hegemonic struggle may be expressed in this way: It developed both material and spiritual forces of destruction to a higher degree than any of its predecessors. These forces were not merely applied, as they always had been, against the hegemonic power itself in the final stage of the struggle, against the aggressor on the verge of defeat. These forces reached to every part of the world, to an extent which had never before been attained. They destroyed, as never before, the lives and work of men, thanks to the technological power of our civilization. At the same time they spilled a corrosive poison into the soul of Western man, thanks to the terror and propaganda which our civilization made reach everywhere. Thus these forces so weakened and divided the forces of the old continent that at last the world powers overshadowed them. The European system, like the hegemonic power which had risen up against it, thereupon split in two. The overthrow of Germany did, in fact, liberate mankind in western Europe from the totalitarian danger. But, for the first time, mankind in eastern Europe was really exposed to peril. This, too, was a result, in the final analysis, of the German striving for power, whatever the specific process was by which it happened. It destroyed that result of the First World War with which Max Weber had tried to console himself in 1918, when he remarked that whatever happened it would be Germany's glory to have shielded Europe from the Russian knout. That glory, too, was expunged by the events of 1939. Finally, the last war accelerated the downfall of the tottering position of the West as masters over the coloured peoples, with all its incalculable consequences.

But let us go on. Great wars in the past had all been fruitful as well as frightful. They took place in a period of vital civilization. The hegemonic powers in them took on positive spiritual missions, sometimes as champions of the Counter-Reformation, sometimes as exemplars of aristocratic life, sometimes as heralds of the achievements of the revolution. The very struggle against them aroused new spiritual life. But if we examine the German struggle in its last phase, was there any aspect of it which brought reconciliation? Engaged in a desperate protest against the course of events in the outside world we did not understand, we did not develop a mission which won other peoples to our side. Our ideology of national Caesarism was not for export. It lost its appeal as it became apparent that in its name the freedom of

other nations was being imperilled, as it began increasingly to
employ Bolshevist methods. The final step in this process came
in 1939 when it reached an agreement with Bolshevism. By that
act it committed suicide.

But during the First World War, too, were we not without an
idea that could have won other peoples to our side? Say what you
will, the expansion of the Prussian system had resulted in driving
a wider cleavage between might and spirit in the rejuvenated
German nation than existed in other peoples. Thus our imperialists fell into perplexity as to how to build a spiritual propping
for the expansion of German power. They tried to find help in
the period of our spiritual flowering, when the life of the individual was glorified. To protect the nations in the many-sided
individuality of their own existences against the uniformity of
Anglo-Saxon society and Russian bureaucracy, was declared to
be our proper mission. But during the First World War we
visibly began to move along the Napoleonic path. The peoples,
of course, thereupon automatically ceased to believe that we had
such a mission. Justifying hegemonic expansion by means of
these ideals, which developed out of the struggle against
Napoleon, gave rise to an inner contradiction.

Germany has in fact twice given birth to ideas which spread
elsewhere: the Reformation, and Marxism. But they did not bring
advantage to German politics.

In summary, this war, so much greater in its destructive force
than previous wars, lacked the beneficial compensations which
were present in them. That is how it seems to us today. But what
will be the judgment of later generations? Probably they will
have to see a compensation in the rebirth of the Western spirit
and in a new organization of the political life throughout the
West. Will our people play its part in such a creative response to
the peril of further destruction? Many Germans will not fail to
have such a hope. But even if others have different hopes for the
future, the prerequisite, in the period of world wars, for *any*
creative response in Germany is ruthless recognition of the frightful role which we have played, as the last and therefore the most
demoniacal hegemonic power of old Europe in decline.

CHAPTER SEVEN

RANKE AND BURCKHARDT

by Friedrich Meinecke

Friedrich Meinecke is not only the Dean of German historians, he was also the first German historian to draw courageous conclusions from the German catastrophe of 1945. In his book, *Die Deutsche Katastrophe* (1946), he pointed out that modern German history presented a deviation from the general Western trend, a deviation which he regarded as a wrong road travelled by his nation. He suggested that Germany should abandon its fateful aspiration of becoming the leading power again and should turn to the peaceful arts which had distinguished her in the more creative and beneficial period of her history, the period of Goethe.

Meinecke was born in 1862. He occupied the chair of history at the University of Strasbourg from 1901 to 1906, in Freiburg from 1906 to 1914 and at the University of Berlin from 1914 to 1928. For more than forty years (1893–1935) he was editor of the representative German historical periodical, *Historische Zeitschrift*. In commemoration of Meinecke's ninetieth birthday the October 1952 issue of the review was dedicated to him and contained a complete bibliography of his works.

Meinecke contributed decisively to the development of the history of ideas in Germany. The most prominent of his many books are: *Das Zeitalter der Deutschen Erhebung* (1906); *Weltbürgertum und Nationalstaat* (1908); *Die Idee der Staatsräson in der neueren Geschichte* (1924) and *Die Entstehung des Historismus* (1936).

The following article by Meinecke is an address delivered by him before the German Academy of Sciences in Berlin in 1948. It represents his last substantial scholarly utterance. It was published by the Deutsche Akademie der Wissenschaften zu Berlin, Vorträge und Schriften, Heft 27, Akademie-Verlag Berlin, 1948. In it Meinecke contrasts the two greatest German historians of the nineteenth century: Leopold Ranke (1795–1886), who joined the University of Berlin in 1825, received the chair of history there in 1834, and became the admired father of modern German, and especially Prussian, historiography; and Jakob Burckhardt (1818–97), who taught at his native University of Basel from 1858 to 1893. After the retirement of Ranke, he was offered the chair of history in Berlin. Although Berlin was then the ranking university of Germany, he preferred to stay in the relatively provincial circumstances of Basel.

Neither Ranke nor Burckhardt has shown a true understanding of the moral and historical resources of Western modern democracy, nor does Meinecke stress their shortcomings in that respect. Instead, he gives a well-balanced picture of these two leading German historians, whose influence he himself experienced. Having almost reached the patriarchal age of Ranke, he looks back with serenity upon these two trends of German historiography, of which the one celebrated the power-state while the other emphasized the forces of civilization. It is characteristic of the present situation that the formerly entirely dominant influence of Ranke is being questioned more and more, and that growing attention is paid to the individualism and pessimism of Burckhardt.

Ranke and Burckhardt are the two greatest historical thinkers produced by the German culture-nation in the nineteenth century. Someone, some day, should do a book on Berlin and Basel— their cities—in the age of the foundation of the Bismarckian Reich. It should indicate how the scholars of these two cities, having brought their achievements to a point of culmination, came into mutual conflict. We should see the development of Berlin and Basel from their historical backgrounds, Prussia-Germany in one case, Switzerland in the other. Yet we should see that both were concerned with the intellectual life of Germany as a whole. One extolled the enhancement of German national power, the other criticized, mistrusted and felt anxiety at that very enhancement. Droysen,* Treitschke† and Dilthey‡ joined their voices with Ranke's, the young Nietzsche,§ Overbeck‖ and Bachofen¶ joined theirs with Burckhardt's. A book such as this might become a symbol of our spiritual fate.

I shall not attempt to depict even approximately these two worlds, or the wider worlds about them, in their varied hues.

---

* Johann Gustav Droysen (1808–84), German historian, professor of history at the University of Berlin (1849–84).

† Heinrich von Treitschke (1834–96), German historian, professor of history at the University of Berlin (1866–67, 1874–86), historiographer of the Prussian state (1886–96).

‡ Wilhelm Dilthey (1883–1911), German historian of culture and philosopher, professor at the University of Berlin (1882–1911).

§ Friedrich Nietzsche (1844–1900), German philosopher, professor of classical philosophy at Basel (1869–79).

‖ Franz Overbeck (1837–1905), German theologian, professor of Protestant theology and church history at Basel (1870–1905), friend of Nietzsche.

¶ Johann Jakob Bachofen (1815–87), Swiss jurist and historian, professor at Basel (1841–43), continued scholarly research there.

All I can offer is a pencil sketch, directing attention just to the essential and substantial elements in the thought and personalities of these two great men. I shall not exhaust my subject.

Since my student days, Ranke has been my guiding star, my pole star. Only later for me did Burckhardt begin to shed his luminescence. First of course was his *Kultur der Renaissance in Italien* (1860) (English translation, *The Civilization of the Renaissance in Italy*, 1878), then the posthumous publications, those long and stupendous works such as the *Griechische Kulturgeschichte* (1898–1902) (History of Greek Culture), the *Weltgeschichtliche Betrachtungen* (1905) (English translation, *Reflections on History*, 1943), and the *Historische Fragmente* (Historical Fragments), which were what remained of the texts of his lectures at the University of Basel. The *Historische Fragmente* first appeared in 1929, in the large complete edition of his writings. In them Burckhardt's own historical ideas are expressed even more sharply than in the *Weltgeschichtliche Betrachtungen*. Finally, his precious letters, especially those he wrote to Preen* in his old age, are not to be forgotten either. In Ranke's case, too, his letters, in so far as we know them, permit us to recognize much more directly and clearly than his works the innermost heart tones of his history. From Ranke's work of youthful genius, his introductory statement on the unity of the Latin and German peoples,† to his *Weltgeschichte* (1881–88) (English translation, *Universal History*, 1884), with its wisdom of old age, his work as a whole, in its coherence and fullness, exerted a stronger influence on historical and indeed historical-political thinking and research in Germany than did Burckhardt's historical works. This difference continued into the very period of the Third Reich. To be sure, Burckhardt's writings, beginning with *Die Zeit Konstantins des Grossen* (1853) (English Translation, *The Age of Constantine the Great*, 1949), viewed as the lonely and unique achievement of a rare genius, did win admiration and had some profound influence as well. But they failed to establish a body of inwardly coherent influence such as that obtained by Ranke.

But today we are beginning to ask whether, in the end, Burckhardt will not have greater importance than Ranke for us as well as for later historians.

---

* Friedrich von Preen (1823–94), German government official and close friend of Burckhardt.

† *Geschichte der romanischen und germanischen Völker von 1494–1514* (1824); Eng. trans., *History of the Latin and Teutonic Nations, 1494 to 1514*, 1887.

You divine the significance of this question. In the historian's mind, historical observation and the experience of living in his own time and sharing in its destiny form an indivisible inner unity. It simultaneously makes his picture of history richer and more limited. It promotes and it hinders the formation of his picture of history. The things we have lived through in the past fourteen years thrust before us quite novel aspects and problems in our own historical past. There is much we must relearn. Yet in such relearning we must avoid falling victim to what is merely happening now and to the emotional impressions of what we have just lived through. But cautious as we may be, still we must say that Burckhardt saw more deeply and acutely into the essential historical character of his own time. As a result, he was able to see the future, too, more definitely and certainly than Ranke could. But does it follow that we likewise have to revise to Burckhardt's advantage our judgment on the picture which each formed of the history of the preceding millenium of Western development? Our reply to this question brings us to a remarkable conclusion. But first I must state the factors comprising Burckhardt's greater excellence in the judgment of the present and the future.

In his lectures to King Maximilian II of Bavaria in 1854, Ranke confessed his feelings, saying, 'It is a happy thing to live in these times.' To be sure, he grew to manhood in the quieter age of the Restoration. Its 'halcyon' atmosphere left deep traces in his nature. But he was far from being a political reactionary seeking to go back to that age. In fully positive fashion he also saw 'a great vital element' in the more powerful movement of all historical forces which was resumed toward the middle of the century. To him the most important thing in that movement seemed the conflict between the two principles of monarchy and popular sovereignty. Though his heart beat for the old monarchy, he was led by his historical insight to what we may call historic dialectic. This was the process by which antagonistic elements may make each other productive and stronger, maintaining each other's vitality and leading to new syntheses. He taught that the old monarchy, in order to meet the needs of the times, should therefore take from the enemy what it could amalgamate with its own nature. It should only combat with determination all the destructive forces latent within the world of revolutionary ideas. He placed 'the continual development of material forces' only in the second rank among the major tendencies of his time.

Then came the age of Bismarck. The Prussian-German federal state was established by the might of the old monarchy. Ranke, with his conservative sensibilities, could keep pace only haltingly with Bismarck's methods of violence and force. But in the end the results achieved by these methods gave him profound satisfaction. In the twilight of his life, on his ninetieth birthday in 1885, Ranke said, 'In the events we have experienced, we may see principally a defeat of the revolutionary forces which make impossible regular continued development of world history. If these forces had stood their ground, there would have been no question of continued creation of historical forces, or even of an unpartisan examination of them. World history in the objective sense would have become impossible. In my littleness, I would not have thought of writing a world history had not the general problem of the two great world forces been decided for me after long struggles and changes, so that it is possible to look back over the earlier centuries in an unpartisan way.'

This is a remarkable admission. Probably only today can we see the weak point it reveals in Ranke's attitude. Is it really true that when the principle of popular sovereignty achieves complete victory—and this happened during both world wars—the continued creation of historical forces, or even an unpartisan examination of those forces, ceases to be possible? Of course, something may be said in Ranke's defence. It is true that he probably had in mind the extreme danger of generalized revolutionary chaos. But the fact remains that he established far too intimate a connexion between the triumph of the old monarchical principle in Germany, which he lived through, and the possibility of writing history from an unpartisan position. Does this not mean just that one is going back to a partisan position in favour of one of the two embattled forces of the century? Certainly any historian in whom there is life will preserve in his heart his own political ideal. His view of history will always bear some tincture of this ideal. But he must also be ready to hold himself above the downfall of his own ideal and to observe with all the power of his mind the changed and darkened world. He must remain poised high over the world as free as can be of partisan outlook.

However, at this point, in a way very characteristic of him, Ranke establishes his own conception of a 'regular continued

development of world history'. In his opinion a victory of the
revolutionary forces would make such development impossible.
But who can give assurance that world history does not sometimes become irregular, that it will not move by leaps and lurches?
We have lived through that history. To an extent which Ranke
neither knew nor anticipated, we have lived the sunless side of
world history. But even during the night, world history remains
world history. It should be understood as such, to the full powers
of our feeble organs of knowledge.

It should not be said in rebuttal that there may no longer be any
objective possibility of writing world history. The true historian,
as long as there is breath in him, will never cease to strive after
inner freedom and at least to think in terms of world history.

In view of all our misgivings about Ranke's honourable confession of faith in his venerable old age, today we are in spirit
closer to Burckhardt than to Ranke. By Burckhardt's own admission, from the time of his youth, his deep-rooted pessimism
kept reminding him of the perishability of all earthly things. This
pessimism prevented him from forming any such ideal image of
regular continued development of world history as that which
Ranke carried with hope and belief in his heart. Indeed the very
pattern of events that seemed irregular to Ranke became for
Burckhardt the gloomy rule controlling the fate of the West in
the nineteenth and twentieth centuries. For Burckhardt saw the
West moving with inescapable necessity into a frightful time of
barbarism. In this respect, however, his inner, his innermost
political desires were entirely in accord with Ranke's. He desired
the preservation of the old conservative world with its authorities,
against the assault of the mass movements threatening it since the
French Revolution. In fact, he rejected the French Revolution
more radically and hated it more profoundly than Ranke. After
all, Ranke saw in the struggle between the two hostile principles
of monarchy and popular sovereignty a positive element of life.
He held the synthesis of the old monarchy with certain specific
demands of the mass movement to be possible. Indeed he
thought it had already been achieved and that it was viable.
Burckhardt would have smiled at that synthesis, thinking,
'*Principiis obsta*' (Resist the very beginnings). It is, in fact, quite
characteristic that, in our present democratic era, this morose
enemy of modern democracy again draws nearer to us than
Ranke. On the other hand, much may be said here in criticism of

Burckhardt and in favour of a healthy and viable democracy. But we may be assured that Burckhardt felt the pulse of his own time more strongly than Ranke, with his safety and security in Prussia-Germany.

Next we must consider Burckhardt's judgment of Bismarck's handiwork. Whereas Ranke, in view of the final conservative result apparently attained by Bismarck's revolutionary methods of violence, later assuaged his dislike of such methods, Burckhardt subjected the basic revolutionary character of Bismarck's handiwork to the light of much sharper scrutiny. For Burckhardt, it was from its inception a revolution from above. He saw it as just the most successful rival of the other revolutions then threatening. 'Bismarck has merely taken into his own hands to do what would have happened in any case in time, but without him and against him,' he wrote in 1872. 'He saw that the rising wave of democratic and social forces would produce, in one way or another, an endless situation of violence. Either the democrats themselves, or the governments would bring this to pass. He said, "*Ipse faciam*", (I myself will do it) and waged the three wars of 1864, 1866 and 1871.' In Burckhardt's opinion, Bismarck had to continue to live according to that law by which he had come up. Thus, speaking somewhere of the *Kulturkampf*, Burckhardt said that it would have 'the effect of encouraging negative and destructive forces of every kind'. New revolutionary institutions stand in a special danger. Having themselves violated law and overthrown old institutions they may themselves face such illegal methods and overthrow. In this regard, he remarked, 'One does not become more secure by driving out one's peers and inheriting their lands.' His profound antipathy for Bismarck did not prevent him from lauding Bismarck, after his downfall in 1890, for having been 'the support and the banner in Germany of that mystery which is authority'. He did not feel that it was in any way an authority in the good old sense, but only a substitute. A substitute authority was better than none at all.

Thus we draw the logical consequences from a series of judgments scattered through Burckhardt's letters. He never did combine them into a coherent general critique of Bismarck, though such internal coherence exists. By no means is this critique the final word that may be said today on Bismarck's work. But after the collapse of Bismarck's work, it is our difficult and painful task to investigate more precisely the internal cleavages and seeds of danger present in it from the outset. It is our task to pass judgment, justly but sternly, and not to shy from breaking with old conventions. In this task, Burckhardt's critique shows us the way.

Now we come to his judgments on the mass movement itself. Like a sensitive seismograph, he senses the possibilities of gravest harm slumbering within it, the appearance as mass leaders of men of the worst sort. He foresaw that, to the horror of some who had joined it at first, the mass assault upon authority would suddenly be transformed, sooner or later, into formation of a terrible new authority by usurpers of power, by *terribles simplificateurs* [terrible simplifiers]. The usurpers, not the old, utterly vanquished dynasties, would take the helm. Relying upon organized military formations, they would command the masses to shut up, to abandon any strong personal desires, to march forward in uniform, while the drum beat, to the misery of daily existence, and then at nightfall be marched back while the drum beat again. In our own lives, we have more or less experienced that future which Burckhardt painted untiringly during the seventies and the eighties of the last century. Today, with some variations and attenuations, we are still in the grip of that situation and do not know when and how a brighter world will come.

But for Burckhardt did world history come to an end with this? Only too often did it seem so, as if his Cassandra eyes saw only as far as the rise and the unrestrainted activity of the new and terrible authorities, and no farther. But it was his way to force whatever hope survived in him of something higher back into his heart, and to reveal it only with utmost modesty and humility. He would not 'cheerfully' trust, as did Ranke in his article, 'Die Grossen Mächte' (The Great Powers), to the genius of Europe to prevent its succumbing to the rule of that one-sided and violent leadership. 'The argument that the spirit is invincible and will always conquer is trivial', he said. He admitted, to be sure, that Europe, in its great moments, had often possessed great men and saviours, and that mankind was not yet doomed to destruction. It was also possible, he averred, that the desire for change which the prevalent optimism now entitled progress, though it was in itself blind, still had 'as its purpose something enduring, or relatively enduring, which *seeks* to do something stronger and higher in us and with us'. How typical is this difference between Ranke's bright-eyed trust that Europe would have a saviour and

Burckhardt's vision of the future, aware of its own blindness and yet with a quiet hope.

Let us again turn our attention from prognoses and return to the diagnoses of the essential character of the nineteenth century given by both Ranke and Burckhardt. Ranke gave principal stress to the antagonism between monarchy and democracy as its vital element. In the second line he placed the unceasing development of material forces. With respect to these material forces, when he republished, in 1879, his book on Serbia and Turkey, he paid homage, in terms of astounding vigour and unanticipated optimism, to the onward-storming civilizing 'genius of the Occident' which put the world to serving it. Burckhardt did not remain unmoved either by the political antagonism between the old authority and the democratic mass will. However, he viewed the material development of the nineteenth century basically with greater profundity and scepticism. He recognized that mankind in general had been transformed since the French Revolution. It was in truth a change for the worse. Firstly, because of the fundamentally false and deleterious doctrine of the innate goodness of human nature implanted by Rousseau in the minds of men awakened their limitless cravings and their belief in unrestricted progress. But also because of the effect upon economic life of the English prototype, resulting from the introduction of machinery, coal and iron. For Burckhardt, these were most unpleasant, indeed hateful, things. Lust for power, money and self-indulgence had broken forth mightily and would drive men to their destruction. While this happened, however, the state, in responding to the demands of the masses, would grow stronger and stronger so that it could satisfy what they lusted for.

We come then to the problem of power and the power-state in general. To it these two thinkers give fundamentally different answers. Of course Burckhardt does not date the modern power-state just from 1789, when it merely received new sources of strength. He views it with unconcealed antipathy from its origins during the close of the Middle Ages. For power in itself is evil, he maintained. That is Burckhardt's terrifying fundamental sentiment in considering the state as such and its significance for mankind. Like a sombre chord struck over and over, it rings forth in his every judgment on the political history of the peoples. He dilutes the state as such into a merely 'necessary institution', a 'negative mantelet', as he says. If things were as he really wished, it would be limited to protection of law, order and quiet in the land. It is, therefore, the night watchman state.

How different is Ranke! The states, he declared in his *Politisches Gespräch* (Political Talk) of 1836, are individuals, 'spiritual essences', original creations of the human spirit—one should say, 'thoughts of God'. Divine inspiration and human impulsion joined together he calls the spirit of the state. To be sure, he knew that the will-to-power of the state could degenerate; he often recognized this in his historical value judgments. But when we look at his works as a whole, power is transfigured and spiritualized in them. 'In power as such,' he says, 'there appears a spiritual nature, a primal genius having its own life.'

Behind the vast disparities in the judgments of the two men lie whole ideological systems and utterly unlike attitudes toward life. Yet they were both rooted in the same nurturing soil—the philosophy of German idealism and humanism. We see that, for such a divergence between these two men to be possible, completely divergent standards of judgment of the state must have been implicit in German idealist philosophy at the beginning of the nineteenth century. . . .

An immense dynamism of creative forces, with ever new antitheses, syntheses and polarities, surges through Ranke's history; everywhere in it reality is elevated to the heights of the spiritual. Thus he came to exalt power, the power-state and power politics. Thus, they too were given too bright a sheen of spirituality. Of course, we no longer think that they deserve to shine so brightly.

Shall we then join Burckhardt in considering power as evil in itself, as the factor of evil as such in history? This would bring us, if we were to remain consistent, to a conception of history just as moralization, so that at every step we would have to condemn the principle of evil. But Burckhardt was not a consistent, but a living, gifted, richly endowed man with a contradiction. In fact, he was also the direct pupil of Ranke; like Ranke, indeed with more attention to esthetic factors than Ranke, he took joy in the infinite multiplicity and variety of historical creation, as if it were indispensable food for his spirit. As a result, he wove together most wonderfully the esthetic and moral elements in his judgment, making them almost inseparable. For, even when he took pleasure in things, the moral law in him never lost its tongue. Now and then the moral law led him into harsh one-sidedness. This happened, for instance, when he passed judgment upon the

Reformation in Germany. He could speak of almost nothing in it but the egoism of those with a passion for innovation, but did not wish to do justice to the impact of true religious feeling. For him, the evil world remained always evil, but none the less it gave rise on occasion to the highest values he sought in history—culture.

This is a mighty theme to which we come now, yet we can only treat it in brief and simplified form. But it would be over-simplification if, as so often happens, we were to consider the conflict between Ranke and Burckhardt only as the antagonism between political and cultural history. For no matter how much the political aspect of events dominates in Ranke's historical writings, how the factor of culture can be maintained and continued amid the rise and fall in the destinies of the peoples forms for him too 'the foremost question in world history'. His profound and enthusiastic attitude to culture and to its 'jewel', the 'immortal works of genius in poetry and literature, science and art', truly does not require special proof. In his presentation he gives preference to the political side of events, first, because it includes the strongest casual elements for the fate of the world of culture, and further, because when, as we saw, he spiritualized power and the power-states, to a certain extent he also merged political history in cultural history.

But here the paths of the two thinkers diverge sharply. For Ranke, creating harmony, throwing a bridge over the abyss, causes the world of culture to include religion, the state, and, in general, whatever is, in the noble sense, human. Burckhardt, however, separates culture from religion and the state, guards it to a certain extent against them, declaring, 'The three forces are highly heterogeneous among themselves and cannot be co-ordinated.' For in his view religion and the state are both stable and, at least for the people concerned, claim enforceable authority. Culture, however, is fundamentally different. 'We call culture the total sum of those developments of the spirit which occur spontaneously and do not claim enforceable authority.' Elsewhere, Burckhardt does not favour such abstract formulations. Yet in this one we have before us, if not the whole, at least the innermost Burckhardt, this individual in himself wholly sovereign and yearning for liberty. We hear him say to religion and the state, 'I acknowledge you indeed to be historically effective forces of the first order and I also acknowledge a particularly close relationship between religion and culture. But you do not create culture, for you claim for yourselves enforceable authority.' Culture is only what arises, freely and spontaneously, out of the creative impulse, in particular art, poetry, philosophy and science. Even work for material ends, in so far as it is done with spontaneous freedom, he still includes in culture. He gives especially high rank to art and poetry, however, in serving his needs. Only the loss of works of art and poetry, he declares in the *Griechische Kulturgeschichte* (History of Greek Culture), is irreplaceable. As for research, later times will make good what earlier times failed to do. Goethe, he once declared in reproof, should have completed writing his *Nausikaa* instead of searching for archetypal plants. For only he could write the *Nausikaa*, but even in his time other investigators could have taken care of the other matter.

The quiet glow with which Burckhardt not merely enjoyed, but also paid honour to the most beautiful of the beautiful, makes his achievement as an art historian as great as it is. Now, however, it sheds a light of conciliation upon his picture of world history in general, otherwise still painted in such dark colours as the battleground of the force of evil and all human egoisms. There came to Burckhardt as he watched this drama in which culture bloomed most gloriously from the very soil which gave rise to the most terrible lust for power and unspeakable calamity, an intimation that a mysterious vital connexion exists between light and darkness. The illuminating picture of the *Kultur der Renaissance*, with its background deep in darkness, already gives us some sign of this intimation. It is expressed even more clearly in the *Griechische Kulturgeschichte*, which he wrote in a mood of intensified pessimism when, after the events of 1866 and 1870–71, he saw the approach of an era of wars, growing mass demands and disasters. The image of the Greek *polis*, with its disruptive struggles, its idea of the state distorted beyond the capacity of the normal nature of man, then seemed terrible to him. That the Greeks were unhappy was in fact one of his principal theses. And yet they also had their miraculous achievements in mythology, art and poetry, which after all would hardly have been possible without the *polis*. Then suddenly we find this sentence, 'Power can have a high vocation on earth; probably only upon it, upon the ground which it safeguards, can cultures of the highest rank grow.' And still more when it came to the fertilizing effect of power which is evil in itself, his ideas dared to meet Ranke's most closely. Ranke begins his *Französische Geschichte* (1852-61) (History of France) with the sentence, 'There are many kinds of war and many kinds of heroic glory; the foremost praise belongs to those who by triumphant weapons have opened new theatres for the culture of mankind.' According to Ranke, Caesar deserved such praise for opening up Gaul. And Burckhardt says in favour of Alexander, 'And now, in terms of our feeble understanding, it is always fortunate when a higher culture, a more gifted people, vanquishes a lesser culture, a less gifted one.'

But another fundamental thought shared by Ranke and Burckhardt belongs here. This is the high satisfaction felt by the two men when they looked at the continuity of world history, from the ancient Near East to the Greek-Roman world and then into the Romanic-Germanic West. For upon this continuity rests Western culture. In this connexion Ranke placed principal emphasis upon the bridge leading from the Roman Empire and Christianity to the Germans, and Burckhardt upon the incredible good fortune that the conquering Romans admired, and were permeated by, Greek culture. Both continuities, however, were only possible by the activity of that power which in Burckhardt's eyes was evil in itself.

For Ranke, it was a confirmation of his belief in Divine Providence. Human motivation was everywhere, but divine inspiration everywhere as well. For him the light in world history came from above—for Burckhardt, it came from within, from the spontaneity of the productive men who create culture. In this connexion, culture as a result and power as a means do not work so harmoniously, so willed of God, as with Ranke; they only form a remarkable and exciting combination of forces working alongside, against and with each other. The spirit of the metaphysically cautious later nineteenth century in which Burckhardt lived prevented him from attaining so pious a faith as Ranke's. But without a chastely concealed religious feeling, without a wholly discreet quiet hope in a super-mundane, even a Burckhardt could not live.

There are several passages, touching in their rarity, which testify that in the end he presumed that there existed, above the rise and fall of world history with all its precipices—all that our feeble eyes can see just ahead—a 'higher necessity', an 'almighty hand', an economy impenetrable to us.

Thus they share their outlook on the final and highest questions, but we may only state this concord lightly. For all of that, they continued to impart form to the material of history in quite different ways. Of the two fundamental conceptions of modern historicism, individuality and development, especially in each entity as well as in the general course of world history, in my opinion, Ranke stresses the second conception, he still tries to be fair in every case. He finally merges all individualities, no matter how brightly illuminated they may stand out in his work, into the powerful stream of a total development. Burckhardt, on the contrary, with his own personal artistic demand for an image and an attitude, thrusts the conception of development far into the background, in favour of the expression of that which at all times can be grasped as the situation and the type of a people and an age. Ranke saw history in long sections of time, that is, in the temporal development of specific historical entities and tendencies. Burckhardt preferred to see in cross-section, which in his own words brought out 'the repeating, constant, typical'. For that reason, however, Ranke, who was immersed in the very course of development and at the same time borne by his objective idealism to that conception which since Hegel has been called the objective spirit, was able to feel more within himself and to detect its beating heart more directly than Burckhardt, who compared and typified. All supra-personal entities like states, peoples, religions, institutions, intellectual tendencies, belong to this sphere of the objective spirit. Burckhardt, with the standards of his conceptions of culture and morality at all times ready, was not always capable of achieving the devoted love and grand impartiality with which Ranke depicted both the special inner principles imparting form to entities and the general course of change which brings them into marvellous interaction. Therefore, as a rule, Ranke's judgments on the true or false values of historical entities turn out to be milder, and often juster, too, than Burckhardt's harsh and sharply incisive judgments. For that reason Burckhardt discloses, with a ruthlessness beyond Ranke's capacity, the *partie honteuse*, the human—all-too-human—in history.

Basically, the two men put different queries to history. If we may state this perhaps too sharply, we may say that one asks, 'What does man mean for history?' and the other, 'What does history mean for man?' Stating this more cautiously, we may say that Ranke, and all those who share his tendencies to this day, ask,

'What is the significance of the historically active man for those supra-personal entities of the objective spirit we are primarily concerned in understanding?' The contrary fundamental question put by Burckhardt and his subjective idealism is, 'What is the significance of these entities, and of world historical events as such, for men, especially for productive men who create culture?' Burckhardt himself gave repeated answers in phrases of classic brevity to this, his query to history. For instance, of all the questions which the history of Greek religion raises, he wished only to answer a single one, what 'this religion and these gods were to the Greeks'. And at another place, 'We are interested not so much to determine how far the Greeks went with philosophy, as how far philosophy went with the Greeks.' The Greek man, the man of declining paganism and ascendant Christianity, the man of the Renaissance, the degenerate modern mass man, these are the strongest and most lasting memories left behind in us by his works and letters.

Two different fundamental attitudes toward history, therefore, each having its inner right and its necessity. Their difference is simultaneously polarity and mutual dependence. For each of these two questions can only be given a fundamental answer when the other is answered too. Whoever wishes to travel down one of these roads must always follow the other road with his eyes; hence, he may not stray too far from it. But when this happens, man is transformed into a mere function in the service of general powers and he loses his divine gift of personality. This was the danger in Hegel's philosophy of history. It remains the ever-present danger in collectivist attitudes toward history. But if, on the contrary, no limits are placed upon the idealism of freedom, then the general forces of history lose their inner necessity and fixity, succumbing to the arbitrary action of individuals.

In praise of Ranke and Burckhardt it must be said that, on the whole, they avoided this danger and did not travel too widely separated roads. One can turn with gratitude from one to the other for instruction. With each, we may breathe in the purer air of mountain heights.

Depending on the historical situation, one or the other query to history will dominate. Periods of advance, security, quiet enjoyment, will subside into a sense of satisfaction while contemplating the works created by the human spirit. Times of defeat and collapse, concerned and anxious as to what may happen in the future, will turn their attention, on the contrary, from what has been created back to the creative force. We Germans live today amid the ruins of state and nation; all that is involved in our culture is gravely threatened. Everywhere new paths must be searched out; everywhere these paths are in darkness. To be sure, as we have said, we should not cease to think in terms of world history even in the night of world history. But in such a situation we are wanting in that tranquillity of soul and clarity of vision which enable us, by means of the experiences of our time, to give new shape to the course of development of the objective spirit, that is, to world history in Ranke's sense. One thing, however, has remained to us, our own German way of being men. It presents to us unanticipated problems of the most sombre hue. The inner difficulties of establishing a scholarly foundation for the solution of these problems is no easier. But, at the same time, the task of finding such a foundation becomes more urgent. For that purpose we must rediscover ourselves by throwing light upon the historical transformations of our own character and the interweaving of our guilt and our fate.

A task of quite great dimensions is thereby placed before historical research in Germany—not only for scholarship but also for educational purposes. But it can only achieve its educational effect if its problems are solved in compliance with the standards of pure scholarship; for the historian that means, with strict criticism and tender sympathy at the same time. Universal history must not be lost from sight in this task. There should be constant comparison with the character and destinies of other peoples, and a constant query also as to what arises out of inherited tendencies and what out of historical experience, the answer to this often showing in fact an inseparably interwoven web.

Such investigation would be the foundation upon which, in a happier time, world history in Ranke's sense could then be built again. In such research, the spirits of Burckhardt and Ranke would live on, united by synthesis. We should not think of merging eclectically. It should result from a new, more profound orientation to the relationship of power and culture, of the elemental and the spiritual in life and history. Today I can look no farther than to the threshold of this problem.

CHAPTER EIGHT

THE GLORIFICATION OF THE STATE IN GERMAN HISTORICAL WRITING

by Johann Albrecht von Rantzau

Johann Albrecht von Rantzau took his doctorate of philosophy at the University of Berlin in 1923. From 1926 to 1934 he worked at the Research Institute on Baltic History in Kiel and has taught since 1945 at the University of Hamburg where he was named, in 1951, associate professor of history. The following essay appeared under the title 'Individualitätsprinzip, Staatsverherrlichung und deutsche Geschichtsschreibung' in the monthly *Die Sammlung*, May 1950, pp. 284–99.

I

Our fateful estrangement from the world brought us Germans to the brink of utter destruction. Desirous now of going on with our lives, we must seek for one explanation of our spiritual isolation in the way we have written history. History indeed is not just an academic pursuit. As Benedetto Croce has again recently emphasized, history is the wellspring of action. Though but a handful among us are beginning to admit it, in Germany this wellspring has long been turbid, because we magnified the idea of the national state out of all proportion. Other scientific disciplines, to be sure, did this too, but history most of all. To go more deeply into the causes of this development is not only a task for theoretical study, but even more one of practical urgency.

The heart of the problem is this: Which way must German historiography look? It must seek today a way to write history that the future will not invalidate. Now as before, our thoughts are engrossed by the state, the sovereign power-state. We find that our field of vision is not extended on any side. We do not take into account together with the state the historically creative energies within society. We do not keep in mind the larger framework, either federal union or shared purposes and spirit, within which individual states exist. In its own tradition, German historiography finds no Commonwealth, no Atlantic community of nations. Because there is too little sociology or universalism in our thinking, we cannot form a picture of the world of history and politics adequate for the needs of our day. In general, such universalism as is still to be found in German historical writing is that of Ranke, an ambiguous and elusive universalism. When it looks toward the Middle Ages, this universalism is aware of the coherent Christendom of Europe. When it looks at modern times, it turns to the study of the individual European states apart from each other. It may probably be said that out of a Christian and ethical universalism arose an esthetic and contemplative universalism.

It is dangerous, as has already been stressed, to concentrate attention upon the state and to isolate the phenomenon of the state, the national state in particular. Foreign experts in German history, like Benedetto Croce, and German historians such as Ludwig Dehio, in his new book *Gleichgewicht oder Hegemonie*, and Franz Schnabel, have gone far forward in the right direction.

II

In the long run, we will more and more come to see that a perilous separation of German historical thought from the West came in with the principle that each state is an individual *per se*, living wholly by its own unique laws (*Individualitätsprinzip*). To recognize this is of the greatest importance in considering the problems now faced by German historiography. The isolation of our historical and political thinking does not start in the age of nationalism. Though they were not nationalists, Hegel and Ranke were worshippers of the state; in this they were, despite all other differences in their spiritual position, at one. They combined the philosophy of individuality of the Romantics with the cult of state power also prefigured in romanticism. At the hands of Hegel and Ranke, the state became an individual autonomous with regard to other states; thus the state ran the danger of falling victim to Machiavellianism. With regard to its own people, the state became independent of Western political aspirations, in particular the demand of the bourgeoisie for liberty under genuine safeguards. As thinking about the state, in the course of the nineteenth century, was more and more transformed into the cult of the national state, two tendencies—in foreign policy, the tendency to unbounded Machiavellianism, and, in internal politics, a free hand for despotism—were driven to extremes.

We will probably have a better understanding of the fateful development of German political thought at the beginning of the last century if we put it alongside the contemporaneous development in Tsarist Russia for comparison. It was, as we know, not without the influence of German science that the same process took place in Russia, which even used the same phraseology for historical and political controversy. By the thirties, the first Slavophiles, linking defence of the autocracy with advocacy of a 'unique Russian character',* emerged, Slavophile scholars and men of letters, using the principle of individuality, maintained that Russia's tradition and Russia's mission were a bar to adoption of Western institutions. In his penetrating study of Russian intellectual development, the sociologist Alexander von Schelting[1] has repeatedly drawn emphatic attention to the conservative state ideology in Prussia in the thirties and forties, and shown an illuminating sociological parallel with Russia. In Russia as in Prussia, there was no stratum able, upon the basis of its own economic strength, to defend liberalism against the crown. The intellectuals, especially the professors, were employees of the state. The nobility, in its majority, was unequivocally a nobility of service; it, too, was dependent upon serving the state as military officers and governmental administrators. In both states, the stratum of the prosperous bourgeoisie was relatively small. We probably can say that stress in the leading Slavophile circles upon 'unique Russian character' had a stronger nationalist accent than in the thinking of the German Romantics and the historical school which, for the moment, stressed the individuality of the state rather than of the nation. In Germany, too, the sentiment of nationality was quickly incorporated into glorification of the state.

For a long time now, the nationalization of German history and the so-called *Geisteswissenschaften* (the humanities and social sciences) has been a much discussed and debated theme. The historian representative of this development, as we know, is Treitschke; his influence upon the broad public was, to a significant and ominous degree, superior to that of Mommsen,† though,

---

[1] Alexander von Schelting, *Russland und Europa* (Berne, 1948), especially pp. 123 ff.

* The English language lacks a word for what the Germans call '*Eigenart*' and the Russians '*samobytnost*'.

† Theodor Mommsen (1817–1903), German liberal historian, whose studies of Roman civilization culminated into a sourcework of fundamental significance for the social history of the Roman Empire.

as a scholar, Mommsen was much more important than Treitschke and was not below him as a writer. In Treitschke's early work, *Die Gesellschaftswissenschaft* (The Science of Society), of 1858, we can already see, in a most informative way, how the problem of 'unique character' showed itself in his thinking, and what consequences it wrought so swiftly. In a polemic against the 'excessively narrow concept of the state' of Robert von Mohl,* we read:

Though, in his brilliant polemic against Haller,† Mohl is able to make the very dubious assertion that, in an existing state, the establishment of a new constitution is the absolute equivalent, psychologically and legally, to the establishment of a new state. This calls to mind Aristotle's remark (*Politics*, III, 3) that the polis will become different when the politeia becomes different. But still it does not stand against the more profound political thinking of modern peoples. Far be it from me to join the latest frivolous outcry which asserts that the constitutions of states are worthless formalities. But would Prussia, once it completed the necessary advance to parliamentarism, really become a different state than the Prussia of Frederick William III? Is the whole field of civil law, the totality of political ideas developed over a long period of time, is the systematic network of trade relationships, is the people with all its history, is (to take the danger of being accused of playing with empty words like a dilettante) the spirit of the state a less essential component of Prussia than the organization of the state power?[1]

It is very characteristic how the liberal in Treitschke stands here locked in struggle with the adherent of the historic school, the champion of parliamentary institutions with the defender of ideas developed over a long period of time, that is, absolutist ideas. Later, under the impression of Bismarck's establishment of the Reich, Treitschke turned against parliamentarism. When Treitschke was an old man, he was particularly fond of spicing his lectures with 'harsh judgments on the sins of parliamentarism'.[2]‡

  This article cannot endeavour to make a detailed inquiry into

[1] New edition (Halle, 1927), pp. 61 ff.
[2] Friedrich Meinecke, *Erlebtes* (Leipzig, 1946), p. 96.
* Robert von Mohl (1799–1875), German jurist and political figure very significant in the field of administrative law.
† Karl Ludwig von Haller (1798–1854), Swiss-German jurist and political theorist; typical German literary representative of the social and political currents of the Restoration era.
‡ On Treitschke and his relationship to English political thought, see a recent work by Hans Kohn, *Prophets and Peoples* (New York, 1946).

the development of German historical thinking until it began to glorify the national power-state. I think there has been sufficient clarification of this process. In this case, we wish to show that the concepts of the state and of the nation's 'unique character', as they were developed in association with romanticism, do not any longer provide a basis for German historical writing. We must warn most emphatically that this traditional point of departure, which still has zealous defenders, is of questionable validity. True, these defenders sacrifice the aberrations of nationalism, but therefore they wish all the more strongly to uphold the idea of the state as the real carrier of history. They support their position with an assiduity worthy of a better cause. Yet the intellectual fragility and inadequacy of their viewpoint has been shown many times, in such important works as those of Toynbee and Croce; and the disastrous political consequences of their position have long been very clear. By the seventies, Constantin Frantz, the wearisome grumbler of the Bismarckian era, saw this when he expressed to the unwilling German public his astonishment that 'precisely Germany, which, because of her natural position, was least able to isolate herself; Germany, which even in earlier centuries when communications were still so difficult, did not go through exclusive national development; Germany, whose great thinkers, poets and writers won fame by elevating their spirit over the merely national to the universally human . . . that just this Germany desires to cut herself off politically and spiritually as a national state', since even 'in the constitution of this purported national state, the largest part is based on imitation of foreign models, so that in it scarcely anything particularly German is to be found.'[1]

III

Only after the First World War did the isolation of German historical thinking reach a high point. To be sure, advocacy of the national state, or, indeed, of nationalism, did not then have the field entirely to itself, as little as before 1914. But the influence of apologetic advocacy of the national state, with its polemics against the West over war guilt and other, more or less justified, causes, predominated among the educated bourgeoisie as well as in the higher schools and universities where they were educated.

[1] Constantin Frantz, 'Deutsche Politik', *Bayreuther Blätter*, 1878.

Historians like Max Lehmann and Hans Delbrück were forced
into the shade when they protested against the fabrication of
patriotic legends. Finally, this apologetics provided weapons for
a nationalism bent on revenge. In any event it assisted this
nationalist movement more than it hindered it.

The works of Gerhard Ritter show the influence of our conservative and national state thinking. Well known after 1920 as a
Luther specialist, Ritter later put out many books on modern and
contemporary history. In no case can he be criticized for having
deliberately supported the National-Socialist movement; it is a
matter of general knowledge that, when the war ended, he was a
prisoner of the Gestapo because of his ties to the honest patriots
of July 20, 1944. His publications after 1945 may be, therefore,
taken as highly representative of the historical scholarship of the
present day. We shall only go back to his earlier works for
several especially characteristic expressions of his purely state-
oriented historical thinking. In his biography of Stein, published
in 1931, we find the following assertion, rich in its implications:

The extraordinary and portentous bequest of the German wars of
liberation from Napoleon to the German politics of the nineteenth
century was that the conception of the state was adulterated and distorted by ideologies hostile to the state. The necessity of the struggle
which Bismarck had to wage against liberalism and romanticism on
behalf of the primacy of the state can be understood only when this
political inheritance is recalled.[1]

Of course, what Ritter here condemns as an ideology hostile to the
state is the influence of the conception of natural law and of the
Western attitude to the state found in Hardenberg and Stein.
Therefore, he is condemning the only way it is possible to make
over the German citizen from one who is ruled to one who rules
and shares responsibility for the working of the state in Germany,
the only way, therefore, it is possible, if not to exorcize, at least to
mitigate the danger of deifying the authority of the state. The
endeavour to use Bismarck in 1931 to correct Stein and Hardenberg is the very contrary of what should have been done since
1871—that is, to rebuild the Reich in the spirit of the idealist
reformers of 1806. This would have enabled it to survive, not just
by the means of its external might, but also by its political spirit
and constitutional forms.

[1] Gerhard Ritter, *Stein* (Stuttgart, 1931), I, p. 5.

IV

Any political situation—including beyond doubt the present German situation—can furnish the occasion for historical and political apologetics. Only if its fundamental conceptions are able to support critical examination is the apologetical way of looking at history justified and effective. Only then can it serve the prestige of a nation and the authority of its scholarship. It is just this which is not true in present-day German apologetics, however, as a closer analysis of characteristic works by contemporary historians will show. The conservative and German nationalist explanation of German history now being put forward, clings fast to nationalist conceptions, which, resting upon the ambiguous basic attitude of Ranke, put German historiography on a false track. German historical scholarship cannot find its way out of the blind alley into which it inevitably ran, particularly in its treatment of modern history. It then became unfit for any service except being the housemaid of national aspirations. Has it not been the fate of German historical scholarship that its influence upon intellectual life has not been at all commensurate with the labours of research it has performed? Is it highly striking that German historians can hardly number any in their ranks but Friedrich Meinecke whose world recognition is comparable with that of Pirenne, Huizinga, Rostovtseff, Hazard, Trevelyan and Toynbee? Where can the cause lie but in the contraction of the historical horizon and the monotony of themes studied? By concentrating rigidly upon the *étatist* tradition, by secluding themselves from all living philosophy and any more inclusive political and social conceptions, German historians have brought this fate upon the history they write.

This can be seen even in the rejection, often only slightly disguised, of Meinecke's *Die Deutsche Katastrophe* by older German university historians and frequently by the young rising generation too. What is the reason? German teachers of history found in this book the influence of a philosophical ethos they found strange, an ethos inconceivable to their purely nationalist ethos, which seemed to be 'in the clouds' and even unpatriotic. They had no desire whatever for a truthful explanation of the German catastrophe; they wanted far more an analysis which glossed over Germany's failure.

V

We find a widely read apologia in Ritter's book, *Europa und die deutsche Frage*, and his essays on the relation between power and morality.[1] In these works, Ritter continues his earlier effort in *Machtstaat und Utopie* to defend German thinking on the state against western Europe. But now, after the frightful experience of the Third Reich, we sense in him a strongly disillusioned apologist for nationalism. He does not merely renounce Hitler personally and the entire National-Socialist movement, he also condemns most sharply the attitude of the political Right in Germany, in particular that of the German National People's Party in the Weimar Republic. He also feels that Pan-German ideologists and militarists like Ludendorff interfered disastrously with German political matters during the First World War. Finally, he puts an equally great distance between himself and the government of William II, and also the boastful nationalism of the seventies. True, he does not try to defend Bismarck's policy in every case. He expressly calls the annexation of Alsace-Lorraine a political mistake. He is, therefore, not at all a chauvinist nor even a nationalist in the usual sense of the word. It is never the aberrations, but, always, only the foundations in the mind of our existence as a national state, which he seeks to shield against foreign criticism, principally the condemnation of Germans as a 'hopeless case' in international affairs.

At the centre of his inquiry, *Europa und die deutsche Frage*, stands the German attitude to the state. It arose in the early nineteenth century from the meeting and mingling of the Enlightenment, idealism and romanticism, and was later transformed into *Realpolitik*. Ritter seeks to uphold this sytem of thought and the corresponding practice as worth while and viable; he defends them against hostility from the West, particularly their identification with National-Socialism. In his introductory remarks he goes farther back into history to consider the political ethics of Luther and Frederick the Great. He finds no difficulty in proving that only things taken out of context, like Luther's expression, 'Be subject to authority', or the demoniacal character of Frederick the Great, can be brought into any connexion with excessive

[1] *Europa und die deutsche Frage: Betrachtungen über die geschichtliche Eigenart des deutschen Staatdenkens* (Munich, 1947); *Das sittliche Problem der Macht* (Berne, 1948).

German nationalism and with National-Socialism, and into opposition with the European West. In fact, only in the nineteenth century can we find a fully-developed, 'uniquely characteristic' German pattern of ideas on the state opposed to that of the West.

Ritter, in his polemic against the West, ends by presenting this German version of political thinking and defending it as a fully justified 'unique characteristic'. In any event, as has already been remarked, there is a question whether Ritter wishes to defend the German 'unique character' in its entirety, through thick and thin. As may easily be understood, this is not so. In the final analysis, he is trying to prove that essential traits in the life of the German state are 'worth while'—worth while by generally valid, normative and universal standards, not by those taken from individualistic and relativistic thinking. This is what must be done if one does not wish to magnify the cult of 'unique character' to the point of the grotesque or the nonsensical. Cannibals, after all, could actually justify man-eating by the simple statement that it is an expression of their 'unique character'.

What is it then that Ritter, who rejects much in the theory and practice of our political history, really wishes to defend? Principally, the developments in Germany leading to Bismarck's foundation of the Reich which did not accord with Western political ideals. He wishes to show the roots of this development in a healthy and completely justified political life and to demonstrate that the series of later events culminating in National-Socialism was fundamentally an un-German phenomenon arising from western European mass democracy. A contradiction then shows up in Ritter. On the one hand he has to affirm that there was worthwhile political life in Germany up to and including Bismarck's establishment of the Reich and his guidance of the state. On the other hand he must show a reprehensible degeneration for which the West is responsible, leading through Darwinism to the imperialism of the era of William II, leading through the mass democracy originating in the French Revolution to National-Socialism. This results in assigning a middle position to the period of William II, since on the one side it was influenced by Anglo-Saxon and French colonial imperialism and therefore had to be rejected, but on the other hand it had to be defended because it was guided by justified traditions and state interests.

In keeping with his initial position, Ritter seeks to justify German thinking on the state against three essential objections from the West. First, we are criticized for lack of readiness to make our public life parliamentary and democratic, in imitation of the West. Ritter uses in rebuttal a common argument of anti-democratic ideologists since Hegel and Ranke; this is the assertion that liberty has adequate safeguards in the state-under-law (*Rechtsstaat*) and that the achievement of popular sovereignty raises many problems and qualms. Against the charge that the ground for terrorism and dictatorship was prepared in Germany in the nineteenth century, Ritter emphasizes the closely-related argument that these forms of political depravity arose in western Europe and were only adopted by Germany. Finally, he would gladly clear German political activity of the slur that it moved past nationalism to an imperialism of world conquest. His defence is that these political tendencies also arose in the West as a result of the French Revolution and Darwinism, and that they should, therefore, be considered as unwelcome gifts to central Europe from western Europe.

We may question whether Ritter's apology for the unique or original character of German politics is persuasive. Does it hold its ground against inquiry into the facts of history and politics?

The way Ritter handles the reproach that Germany was not completely parliamentarized is, unfortunately, very characteristic of our German political thinking. He beats around the bush. Ritter assails the foreign critics of German history with over-looking the many forms of local self-government existing on German soil both in the time of the old Holy Roman Empire and afterwards. 'The abundance and multiformity of autonomous local, cantonal and provincial agencies of administration served the German burghers and peasantry as the seat of activity for the common welfare and as a preparatory school for political life . . . long before there were mass political parties', he argues. ' . . . among us the corporate bodies of communal autonomous administration offered the opportunity to develop a sense of free citizenship and free civic pride.'[1] This is the favourite argument of numerous German historians inclined to apologetics and desirous of replacing self-government of the people by self-administration of the burghers. Viewed politically, this is the

---

[1] *Europa und die deutsche Frage*, p. 38.

typical attitude of our National-Liberals. They, too, believed that civic and political freedom were sufficiently protected without a thorough control over the state power. Hence, too, Ritter's defence[1] of the Bismarckian imperial constitution, which reserved to the crown broad independent control over the foreign office and the armed forces. If Ritter, and many German historians with him, considers this so-called constitutional monarchy to have been a viable form, we need only inquire what answer Ritter gives to Max Weber's stricture on Bismarck that he left behind him a nation 'without any political education or political will-power'.[2] We need merely see how Ritter treats the personal government of William II, made possible by the provisions of the Bismarckian constitution. It must come as a surprise, however, to see Ritter's pained astonishment that, to this very day, all the zealous efforts of German constitutional lawyers to show that Bismarck's constitution provided adequate safeguards for liberty, have failed to persuade foreign scholars. For the West, the only choice is between the sovereignty of a monarch and the sovereignty of the people. Fortunately for politics in the West, it has not seen the sense of splitting hairs in an attempt to reconcile the irreconcilable.

Ritter's analysis makes it quite clear that he rejects the principle of sovereignty of the people as well as its dominant form in western Europe, parliamentarism. He laments over the symptoms of mass psychology spread over the Continent by the contagion of the French Revolution. In his opinion the French Revolution was a 'daring effort' to found the state exclusively upon rational principles easily intelligible to any citizen, instead of upon the antiquity of its origins and the religious injunction of obedience. Ritter then perceives an immense resulting process in which all strata of the people became involved in politics. This process culminated in the demand for direct participation by all and sundry in the affairs of the state.[3] The classic figure of English liberalism, John Stuart Mill, in his celebrated essay *On Liberty*, once said that the English still were in the habit of looking on the government as opposed to the interests of the public. Such a conception is at utter variance with Ritter's idea of the state, when he writes, 'Whoever reproaches the Germans simply for a deficient tendency to opposition, dissatisfaction and

[1] *Ibid.*, p. 21, n. 15.
[2] Max Weber, *Politische Schriften* (Munich, 1921), pp. 19 ff.
[3] Ritter, *Europa und die deutsche Frage*, pp. 43 ff.

revolution, reveals a curious notion of the nature of the state community and civic virtue.'[1]

If, then, Ritter is sceptical of Western democracy, what is the kind of state to which he gives his sympathy? What kind of state would he keep as 'the uniquely German kind'? Certainly not despotism. Nor does it seem to be monarchy, in either its absolute or its constitutional form; at least there is no evidence that he does. A witty comment from the eighteenth century probably gives some explanation. Justus Möser* said that the king ruled in France, the free men in England, but the 'servants of the Crown', that is, the government bureaucracy, in Germany. It is evident, then, that the old German authoritarian and bureaucratic state remains close to Ritter's heart, and that he cannot break with it. Even now he tries to justify it, to the undoubted satisfaction of many educated Germans. When Ritter finds sovereignty of the people to be of dubious value, parliamentarism superfluous, and the tendency to dissatisfaction and opposition incompatible with civic virtue, he can only be speaking in the name of this authoritarian state. His judgment, in fact, resembles that of a member of the Prussian government during the thirties of the last century, who said that it did not behoove the subjects to judge the actions of the government by the measuring-rod of their own limited insight. This dictum later became famous in the cruder notion of the limited intelligence of the subject.

We must expect a historian who wants his voice to be heard by the public, and Ritter's will be, to advocate a viable conception of the state. The traditional authoritarian state long ago lost its viability. This is clearly demonstrated by the course of history in the nineteenth century, and especially by the German catastrophe in the First World War. The mental prerequisites for the authoritarian state have long since disappeared among the people in Germany as well as elsewhere. More than one hundred years ago, Jakob Burckhardt saw that this was how matters stood. In 1842 he wrote from Berlin:

The so-called historic foundations underlying almost all European states, including Prussia, have been undermined. The complete negation which took place at the end of the last century in the state,

---

[1] John Stuart Mill, *On Liberty*, chapter I, para. 9 (ed. Alburey Castell, New York, 1947), p. 8; Ritter, *Europa und die deutsche Frage*, p. 195.

* Justus Möser (1720–94), German man of letters and historian, one of the fathers of the historical school of law, economics and ethnology.

in the church, in art and in life, has poured such an enormous mass of objective knowledge into all minds at all awake (and developed it among the better ones), that a re-establishment of the old status of legal minority is no longer even to be thought of . . . the terribly expanded sense of power in the individual consists in this: *cogito* (whether rightly or wrongly does not matter) *ergo regno*.[1]

The development which young Jakob Burckhardt saw occurring did destroy the viability of the authoritarian and bureaucratic state. Nor did Bismarck succeed in the effort to maintain it. The Chancellor himself recognized this when, shortly before he stepped down as Chancellor, he toyed with the idea of a *coup d'état*, which meant maintaining the authoritarian state by violence.

Another and broader reason why Ritter prefers the bureaucratic state against parliamentary democracy is that he thinks democracy inevitably leads to dictatorship and terror.[2] Instead, he is obviously confident that the officialdom embodying the 'unique character' of Germany has the capacity to protect the state-under-law (*Rechtsstaat*) and thus to assure a certain measure of freedom. It may well be argued in rebuttal that the bureaucracy stands ready to serve any formally legitimate government. Let us disregard this question for the moment. Analysis of Ritter's assertion that terrorist Caesarism, and hence National-Socialism as well, is a child of Western democracy and has nothing to do with the 'unique German character', is much more important for present-day historical judgment. With regard to Ritter's thesis, let us first note, since Ritter has not called attention to it, that German movements and parties do exist which cannot in any way deny, and do not wish to deny, their derivation from the French Revolution and Western mass democracy, but have no responsibility whatever for the seizure of power by National-Socialism. This is true of German Social-Democracy in particular. Formal democracy just provided the technical opportunities for the seizure of power by National-Socialism. The force to which Hitler's movement owes its triumph is without question nationalism. As for Jacobinism, Bonapartism and Fascism, it is indeed doubtful whether their rule would have been possible without the influence of nationalism and imperialism.

[1] Jakob Burckhardt, *Briefe* (Leipzig, 1935), p. 57. For criticism of Burckhardt's later attitude of political withdrawal and his flight to 'authority', see Croce, *History as the Story of Liberty* (London, 1941), pp. 100–10.
[2] *Europa und die deutsche Frage*, pp. 46 ff.

Ritter pays heed to this fact. Therefore he introduces modern nationalism into his inquiry, in the conviction that he can blame it, too, upon the French Revolution and hence upon the Western world. This means assigning to the evil, non-German world around us, responsibility for the two components of the National-Socialist movement, terrorism and nationalism bent on conquest. Exactly as Ritter, in this apologia, places the German state-under-law of the nineteenth century in contrast to Western democracy, so he seeks to differentiate the moderate *Realpolitik* of a Bismarck from aggressive nationalism and imperialism. Just as he traces back the seizure of power by Hitler to parliamentary democracy, so he derives nationalism and imperialism from Western trends.

For two very strong reasons we must resist this repeated effort to exonerate the German 'unique character'. Ritter admits in one place that the cult of nationality in the French Revolution, at first hailed with enthusiastic goodwill by most European intellectuals, was carried by an idealism which successfully won mankind to its side, exactly as happened later with British imperialism, whose world-winning might was most brilliantly portrayed by Seeley.* In contrast, as Constantin Frantz expressed it, German nationalism was completely self-centred and represented only itself. The profound and portentous difference between the two nationalisms goes back to their origins. It is well known and has been emphasized by such far-sighted observers as Ernest Renan and Dostoievsky, in their critique of culture, that German nationalism, like the Slavic nationalism derived from it, is a different and more dangerous movement than Western nationalism because it has its roots in the naturalistic soil of speech and folk. For such nationalism leads to cultural isolation and finally to the claim of biological superiority, while Western nationalism is essentially founded upon the political conception of the sovereignty of the people. Furthermore, Ritter overlooks the fact that aggressive German nationalism and the National-Socialist movement descended from it replaced what they lacked of civilizing idealism, by nihilism in thought and feeling. By means of Nietzsche's influence, the Germans contributed to the rise of this nihilism, which broke into Western history in the twentieth century. Ritter does not seem to recognize German nihilism as an equally disastrous and decisive factor in the social and political life of

---

* Sir John Robert Seeley (1834–95), British historian who wrote *Life and Times of Stein* (1878) and *The Expansion of England* (1883).

Germany after 1918. To overlook this modern phenomenon, as terrible as it is powerful, signifies a major shortcoming in his analysis of the present. Clearly the political historian cannot go far forward if he pays too little regard to philosophy.

To ignore, as Ritter does, the nihilist depravity in German National-Socialism, in the final analysis, to charge it, and all German nationalism with it, to Western mass democracy, is to do disservice to the necessary political reorientation in Germany and to increase the confusion in nationalist thought which is still current. Today it is anything but helpful to our political rebirth to dismiss the criticism of the Germans by placing the main weight of blame for the moral lunacy of the National-Socialist system upon Western ideology and the modern rule by the masses, thus relieving of responsibility the authentic 'unique German character'.

It would add nothing essential to demonstrate here in detail that Ritter's comments on Bismarck, William II and his era, and German annexationist policy in the First World War, are exonerations of aggressive German nationalism undertaken in a kind of conventional apologetic zeal. They are essentially superfluous with regard to his fundamental theses.[1] As a matter of fact, Ritter fundamentally removes blame from the entire German nationalist movement and ascribes its aberrations to contamination by an un-German mode of thought. The doubtful validity of such exculpation had to be proved, while preserving the uniquely German way of driving nationalism beyond all bounds, till it degenerated into nihilism.

VI

As has already been indicated, Ritter, in the study with which we are here concerned, does not try to prove that German thinking on the state was completely autonomous and 'unique in character'; he does not try to exempt it from any judgment by general human standards in the realm of political and state action.

---

[1] See, for instance, his retouching of all the brutal traits of character in Bismarck, who is portrayed by Ritter's pen more like a Richelieu or indeed a Talleyrand, without his own typical fury (*Europa und die deutsche Frage*, pp. 82 ff., 100 ff.); the endeavour to discharge the Prussian General Staff of responsibility for the outbreak of war in 1914 (p. 162); the treatment of German annexationist policy in the First World War as a bagatelle (p. 171); finally, the wide separation he draws between Hitler and his supporters in the nationalist big bourgeoisie (pp. 191 ff.).

Because the Christian tradition survives in him,[1] Ritter is invulnerable to the peril from our nationalist enthusiasts who, in their boundless subjectivism, have forgotten the time-honoured warning: What is felt by all men or a majority of men to be right . . . must be the limit of human reason, and he who would withdraw from it should beware lest he withdraw himself from all humanity.[2] Ritter consciously states, and attempts to prove by the facts of history, that the Germans shared in the values of the European civilization.[3] But all Ritter's efforts to prove his point merely demonstrate that, characteristically, the sense of political values possessed by all our Rightist historians since the beginning of the nineteenth century was never applied in practice by the institutions of our state.

This is shown most clearly, as we have noted, in Ritter's overly great readiness to accept authority, and in the restraint, or rather inadequacy, of the claim he puts forward on behalf of political liberty. This is precisely why he prefers to overlook the weaknesses in the development of our state, instead of exposing them. Finally, it explains Ritter's assertion that he cannot discover a noteworthy degree of excessive delight in obedience or indeed of servility among the Germans. From which we can only conclude that preserving the mentality of the old authoritarian and bureaucratic state saves one from seeing many a sorry spectacle.

Ritter's philosophical and political concepts of value are not really powerful and thorough. A simple comparison of his book with Meinecke's work on the same problem, *Die Deutsche Katastrophe*, makes this clear. In Meinecke we find just that intensity of ethical consciousness required in a historian equal to his tasks and all too seldom found among German historians. Many works of German historical scholarship would be impelled by a more powerful spiritual drive, and therefore be both more arresting and more effective, if the author's spiritual consciousness, in particular his sense of political ethics, were more strongly developed. The pull exerted upon each other by devotion to the factual and the sense of spiritual values makes each more productive. Realizing the danger that many historians of our day were not meeting this basic requirement, Meinecke, by 1927, called attention to this

---

[1] See his controversy with Nietzsche in *Das sittliche Problem der Macht* (Berne, 1948, pp. 136ff.).

[2] Giambattista Vico, *La Scienza Nuova* (Opere, IV-iv) (Bari, 1928) book I, sec. 4, p. 131 (trans. T. G. Bergin and M. H. Fisch, Ithaca, 1948, p. 94).

[3] *Europa und die deutsche Frage*, p. 200.

fundamental demand in his article 'Kausalitäten und Werte in der Geschichte'.[1] With his typical vigour, Meinecke demonstrated that we can understand historical relationships not just by stripping the outer layers from reality, but only by taking hold of the value in it. In fact, he sees, unabashed, the distinctive marks of a true historical work to consist in the attitude toward the primal ideas of the good, true and beautiful, hopelessly antiquated as they must seem to many of his positivist and nationalist colleagues.

This idea of Meinecke's ought to assist somewhat in reorientation. Historical scholars come to a parting of the ways in their attitude to these demands. They are, in truth, the authentic demands of an idealism which has been so often misused on so many lips. A positive or negative decision carries with it proof of the presence or absence of a true feeling for liberty. Only by freedom do we come to authentic ideas so that the struggle for freedom stands in the centre of history. Despotic institutions and conditions of every kind, even in the form of national power-states, are worthy of study only as deviations from man's true destiny. Their 'unique character' is never historical in the full sense, however much it may impress the superficial observer by its enormous scope.

If the idea of freedom is a prerequisite for historical activity of the human mind, then German historiography today needs true and clear ideas of spiritual and political liberty. If today, by pressure of the Western world outside, the word 'freedom' is used far and wide in German historical education, while German historians try to hold fast to that feeble and falsified notion of liberty which penetrated German political thinking in the days of Hegel and Ranke, to the delight of Prussian absolutism, the situation will be both ridiculous and sterile. It may be hoped that, with the aid of an authentic and revivifying idea of freedom, the narrow *étatist* and national horizon of our conventional historical consciousness will be extended more widely. Authentic national aspirations are always and only, aspirations to freedom. In truth, they essentially consist in nothing but the right of each individual nation not to be suppressed by any foreign national or multi-national state.

Thus, thanks to vital liberal thought, our historians would cease to stare monotonously at the operations of the state. Liberal

[1] *Historische Zeitschrift*, CXXXVII (1927).

agitation and movements do not flourish within the confines of the government services, they grow upon the soil of social groups and their varied activities. The charge that German political historians have long pushed society into the background behind the state, that they prefer to portray the deeds of military men and state officials rather than the workings of sociological groups, is still to the point. Of course, the advice we are now getting, especially from America, to concern ourselves with sociology, may often ring wearily in our ears. But it is not just a crotchet. It arises because German university scholarship, with its tradition of regarding the study of state documents as the alpha and omega of history, has incontrovertibly entered a blind alley. We see again today, in the work of Arnold Toynbee, who also began his researches as a political historian and certainly does not fail to recognize the historically creative importance of the state, that the introduction of sociological and religious-psychological processes open wide the historian's horizon.

German historiography must expand the range of its investigations beyond the national state. Among our scholars in the field of history, above all modern history, only a few show an inclination and capacity to leave the basis of the national state and to understand political happenings upon the basis of broader relationships. Even though the present German situation, which doubtless is in part the product of mistakes of the Allied powers, compels the German people and German political leaders to concentrate upon national problems, German historiography must cultivate and strengthen its ability to study problems in a supra-national spirit. Only in that way will it help us to better our historical and political understanding of the world situation and of the problems of our individual state. In the twentieth century, scholarship hemmed in by national formulation of its problems, offering nothing to the world and therefore of no value to the world, no longer brings advantage even to its own people.

CHAPTER NINE

MODIFICATION OF THE GERMAN-POLISH RELATIONSHIP

by Ellinor von Puttkamer

Dr. Ellinor von Puttkamer was born in 1910 and is at present lecturer (Privatdozent) for comparative constitutional history and east European history at the University of Bonn and an official (Oberregierungsrat) in the Federal Ministry of Justice in the Division of International Law. Among her books are, *Frankreich, Russland und der polnische Thron 1733* (Königsberg, 1937) and *Die polnische National-demokratie* (Cracow, 1944).

Her article on the revision of the relationship between Germans and Poles appeared in *Die Wandlung*, III (1948), pp. 206–15. While German historians now pay much attention to the relations between Germany and the West, little attention is paid so far to the question which was so important before and after the First World War, namely, the relationship of the Germans to the neighbouring smaller Slav peoples. There a revision seems as much needed as in the relationship to the West.

★

In 1944 the Polish author of a well-known book on the German terror rule in occupied Poland[1] made the gloomy forecast that hatred in Poland 'will continue for many generations and last very long after the war until Polish-German relations become normal again'. In his opinion, 'during the twenty to thirty years following the conclusion of peace . . . no German (will) be able to show himself in Poland, for no one will be able to take responsibility for the attitude of the population'.

Whoever, with alert conscience and clear discernment, breathed in for just one day the air of the *'Generalgouvernement'* or the *'Warthegau'* will have to share this pessimism. After the war the whole terrible burden of feelings generated by the present frontier line and its resulting cruelty, has been added to the hatred sowed by Germany. None the less, an effort must be made to spin threads

---

[1] Stefan Tadeusz Norwid, *Martyrium eines Volkes* (Stockholm, 1945), p. 270. German trans. of Swedish original, *Landet utan Quislings*.

of communication between them. Even the rare person-to-person connexion which did exist between individual members of the two peoples have been sundered by the outcome of the war, which practically included Poland within the Soviet Union. Even if there are in Poland persons of good sense wishing to converse with Germans, their voices cannot break through to us. We have virtually no contact even with the 'other Poland' of the emigration, and we should have no illusion about its readiness to come to an understanding. There remains nothing else for us to do at this time, therefore, but to clean our own house without hope of immediate effect upon them, and thus prepare in advance for the time when—perhaps—improvement in the relationship of people to people, or indeed of state to state, will be possible. Only in this way may one of the worst situations making for European conflict be reduced. This rather resigned statement is necessary before we can even attempt to probe into the old, hardened and recurrently inflamed abscess of German-Polish relationships.

Scarcely any question in European politics has been constantly handled by both parties with such frightening lack of objectivity, such disfiguring resentment, as the problem of the relationship of Germany to her Slavic neighbours, most of all to the Poles. It is well known that here, on the German side, the pendulum has swung back and forth between hatred and enthusiasm. Also as regards Russia, we find this oscillation of feelings, with the fundamental difference, however, that in this case generally the honest desire of the Germans to reach objectively accurate judgments, can be taken for granted. But precisely this is almost completely lacking so far as the smaller Slavic peoples are concerned, with the only exception—perhaps—that one or another of these peoples for a time—as for instance the Ukrainians, Slovaks and Croats quite often—has been used by Germany for her policy. For the Germans, Russia remains the interesting great unknown; it does not seem worth the trouble, however, to understand the Poles, Czechs, Serbs and others. In the final analysis, this seems to rest upon a denial that these others have individual value. A symptom of this is the fact that on the lips of Germans, to call the Poles by their national name 'Polak' has become an expression of this contempt; it is even stronger in the bungled plural form 'Polacken', which has a hard and offensive ring in German pronunciation instead of the soft and melodious correct form 'Polacy'.

It is not principally real differences of opinion which stand between the two peoples, but psychic reactions crystallized into 'complexes' in the truest sense of the word. Occasional admissions that the other party has 'good qualities' recede wholly into the background behind these reactions. Most Germans consider Poles to be negligent (note the phrase *'polnische Wirtschaft'* for an ill-managed home or government) and incapable of governing themselves, uneducated and uncivilized, careless, wasteful and corruptible, false and servile to the point of hostile duplicity (*Hinterhältigkeit*), and cruel to the point of sadism. Most Germans consider as absolute truth the assertion that all culture in Poland simply comes out of Germany. This belief, one of the most dangerous, has worked particular harm. (Responsibility for this belief rests upon a school of petty-minded historical writing which always gives central importance to the service of its own nation. However precise its scholarship, its political tendency has contributed essentially to poisoning the atmosphere.) On the other hand, on the Polish side an icy hatred, coupled with a scorn certainly in no way inferior to the Germans' contempt, appears the fundamental feeling toward the German.s The Poles see the German as a bureaucratic 'bicyclist' (*Radfahrer-typus*: obsequious to those above, scurrilous to those below), wanting in *savoir-vivre* and true education, and stupid because so easy to dupe. In addition, there is, even when the German is well intentioned, a feeling of a permanent threat resulting in mistrust. This is probably the principal source of the hatred; for, as Max Scheler[1] observes, hatred rests upon a feeling of powerlessness. Perhaps the reversal in the relationship of political power today can lessen the Poles' hatred, together with their feeling of powerlessness. But we should not be too optimistic, for we are not at all concerned here only with the effect of political pressure, but to a large degree with the reaction to German passion for work. Its ethos, understandable only to the Germans themselves, always fills other peoples, and particularly the Poles, only with mistrust.[2] The judgment with regard to each other may be partially founded or may only rest upon misunderstanding. Both are actually right, *cum grano salis*. But fundamentally this does not help us much, for aspects of feeling cannot be correlated at all with rational explanations. It is of much more interest for us to ask what were the causes which led to such an accumulation of negative feelings and

---

[1] *Die Ursachen des Deutschenhasses* (Leipzig, 1917), pp. 20 ff.
[2] Cf. *ibid.*, pp. 65 ff.

whether these must still continue to be operative even under present-day conditions.

An effort has often been made to explain all difficulties upon the basis of the two 'national characters' and to characterize them, therefore, as imponderables, themselves beyond change, basic to any investigation of the problem. Reflecting this view were a 'Historical Primer for Army and People'[1] and a pamphlet[2] on the Polish national character written and published during the last war with the specific purpose of establishing such judgments as a foundation for administrative tasks in occupied Poland. It is beyond debate that between nations as between individuals sympathy and antipathy can determine attraction and repulsion as if by a law of nature. It is, however, equally certain that such psychic preconditions do not remain constant in the course of history. That any such simplified thesis is untenable follows from an instance close at hand within our European family of peoples, the relationship precisely between Germans and Frenchmen, which has been subject to so many repeated alterations. If there really were such a fundamentally insuperable aversion between Germans and Poles, or, in general, between Germans and West Slavs, then the complete amalgamation of both elements in the German East which has taken place without compulsion since the Middle Ages and has produced the specific type of the East German, would be as inconceivable as the gap which separates precisely these East Germans, despite their overwhelmingly Slavic blood, from their Polish and Czech neighbours. Therefore, any attempt to explain the bad relationship between Germans and Poles upon the basis of biology and a resulting fixed national character must be firmly rejected.

The same arguments also fundamentally refute the method of seeing this friction as the expression of a social struggle between the German 'master people' and the Slavs under their yoke. At the level of the subconscious, the accidental similarity of the sound of the words *Slawe* (Slav) and *Sklave* (Slave) has sometimes contributed to it, however astounding the simple-mindedness involved may be.[3] It is not at all true, as later German historical

[1] Franz Luedtke, *Ein Jahrtausend Krieg zwischen Deutschland und Polen* (*Geschichtsfibeln für Wehrmacht und Volk*, III), Stuttgart, 1941.

[2] Karl C. von Loesche, *Der polnische Volkscharakter*, Berlin, 1940. (*Schriften für Politik und Auslandskunde*, LXVII–LXIX.)

[3] Even Grimm's Dictionary, x, 1899, *c.* 1309 ss., brings the expression used by Byzantine historians for the Slavs, Σκλαβινοι, Σκλαβοι, in connexion with the Latin *sclavus*. Modern Slav philologists consider the derivation from the Slavonic

writers were pleased to put it, that in the German East a German ruling stratum, by which culture was transmitted, made itself the sole masters of the land. The Slavic population at the base was always quite open to Western culture. Therefore they also maintained in part their own higher stratum in society which could merge with the similar stratum of immigrant Germans. On the contrary, since the end of the late Middle Ages, the German townsmen settled in Poland, as soon as its own separate sphere ceased, together with the disappearance of German law (*Stadt-rechte*), more and more came into line with Polish conditions and customs. And the sons of German noble families who emigrated to the Polish aristocratic republic in its Golden Age, became the ancestors of Polish nationalists who often showed themselves to be more hostile to Germany than ethnic Poles. The situation in Poland was wholly different from that in Bohemia, where, after the political connexion with Austria was established, the Slavic nobility was thoroughly Austrianized, the German inhabitants of the cities, however, maintained themselves as such, and thus, in fact, at the same time social stratification also became national. There can be, therefore, no question of an original social tension between the two peoples in Poland. Beyond doubt, however, the Germans' scorn for the Poles was nurtured by an impoverishment of the great mass of the Polish population, unlike any known to Germany in the period, resulting from lack of political freedom in Poland in the nineteenth century. The Poles, therefore, were compelled by economic hardship to go as agricultural seasonal or permanent industrial labourers to foreign countries, where they formed a group of blatantly unimpressive representatives of their people; meanwhile the aristocracy and the intellectuals held back very strongly and scarcely came into contact with Germans except in the Austrian multi-national state. Present-day Germany, finding herself in a similar situation of difficulty, will pass judgment less presumptuously.

The application of a kind of class struggle theory to German-Polish relationships is an invention of modern chauvinism. It was apparently supported by the economic poverty of the Polish people, but today is not a tenable thesis any more.

Much more, the difference in religious affiliations can afford explanation of the failure of the two peoples to understand each

slovo (word) to be probable. According to this analysis, Slavs are those whose speech is comprehensible (to themselves). Cf. Paul Diels, *Die Slawen* (Leipzig–Berlin, 1920), p. 6.

other. In any case, the Germans on the frontier felt the special, nationally-modified character of Polish Catholicism to be a sharply divisive element; indeed, 'Polish' and 'Catholic' were considered equivalent. In fact, the hatred of the border populations in Silesia, which is Catholic on both sides of the frontier, was also never as embittered as on the east Prussian, Pomeranian or Brandenburg frontiers. To some extent the relatively good understanding between Austrians and Poles may result from the common religious basis. Many 'faults of character' for which the North Germans in particular reproach the Poles may be reduced to a misunderstanding based on the different religious peculiarities. There are some stupid prejudices—especially that of falsity ('shifty eyes')—shown on occasion by the Protestant toward the Catholics of his own people. This may be due to the fact that the Catholic, confronted by Protestants, prefers to withdraw into a realm which offers final refuge; however, he neither will nor can give any insight into this refuge to the Protestant, who, in his opinion, does not participate in this security. The kinds of piety shown by Poles and Germans of both religious faiths are very dissimilar, however. Here the middle position of Poland, between East and West, finds expression in a strong tendency toward external demonstrativeness and in a divergence between profane and sacred life incomprehensible and often repulsive to the western European. Whoever has attended the service in a Polish church will scarcely imagine this difference. These facts are made clearer than by words in well-known descriptions, for instance those given us by Daniel Chodowiecki in his informative sketch, 'In a Danzig Church'. There we see a woman lying on the floor in prayer, in penitence and piety, and beside her a *Szlachcic* twirling his moustache and staring at the ladies. Very essential for the characterization of Polish Catholicism is its firm position as a national church, exceeded if at all only in Spain. This national church was always intolerant. Protestants were scarcely considered to be Christians; this was significantly expressed by the fact that they were known in old Poland merely as 'Dissenters', that is, they were understood only in terms of a purely negative conception. The increasing religious rigidity of the Poles, on the one hand, and the neighbouring Protestantism in North-east Germany, on the other hand, has made an understanding between them considerably more difficult since the Counter-Reformation. None the less, we cannot comprehend why the religious difference must work so much greater psychological damage here than on other Catholic-Protestant frontiers. Finally, only about half of the frontier between the religious groups coincides with the border-line between the peoples. Religious developments, therefore, can explain the differences only in part.

In addition to the differences in the form of religious life, the divergent political and constitutional development of the Polish and German states has had its consequences. For centuries the Polish ideal of government has consisted in laissez-faire on the largest possible scale, the German in political-bureaucratic organization. We must add the observation that the position of freedom as men strove for it in old Poland by such laissez-faire brought benefit only to the nobility, who alone were considered to be the 'nation'. The 'anarchy' of old Poland was criticized by all European peoples and by the Poles themselves, too, but there was no lack, however, of those who admired their freedom. In Poland, in fact, an effort was made to reinterpret it as a principle of state preservation ('*Polska nierządem stoi*'—'Poland exists upon the very basis of anarchy'). Only the Germans, the Austrians included, looked at it wholly without understanding. It made them feel a sincere conviction of their right to intervene, to destroy the state and the system, and to introduce their rational, thoroughly organized 'order'. In the period of the elective monarchy, in the main political ideas of the period of partition, and in the time of the new independent state, the Poles always felt themselves to be exemplars of democratic orientation. Their practice often had a very slight 'democratic' aspect. But this is not decisive for the *feeling* toward the state. This was directed at all times toward freedom at any cost. Therefore, throughout the course of modern history, it has stood in sharpest contradiction to the rigid new monarchical establishments of the East German territorial states and the empire founded on them. So different was the course of development of political purposes in the two nations as a result of the difference in the character of their political ethos, that it must be looked upon as one of the principal concealed dangers imperilling revision of the German-Polish relationship. To be sure, in the political situation at the present time, this Gordian knot has been cut in simple fashion: a politically independent Poland no longer exists on Polish soil and the border-ing German territory bears the same stamp. If these conditions are accepted as final, then, in any case, it is idle to consider at all the problem of the German-Polish relationship. If, however, this situation of Poland, like that of our own political dependence, in our opinion is transitory—then, and only then, is there still in general any possibility of a neighbourly discussion—one day the difference of state conceptions will again make itself felt. To the degree that an official rapprochement of ideology may develop, the situation will be altered, but the discordant traditions will scarcely be repressed completely, and the diametrically opposed tendencies on their part to seek the greatest possible freedom, and on our part to achieve strict cohesiveness, will continue to exist in the subconscious and will raise difficulties for neighbourly relations.

A great difficulty in clearing the way for a better German-Polish relationship consists in the circumstance that the Germans, for failure to learn the language of their Slavic neighbours, in general lack any conception of their cultural life. But this technical difficulty ought not to have as troublesome results as have taken place. It would have been sufficient, in fact, if the small number of those who knew the language had played the role of mediators and brought closer to their own people in translation something of the intellectual life of their neighbouring peoples. But the contempt we have already spoken of stood in the way. Place the level of our Eastern neighbours where you will, you cannot criticize it till you know it. The feeling that western Europe is the direct inheritor of ancient culture, while only its radiations reached the East, probably lies at the root of this prejudice. But it should not be forgotten that, from this point of view, the line of demarcation definitely runs not primarily along the eastern frontier of the Germans, but along the *Limes* and the Rhine, and secondarily along the Elbe. One must further be aware that precisely Poland was in very intense relation with papal Rome, and later also with France and Italy, and established a closer contact with the civilization of ancient Rome than did Eastern Germany. However, the social stratum upon whom these influences worked was relatively narrow. One of the best known of present-day Polish historians, Oskar Halecki,[1] has spoken of the fact that the difference between 'Old Europe' and 'New Europe' did indeed exist, but for a long time was not a qualitative but only a quantitative one. One can scarcely measure

[1] 'Der Begriff der osteuropäischen Geschichte', *Zeitschrift für osteuropäische Geschichte*, IX (1935), pp. 8 ff.

the mistakes Germans made as a result of their studied under-estimation of Poland, during recent years in particularly shameful fashion. All too often Germans have fallen into the awkward position of having their ignorance put them at the mercy of the superiority of educated Poles obviously conversant with Western culture. Greater attention to knowledge of the East is one of the preconditions for improvement of the political relationship.

Here belongs as well the demand for neutralization of historical consciousness on both sides. The poisoning of this historical consciousness is more responsible for the bad relationships than any real differences. The historicism of the nineteenth century, a child of the awakened national feeling, fell on especially fertile soil among the nations of the East, precisely those peoples which had reasons to feel themselves threatened or even suppressed in their political autonomy and independence, since romanticism found self-justification in historical events. It is striking how well informed about the history of their own country are most Poles, and not only those with an education. The Germans did not view with pleasure the claim of the Eastern peoples for their own historical tradition, however, even though the very stimulus for it actually came from Herder and the German Romantics. This feeling was justified if it was a case of glorification rising out of national pathos, but only then. Unfortunately, not enough objectivity was maintained. Most German historians had in-sufficient linguistic knowledge to be able to give serious con-sideration to the history of the Slav nations. Thus this task automatically slipped into the hands of those who themselves originated in Slav territory, and therefore seemed to bring with them the necessary conditions for studying Eastern conditions. But this group of German scholars for the most part felt com-pelled to take part in the struggle of nationalities (*Volkstum-kampf*). On both sides, therefore, arose the notion that historical writing had to serve the controversy between the nations. Emotions waxed hot over questions, secondary and even inci-dental for the life of the peoples, which it could only do harm to discuss. Is there really still such importance today in solving the debated vassal relationship of the first Polish princes to the Emperor, or to debate the 'nationality' of Copernicus, the resident of Torun (Thorn)? Why is it demanded that Veit Stoss be accepted as 'German' or 'Polish', just because he worked in

Nuremberg *and* in Cracow? It is shameful that respected historians
in both countries put themselves at the disposal of this struggle.
It is not to be doubted that this historical writing was done with
the usual erudite precision and resulted in many correct individual
achievements. It was not its method which was false, but the way
of posing the problem. Thereby it made ready for the time when
National-Socialist pseudo-scholarship, by seeking to conceal its
policy of conquest in the East through falsification of the mediaeval
conception of the Empire and asserting that it abolished the
existence of an historic Poland simply by forbidding the use of
the word 'Poland', replacing it by 'Vistula space' (*Weichselraum*),
carried this spiritual tendency to its end. Thus German historical
conception of Poland was carried *ad absurdum* and fell victim to
being ridiculous, a deadly malady. On the contrary, however, the
objectivity of the Polish picture of history is especially endangered
at the present time by convulsive efforts to establish historically
the possession of the eastern territories of Germany. From what
we have been able to see of the latest Polish historical writing, the
old national standpoint seems to prevail. The Baltic Institute at
Torun (Thorn) and the Western Institute at Poznan (Posen) have
published various works in defence of the new western frontier.
In any case, there seems to be some preference for supporting
their position by political and strategic arguments.[1] On both
sides the road to a dispassionate historical approach appears very
long. However, if we want ever to approach our goal, we must
at least start our journey on that road.

If, then, the differences between the two peoples prove, in the
event of sober analysis and some good will, to be not at all
insurmountable, if the achievement of political and historical
objectivity proves in any case to be a possible goal, the important
question still remains open, however, whether the realities of the
foreign political situation do not make all these fine theories of a
revision of the German-Polish relationship into speculation without contact with the real world. The fate of the German-Polish

---

[1] See *Wiadomosci Polskie*, I, no. 45 (Frankfurt-am-Main, 1947), p. 5, and the review
of Zygmunt Wojciechowski (ed.) *Poland's Place in Europe* (Poznan, 1947) in the
American Historical Review, LIII (1947), pp. 105 f. See the report by Alexander Werth
in the *Manchester Guardian Weekly*, September 25, 1947, about the slightly ironic
attitude of some Poles to this interpretation of history: 'the Poles love giving us . . .
little lectures in etymology. Archeology is also sometimes invoked: I was thus
shown the eleventh-century Polish foundations under a German fifteenth-century
castle at Stettin. I suspect, however, that many Poles who use these etymological
and archeological arguments do so in fact with their tongue in their cheek.'

relationship will depend upon the way the position of the Soviet Union develops. Since Russia entered the European world, the German-Polish relationship has been fundamentally only a portion of the problem of Russian-European relationships. This fact constitutes the obvious background for all discussion of German-Polish affairs. If we start from the present situation, we come out with little hope only. An honourable understanding between Germany and Poland is very improbable upon the basis of the present radical solution supported by Russia. Illusions on this score are as far off as the erroneous belief of earlier generations wishing to follow a policy of equalization without touching the status of the partitions. But every German who has realized how new the present international situation is will see that the dream of a complete re-establishment of the old conditions is impossible, and that this is not even the point if we learn to be Europeans. This is an inexorable fact. It does no good not to accept this truth, though for Germans, pain over their losses results in a constant temptation to avoid recognizing the facts. Only such soberness can give courage for the new tasks and patience to see them with eyes that peer far into the future. We are now at a turning-point. It is evident that the idea of the national state was carried to excess, and that its day is past. Before it began to develop in the declining Middle Ages, the only quarrels between Germans and Poles were those usual among close neighbours. As late as the thirteenth century, a Polish prince brought the Teutonic Order into Prussia, and in the fourteenth, Polish kings began the planned immigration of German citizens. Poland, by its entire tradition a part of the sphere of Western civilization, has never doubted that also politically it has to be a part of Europe. But in recent centuries it sought its support not from Germany, but from the Western powers, seeing in them allies precisely against Germany. The rapprochement now taking place between the Western powers and Germany destroys the value of such a policy for Poland and permits hope that, if Poland is able to find her way once more to union with the West, the German-Polish antagonism will be lessened. The alignment of forces is new. Its realities can operate more powerfully than the appeal to reason alone, which is never able to control political passions of such intensity as now exist between the two peoples. The demand for revision of the German-Polish relationship is therefore today less fantastic than the degree of mutual incitement would seem to indicate.

We ought not to abandon the effort to reach an equal settlement by agreement of the immediate participants. Until this can come about, decades and probably generations will pass. If the feelings of hatred and revenge are to be overcome and an agreement based on mutual respect is to be possible, such a period of waiting will in truth be necessary.

CHAPTER TEN

TOWARD A REVISION OF THE GERMAN CONCEPT OF HISTORY

by Walther Hofer

Walther Hofer was born in Switzerland in 1920 and studied at the Universities of Berne and Zürich. He received his doctorate with a thesis on 'Friedrich Meinecke as an Historical Thinker', which was later expounded into his important book on Meinecke's *Geschichtschreibung und Weltanschauung* (Historiography and Ideology), which was published in Munich in 1950. He has been *Dozent* at the Free University of Berlin since 1950. His forthcoming book, *Die Europäischen Mächte und der Ausbruch des zweiten Weltkrieges* (The European Powers and the Outbreak of the Second World War), which will appear later in 1954, promises to become the first comprehensive and objective study of this problem in Germany.

The following essay is a somewhat shortened version of a lecture which Dr. Hofer gave in Zürich in December 1947, and which was reprinted in the *Schweizerische Hochschulzeitung* in March 1948.

The problem under discussion here is beyond question at the centre of the debate on the so-called 'German question'. Already before us are a multitude of critics of German historical thought and their programmes for its revision. In this connexion it is significant that among those who have come vigorously to grips with the problem have been chiefly sociologists, theologians, psychologists, philosophers and journalists, but hardly any historians. The historian's reticence is understandable, for the specialist's limitations are at work. Where the thinker with a more systematic methodology comes forward at once with radical solutions, the historian sees above all the fullness of historical life, its complicated and intricate structure, and the manifold possibilities for its interpretation. When the historian speaks of revision of a picture of history, he is thinking above all of the reworking of a vast mass of historical material. But to do this requires work, still more work, and therefore time. Nevertheless, the historian already has something decisive to say. He must speak up, before catchwords and commonplace works too much harm. The problem of revision of German history penetrates to the very core of the historian's responsibility to life. A principal task of future historical writing is involved. But, in general, in order to be able to undertake this task, one thing above all is necessary. That is a genuine *historical* analysis of German history, and its criticism in a true *historical* spirit. Indeed, in accordance with the nature of a concept of history, we are concerned primarily not with criticism of all the concrete historical notions present in this concept of history, but with analysis and criticism of its ultimately determinative *ideological* elements. This is the task we have accepted today.

Though concealed in the conception of history is the notion that we have in our mind a picture of the historical past, the theory of historiography has long since recognized that we should not take 'picture' here in the sense of a faithful copy of the past. Naïve historical realism, according to which something like recognition of an historical object 'in itself' (*an sich*) is possible, has long since been overcome. The picture which we form of the past must not be compared to a photograph, but to a painting. And, just as we can only see a landscape from a given place, similarly all historical vision is determined by that place from which we view it. It means seeing *in perspective*. Broadly conceived, a historical problem, therefore, is always a question by the present to the past. Hence, in point of fact, the questioner's interest and principle of selection, and in the final analysis, his value system and his ideology are decisive factors in the definition of the question. An understanding of history is never achieved by cognition without prior assumptions, but with understanding of the specific assumptions. Only when these assumptions enter into our calculations as conditions, can we speak of historical objectivity.

But then a broader question is raised. This is the question of the *person* (*Subjekt*) who forms a picture of history. In the end it is the individual man, having his own individually differentiated historical conception. But we are now concerned with the picture of history of an entire people, of a civilization as such, and hence of a subject or person of a higher level, definable only by some abstraction, by typification of individual attitudes. We recognize at once the difficulties which must arise when we introduce the idea of a 'German' as a person of this kind who forms a specific picture of history. All sorts of differentiations must be made. The notion of a specifically German concept of history is admissible only if we recognize that *typical* characteristics, crystallized out in the course of time, are involved. Only on this assumption can we speak meaningfully, without impermissible generalization, of a *German* picture of history as such.

Therefore, the typical characteristics to be set forth here in detail as the German picture of history cover approximately what used to be called *official* German historiography. The official German picture of history said to require revision is the picture of the German past created by scholars in the universities, then popularized, and finally hardened by successful propaganda. Even though a formal restatement is difficult, we can probably best say that the historiography involved supports and gives sanction to national policy, from which it then receives in turn its determinative impulsion. Such a close reciprocal effect between politics and history in German thought is indeed confirmed by the common fiasco of political action and historical thought. It becomes clearer than ever that there really was such an officially and generally recognized picture of history in Germany when German historians speak of the 'conventional' picture of history. Finally, although the conception of a 'German picture of history' ought to be fixed more exactly in time as well, it has not essentially been transformed within official German historiography. Thus, for instance, Droysen's purely Prussian picture of history was revealed as contrived history (*Geschichtskonstruktion*) and corrected. The *kleindeutsch* picture of history derived from Treitschke was weakened in favour of the *grossdeutsch* aspect, and then, in the period of the Third Reich, was proclaimed as antiquated by historical developments. The typical characteristics involved, therefore, track back in time. Ranke's period may serve as the point of departure of our summary observations. But in investigating these typical characteristics, we must always keep in mind that different currents were always present in the historical thought of Germany, and that many individual aspects must be neglected in the investigation of typical characteristics.

This official German picture of history, for the time being defined more in a formal way, has now been proclaimed, indeed by competent German historians themselves, to require revision. Thus, Gerhard Ritter, in his *Geschichte als Bildungsmacht* (History as an Educational Force), writes: 'Nowhere, after the great collapse of 1945, is reconstruction more urgently required in the German educational system than in historical teaching. The first and principal reason is that the entire foundation of instruction, our very picture of history, has suddenly fallen into uncertainty. For, after the shameful misuse of the finest ideals of German history, its honourable traditions as well as the belief in the nation and its future, what still remains firm of the historical and political convictions and the traditional values of German history? Perplexed and distracted, the Germans stand today at the grave of their past.' And elsewhere the same historian writes: 'In the question of the handling of material, we are proceeding free of any restraint by the conventional, in the conviction that the new times require a fundamental revision of the picture of history accepted in Germany.' Much in the same vein, Friedrich Meinecke writes in *The German Catastrophe*: 'Our traditional picture of history, with which we grew up, now requires a fundamental revision, in order clearly to distinguish from each other the true and false values of our history.'

The necessity of a fundamental revision is therefore beyond argument. Naturally, revision does not mean that an effort will be made to portray what has happened as not having happened. Despite any effort at revision, Bismarck's foundation of the Empire remains a fact. Meinecke makes what is at stake wholly clear. It is a new division between true and false values. Ritter, too, speaks of values, ideals and convictions. Obviously it is a question of their revision and not of the revision of facts. Facts as such cannot be revised. True and false values can only be recognized and classified upon the basis of a *value system*. The person who makes his own picture of history, therefore, also in the last analysis determines what shall be given a place within a given historical connexion and thereby shall be meaningfully identified. He determines the place things shall take in the picture of history.

It is not because the past has changed, therefore, that a picture of history can come to require revision. The past in itself is a disordered, amorphous and indeed unrecognizable mass. Only because the relationship between the present and the past has changed can revision become necessary. The position from which history was seen and created is no longer valid. The value system upon which the picture of history was built has collapsed. We must go one step farther. A picture of history can also come to require revision because it ceases to answer responsibly not only questions connected with the past but also with the present and the future. Finally, revision becomes a necessity because of recognition that the nature of a picture of history has a decisive influence upon the shaping of active life. Only in this case can we meaningfully speak of history as an educational force. Our argument hinges on recognition that historical thought leads to historical action. History as thought and as deed, Croce* calls it. And Meinecke, too, when he writes that the lofty vocation of German history at the present time is to maintain the true values of the German past, to discern its false values and 'when it comes to action, to warn against them', emphasizes the internal relationship between thought and action.

Revision of a historical picture, therefore, means differentiating anew between true and false values in history by means of a value system already transformed or still to be transformed. It means differentiating anew between light and shadow by changing the direction of the searchlights into the past. Thereby we are saying, too, that the standards by which true and false values of the past must be differentiated anew can arise only out of the present. We are also saying, in addition, that a revision of the German picture of history can only succeed in connexion with a revision of the *ideology* which precedes and determines it.

It is precisely our own concrete example which proves that special attention must be paid to the ideological elements constituting the picture of history. Until the Third Reich, German historical scholarship was always exemplary in methodology and detailed research. None the less, a distorted picture of history resulted. The source of error, therefore, clearly lies elsewhere, in the ideological foundation.

How then should revision proceed concretely? Which standards should it employ? The danger that we will fall from one extreme to the other, that we shall burn today what we adored yesterday, is great. Simply to declare that all German history since Frederick II of Prussia, or indeed since some earlier period, has just been on the wrong track and ended necessarily and logically in the collapse of the Third Reich, is naturally by far the simplest way and demands the least exertion of mental energy. Because this thesis is so simple, and, like anything simple, attracts at first

---

* Benedetto Croce (1866–1952), Italian philosopher and historian; see his book *Germany and Europe* (New York: Random House, 1944).

glance, it has been widely adopted and is wholly alive in popular thought. What they have done is to replace one historical artifice by another, by simply changing the sign of value. In this respect what was represented as a fascinating rise, willed by historic destiny, now appears as a frightful fall, equally the work of destiny. It is scarcely remarked that such a theory of necessity permits the historical responsibility of the leading Germans to slip through the mesh of history. But there also occur individual generalizations and simplifications having frightfully little to do with historical thought. Thus, for example, the developmental continuity of intellectual history is simply rolled back. It is understood as a causal chain and then is supposed to support the newly created artifice. There is a rummaging about throughout Germany's past for witnesses who will prove, as far back as possible, that disaster was inevitable. Obviously, in such fashion, anything can be proved by history. It is equally clear that to do so is the exact opposite of true historical thought. Formally, this method has no distinction whatever from the method of National-Socialist historical writing, which sought throughout the German past for spiritual ancestors of its ideology. This way of thinking is all the more dangerous because it includes a kernel of incontestable truth, that ideals continue to work in history as spiritual powers and can still bring forth great historical effects after the passage of centuries. By applying a wholly inadequate operating principle to history, which is always chiefly intellectual history, this way of thinking becomes false in its very essentials. It uses the operating principle of cause and effect; in so doing, it believes that it simplifies historical connexions, but in fact destroys them. Following Jakob Burckhardt, we best may call those who apply such a way of thinking to history '*terribles simplificateurs*'. All genuinely historically thinking persons reject such artificial constructions. And therein lies, it seems to me, the essential task and responsibility of historical scholarship in the immediate future.

In accordance with the nature of a picture of history, the only correct way to engage in an enterprise of revision, therefore, can be the following:

1. The analysis, criticism and revision of the ideological, that is, the metaphysical, ethical, historical and political philosophical assumptions on which the picture of history rests;

2. The criticism and revision of the picture of historical development itself.

The problem of revision, therefore, is primarily an ethical and ideological problem, a problem of education, and only secondarily a problem of scientific historical criticism. Let us therefore now endeavour to make our analysis and criticism of the ideological assumptions of the traditional German historical interpretation. The traditional German picture of history appears open to attack of critical examination principally on three grounds. These are:

Power is idealized and glorified.
War is made heroic and moral.
The national idea is radicalized and made absolute.

We are therefore concerned with the broad problems often indicated by the trinity of imperialism, militarism and nationalism, except that these catchword ideas do not in any case really describe exhaustively that complex of problems. We mention them here only in order to make clear that, in discussion of these questions, we must extend our view to European history. For nationalism, militarism and imperialism have been recognized as just the three principal forces which more and more clearly determined political, economic and (since it is also a question at all times of intense spiritual currents) spiritual development since the middle of the nineteenth century, and finally led into the period of world war. If we therefore have borne in mind that general phenomena of *European* history are involved here our question must then be modified in this direction: How it became possible that these three forces determined German history more strongly than that of other European countries. And, what concerns our essential problem, how it came about that the German picture of history received its characteristic shape all the more distinctly from these three forces.

We can best make this clear to ourselves by tracing the development of German historical thinking since Ranke formed his picture of history. Beyond question, power, the political power of the state, plays a significant role in Ranke's historical interpretation. But it could not dominate his picture of history because religion faced power as an equal, indeed in the final analysis, as a superior force in determining history. Only as this duality

13

increasingly broke down in favour of state power, only as so-called 'political history' became possible, did the road open for the well-known disastrous one-sidedness of the glorification of power. Indeed from our present viewpoint, Ranke is criticized for a certain degree of idealization of power. In this respect, the preferred citation is his remark, 'A spiritual nature appears in force as such.' But Ranke was far from mere glorification of force. The Christian humanist foundations of his historical interpretation guarded him against such one-sidedness. His most deep-felt credo was a firm hierarchy of values and life functions. The celebrated, and later so notorious, synthesis of spirit and power which Ranke saw being broadly worked out in history, did not arise out of any intention to conceal the nature of power, but from recognition that power, in the end, depends upon spiritual forces and cannot endure by physical means alone. Is this a false, or indeed a disastrous, recognition? Is it not rather the decisive political and philosophical assumption corresponding to our value system as well? There may be those who reproach Ranke with not seeing historical reality on its true foundation, and in itself the reproach is justified. But it must be said in rebuttal that such historical foundations in the last analysis can be understood only as *ethical* postulates. Nor should it be forgotten that Ranke in his time knew nothing of the modern excesses of power politics since the period of imperialism. Sybel* and Treitschke, however, persisted in a wholly altered period in a subjectively sincere belief in the synthesis of power and spirit, state and civilization, politics and ethics. But they did not wish to perceive that the principal stress had visibly shifted to power and its manifestations. Thus there came to be spiritual motivation for the high estimation and over-valuation of power. Thus, in the final analysis, room was given, in spite of all idealistic and moral reservations, for the rise of a crudely naturalistic and biological ethic of violence.

Quite like the concept of the power-state, the celebrated formula of the primacy of foreign policy was radicalized. This profound idea, likewise, has incontestable value as an insight, so long as it is understood and applied in correct proportions. Indeed we can in general interpret the degeneration of German historical thought as the loss of the sense of proportion.

* Heinrich von Sybel (1817–95), German historian, pupil of Ranke, later became one of the leading representatives of the Prussian school of historians; established in 1859 the *Historische Zeitschrift*.

What we have called making war heroic and ethical arose in a similar way: The new romanticism, and Ranke's celebrated observation in the *Politisches Gespräch* upon the basis of this psychological situation: 'You can tell me of few important wars of which it cannot be proved that true moral energy won the victory.' After the experience of the Second World War, this, too, is certainly an observation from which we can derive some profit! But in Ranke's mind is concealed much more, his own metaphysical assumptions: the belief that good must in the end win over evil in history. However, only when the original idealist philosophy was combined with the traditions of Prussian militarism could such attribution of ethical value to war become dangerous for German thought. Treitschke is the prototype of this 'synthesis'. Listen to his apodictic justification of war: 'The justice of war rests simply upon the awareness of a moral necessity.' Clearly the ethical element stands in the centre of this justification and sanctioning of war. What Ranke still expressed in contemplative observation of the historical world, became in Treitschke's activist historical writing the call to historical action. The essential danger in this metamorphosis of romantic conceptions is the continued use of so-called idealist categories no longer applicable to a totally changed reality. The romantic Christian German circle around Frederick William IV, was replaced in German history by the 'realistic' policy of Bismarck and of the neo-Prussian militarism of Roon and Moltke. Thus an ever-widening discrepancy between the concrete historical development and historical thought resulted. The categories of thought were no longer able to express the forms of living events. Just as the conception of power established its independence, breaking loose from the hierarchy of values within which alone it can hold a meaningful place, so, too, this happened to the military idea. The idea of general military service as conceived by Boyen* had originally a thoroughly defensive tendency and hence could lay claim to great ethical importance, as precisely we in Switzerland must affirm. But, during the course of the nineteenth century, it became constantly more and more an offensive means of power politics, and finally grew into modern militarism. Military thought took in tow the already emancipated concept of power. For militarism is, expressed in the briefest of formulas,

---

* Hermann von Boyen (1771–1848), Prussian field-marshal and the founder of universal military service; Meinecke wrote the authoritative biography of him.

the subordination of political as well as economic to military thought and action. The sanctioning and attribution of ethical value to the conception of military defence, however, which was well justified in wholly different historical conditions, remained also with its militaristic aberration.

Finally, the radicalization of the national idea was added to this over-valuation of power of war. In Ranke's case, it was completely controlled by the dominant idea of a common Western civilization, or, more typical of Ranke, of a common civilization of the Romanic-Germanic peoples. The development of the national idea is characterized by the gradual elimination of cosmopolitan and humanistic foundations on which national feeling originally rested and out of which it arose. Herder proclaimed humanity and nationality together. Even for Ranke the national factor receives its historical meaning and its higher worth only by its place in the universal order. A French historian has emphasized how important it was that in Germany the ideas of nation and nationality were gradually displaced by the words folk (*Volk*) and folkdom (*Volkstum*), which he calls '*termes intraduisibles, parce qu'ils répondent à un autre ordre de sentiments!*' (terms which cannot be translated because they correspond to a different level of feeling). By this he can only mean that these words are merely the conceptual expression of the loss of the cosmopolitan factor. The universalist aspect of the Rankean picture of history was constantly narrowed down to a nationalist picture of history visibly without the meaningful relationship of the national factor to a higher general system. In this case, too, the sense of proportion was lost. Power authority and prestige of the nation became the supreme values, to which all moral, spiritual and economic values and life functions were subordinated. The German picture of history became Germano-centric. It is remarkable and undeniable that the very land most productive of world history has possessed the least understanding of the deeper nature of other nations. Hence, in the work which we have mentioned, Gerhard Ritter must now name as one of the most urgent tasks of the new German historical writing 'to draw at last a picture of western European history in the nineteenth and twentieth centuries, or preferably since the Middle Ages, which shall be soberly clear and free of national prejudices. It can only be of use,' he continues, 'if we learn to observe the modern history of Europe from the other side of the Rhine-Vosges frontier as well.' The principal sin for which German policy after Bismarck's departure has been criticized was disregard for the factor of the world outside. To exactly the same degree, the same was true of the corresponding picture of history. Here we see clearly the negative aspect of the close connexion of politics and history in German thought. Instead of encouraging each other to extend the horizon, they confirmed each other in making national existence and national claims absolute.

We have thus characterized the situation approximately as of the year 1900, when the definition of the German picture of history by the three forces, nationalism, militarism and imperialism, was obvious. We have already emphasized how efforts were begun for fundamental revision in the historical thought of Germany after the experience of the First World War. Basically, what the best minds then produced in historical and political reorientation remains quite valid for the revision now urgent. In contrast, the effect of the rise of National-Socialism upon historical writing must be fundamentally characterized as reactionary. It was a return to that partiality already described, but immensely magnified. Essentially the picture of history of the Third Reich is also characterized by the same three forces. These were now rapidly transformed by extreme intensification to the point of excessiveness. A *reductio ad absurdum* resulted. When these forces were reintroduced in the Third Reich, it was not realized that they had become profoundly anachronistic, since the other civilized peoples in the West set about gradually to overcome precisely these forces and to apply themselves to other tasks. In this sense, nationalism was still more intensified and became the apotheosis of the doctrine of folk and race; imperialism became the geopolitical planning of large spaces and finally the hallucination of world rule; militarism, further intensified, became the waging of war for its own sake, engaging in its final orgies in the militarized party formations.

Now that we have come this far, we must once again take up the question of how this convulsive and diseased over-intensification of general European tendencies in German thought and action could happen. For it is a commonly established conclusion of every analysis that the picture of history of the Germans, in the final analysis, displayed diseased characteristics. In this regard, such expressions as psychosis and neurosis, pathological and psychopathological, are typical. Instead of criticism and revision, various authors prefer to speak of diagnosis and therapy. Are these only words? Certainly in part it may be a question of fashionable ideas, understandable in the age of psychoanalysis. Beyond this, however, there is an undeniable tendency to apply psychoanalytical procedures to whole nations. But even a Benedetto Croce, who is so strict in his definitions and formulations, often speaks of phenomena of disease in connexion with German developments. Where do we get the right and the standard by which to characterize the German development, that is, the development of German mankind, as diseased?

In his lecture, 'Deutschland und die Deutschen' (Germany and the Germans), Thomas Mann has borrowed Goethe's remark that classicism is the healthy and romanticism the diseased, with the Germans, however, as the eternal romantics. The logical conclusion is easy to grasp. But in fields such as this, formal logic has no place, as is not always recognized. If we must characterize all German history, and with it German mankind as such as diseased in its inmost nature, no cure would be possible any longer, then, unless the nature of a people can be transformed. For this reason, Thomas Mann calls the history of the German spirit, or, in his terms, German 'inwardness', not a diseased, but a melancholy history. He does not call it a tragic history, for misfortune ought not to swagger. According to Thomas Mann, the possibility, though not the *necessity*, that the history of German mankind would become such a melancholy history (other Germans would not shy from saying a tragic history) lay concealed within the nature of the German soul. That sins and depravity are to be found directly next to the highest and most fruitful ideas, that even in the most pleasing and ethereal manifestations the seeds of disease may be concealed, like a worm in a rose, belongs to the essence of romanticism. Thus all possibilities given to German mankind are laid down in the nature of romanticism, from the creation of the loftiest and most sublime ideas to the full release of the basest drives. Upon the basis of this recognition, Thomas Mann rejects the thesis of the two Germanies. There are not two Germanies, one good and one evil, 'but only one, which by its devilish cunning made its best do the service of evil. Evil Germany is the good Germany gone astray, the good in misfortune, in guilt and destruction.' Benedetto Croce reaches exactly the same result. He calls the history of the German spirit demoniac and tragic, because it brings forth from its most intimate nature the highest as well as the lowest. On the one hand he speaks of the pure fruitful ideas of romanticism, on the other hand of its diseased parallel phenomena. Long before the rise of National-Socialism, intellectual history generally recognized that the solution of the riddle of German development lay in the nature of romanticism. I will only refer here to the French philosopher of history, Ernest Seillière. As early as the twenties, he sought to make a comprehensive interpretation of the phenomenon of romanticism. I refer also to the work, by Fritz Strich on *Klassik und Romantik* which appeared at about the same time, in which he defined classicism as the search for completion and romanticism as the drive for infinity. 'When the German spirit follows its own path', he wrote, 'it is the spirit of romanticism. Its classic ideal can only be realized with foreign assistance.'

Now if, in addition, we characterize romanticism as the irrational, the yearning, the visionary, the boundless, then we have a clue to the over-intensification of the currents of ideas which determined the German picture of history. The history of the German spirit and hence of German historical thinking is principally characterized by the continuing disintegration of originally idealist conceptions. Concretely, disintegration means secularization, materialization, naturalization, biologization. That is the road from national feeling to race delusion, from cosmopolitanism to the dream of world rule, from a war for freedom to world conquest, from the national state to the organization of space, from humanism and Christianity to exclusive or tribal religion and ethics. The same path was travelled by the total historical metaphysics of German idealism. The 'higher historical necessity', which in Ranke's case was the expression of divine world government, became a mechanistic and causalistic principle in the age of naturalism and a mythological principle in the Third Reich. In it all personal responsibility was blurred, appearing more and more as historical determinism. The concept of fate, but only more extreme than before, is torn loose from its foundation in the treasury of ideas of Christianity and humanism. Under a mythological adornment, it is equated with the leader principle in the Third Reich. Destiny became the leader, and the leader destiny. Thus the concept of destiny led *ad absurdum*. Understood in this way, it became a central feature of the 'Germanic' picture of history, as a theoretician of the Third Reich expressed it, while the ideological background out of which it arose, the tradition of antiquity and Christianity, was abolished as an 'alien superstructure' above the substance of German life.

Against us it could probably be argued that, in our analysis of the German picture of history, we have used the same method that we so strongly wished to pillory. In following the development of certain ideas from Ranke until the Third Reich, have we not combined impermissibly heterogeneous elements, have we not drawn a totally inexistent line in intellectual history? None the less, I do believe that there is a clear line of distinction between our analysis and the method I have criticized. I admit that it is probably ambiguous even to speak of *development* in the degeneration of the historical thought of the Germans. In any case, we must be clear what the conception of development can and should mean in historical thinking. Development should not be meant either mechanistically or biologically. The conception of development should not be combined with the image of a progress from cause to effect, or with the image of growth from seed to fruit. If we are to apply the conception of development to the phenomenon of historical life, two things ought not to be excluded from it—the spontaneous working of the free and creative spirit, and the influence of external factors. Ideas permit, because of their innermost nature, the most divergent individual interpretations and hence realizations. That they can degenerate need not be a reproach against their creators. For the most part, it is unforeseeable developmental forces coming later into operation which impel them to move in another direction or to exaggerate their own true selves. If, in stating our problem, we make this small digression, we come to the conclusion that, in the case of the degeneration of historical thought in Germany, we ought not to speak of a logically consistent development toward inescapable disaster. The seeds of disease were indeed present in the German nature, but they did not *have* to result in an acute crisis. The diseased and disastrous development which the German nature later took in actuality was contained in it not as a necessity, but as a possibility. Belief that German mankind, too, had different possibilities than those which became the fact of history, belief that German history could have taken another course, gives a more profound right to talk of tragic development as such to those Germans who today practice self-criticism. If we here today did not have that belief, then we could spare ourselves the trouble of analysing and criticizing the German picture of history. For what criticism should make possible and what revision should undertake, is nothing else than the search for those wasted possibilities, when all revision would become an illusion. Patients whose bodies no longer show signs of becoming healthy must give up their doctors. But before we begin our search for those healthy forces, those other possibilities in the German nature, we might well throw light upon the problem of the diseased German development from another angle, which seems of great interest to me.

Though this aspect stands in closest connexion with the explanation of the degeneration of German mankind upon the basis of the nature of romanticism which we have just given in terms of intellectual history, it arises even more from a concrete historical situation. This means that the typical characteristics of German historical thinking, as they were finally established, can be understood under this motto as well: Historical destiny treated Germany and Germans badly. This amounts to saying: In its historical development over the centuries, Germany remained behind, indeed was kept behind, the other European nations, particularly those of western Europe. This very conception as well narrows historical consciousness to political factors; it is, however, wholly understandable upon the basis of the historical situation around and after 1800. The German spirit first truly realized this specific German position in European history when roused and alarmed by the ideas of the French Revolution and Napoleon's invasion. Only then, with a weirdly pleasing suddenness, German thought became aware of Germany's position with regard to the civilized peoples of the West. Hence the feverishness with which so many German spirits seized upon the new ideas. Thus the situation in which Fichte made his *Addresses to the German Nation*, the time when the specifically German national idea and state conception arose, is psychologically wholly similar to that in which Machiavelli created his theory. This psychological concordance, from a certain point of view a historical concordance as well, enables us for the first time to see in a correct light the formation at just that time of a Machiavellianism of German origin. That was the historic moment when the alliance was formed between idealism and Machiavellianism, so promising in appearance but in actuality so disastrous for the future of Germany. Over this alliance, as a verdict, this phrase could be placed: An extraordinary situation calls for an extraordinary theory, and this theory demands extraordinary measures in turn. At this point the idea that German development permitted, indeed demanded, the extraordinary, entered German historical thinking and soon became a political axiom. From the notion that destiny had treated Germany badly arose an axiom in German thought that destiny must be coerced. This idea indeed was already quite strong in Machiavelli when he called Fortune a woman who, to be had, must be beaten and bullied.

The dissatisfaction of German thought with destiny extends, however, not only to historical development, to the dimension of historic *time*, but also to the geographic situation, and therefore to the dimension of historic *space*. If the first notion is illuminated by the refrain, 'We came too late in history', then the second notion can be expressed in the words, 'We have an unfavourable position in the historical world.' Both thoughts, however, justify the conviction that the extraordinary, that is, that which cannot be measured by European standards, is permitted, or rather even more, required, for Germany. After Ranke, historical thought comes increasingly under the spell of these two ideas. The idea that supposedly history had treated them badly, that they were the dupes among the peoples of Europe, became intolerable for a Germanism rising to ever higher levels of self-consciousness. It finally was intensified into an essentially compulsive notion. Above all, it explains the restless, hurried, excitable and irritable qualities of German politics in the latter part of the nineteenth century. It is not the least explanation of so anachronistic a measure as the annexation of Alsace-Lorraine. The idea that, when the roles in the drama of world history were distributed, they received only a secondary part, became a veritable complex. In it, once again, we may speak in particular of a time complex—the thought of having come too late; and a space complex—the thought of having to live in too exiguous and perilous a position. We do not wish to develop this theory any farther, however interesting it may be in itself. Certainly these fixed ideas furnish a broad explanation of the fact that the three forces of nationalism, militarism and imperialism took on especially radical forms in Germany. On the other hand, in historical writing they served as justification for German action and thought before the forum of world opinion and history. Thus a more extreme form of nationalism was justified by the argument that national unification was achieved late in history, and hence under particularly unfavourable circumstances. Hence it seemed evident that power and unity had to take precedence before liberty, and it became, so it seemed, an historical necessity that nationalism, instead of allying itself with liberalism as elsewhere in Europe, sought to crush it. The hurried, restless and irritable character of German imperialism, including its naval policy, is precisely the policy of expansion and world-wide economic activity of a late-comer who, if he still wants to snatch something for himself, if he still wants a place in the sun, in the much-preferred graphic expression, had to have a tighter grip than his more fortunate rivals. Strict military order and more energetic military thinking are also a necessity, arising inescapably out of the difficult geopolitical situation and un-favourable frontier conditions. Germany is the central power, held by virtue of a geopolitical law of nature between the pincers of the powers on the flanks. One after another, this and similar theses are encountered in German historical writing, of course especially after the foundation of the Bismarckian Reich, at every turn, until one is fed up with it. It is easy to see that such arguments which finally become compulsive notions gravely influence politics. The question, however, was whether men would succumb to the compulsive notion or expel and extenuate it by proper political action. Bismarck did not succumb to this complex. It was already evident in the case of William II that he did, and in Hitler the case became pathological.

Let us look back from this point. We have endeavoured to throw critical light upon the decisive ideological, that is, meta-physical, ethical, political and historical philosophical assumptions of the German picture of history. In this respect we had to keep the European scene always in view in order to maintain a stan-dard for judgment of specifically German traits of character. We now recognize that such a development of German historical thought had to lead to estrangement from Europe, especially from western European spirit. It led to what Benedetto Croce has called 'spiritual dissension between Germany and Europe'. In his view, the 'most urgent and immediate future task' is to investigate the basis of this dissension and to lay clear its preparation deep into the past. But we have also mentioned that our generation is not the first to set itself to revise fundamentally the German picture of history. The First World War already created a spiritual and political situation for German mankind similar to that existing

today. Together with Ernst Troeltsch* and others, Friedrich
Meinecke then sought to establish some rapprochement between
Western and German political and historical thinking. Even
from our present-day point of view, the achievements of these
men in intellectual history are still thoroughly valid, and much
in their thesis can be adopted in the revision incumbent upon our
generation. Even then it was already clearly realized that the
central problem of revision was the romantic-idealist world of
ideas as the ideological source of nourishment for German
historical thinking. Such self-criticism first became really
possible when German scholars began to take lessons from
Western rationalism. It was precisely the French who, from the
counter-position of rationalism repeatedly called emphatic
attention to the ferments of romanticism, of the irrational and the
mystical, working in the German picture of history, and hence
to the dangers latent in it. Only now, the more rational historical
and political thinking of the West made a new evaluation of the
German historical traditions and ideals possible. Now the dangers
of the romantic idea of identity, which sought to constrain the
opposing elements into unity and inoculated German thinking
with its symptomatic addiction for synthesis, were recognized.
Men learned to see that the supposed syntheses were vast illusions,
that alongside power ever less room remained for the spirit, that,
alongside politics, ethics made out badly, that freedom was an
equal partner alongside the authority of the state. It was recognized that men, hypnotized by the growth of political power, had
wholly forgotten to give cultural traditions and values their
proper place in history. Thus, the cry arose, 'Back to Goethe and
Humboldt, to Schiller and Kant.' Naturally it was not meant that
it was desirable or possible for the Germans again to become a
people of poets and thinkers, but that the Germans should again
seek direct spiritual contact with the great cultural figures of that
time. It was recognized that the developments which permitted
the national idea, in alliance with the conception of the power-
state, to become its own end and the supreme value, was an
aberration of the German spirit. Men learned again to look up
to a higher idea which would give direction to political and
historical thought: the idea of the common civilization of the
West. That is why it is important to search out those men and

* Ernst Troeltsch (1865-1923), German Protestant theologian and social
philosopher.

those ideas which warned that the wrong path had been taken, and sought to direct the German spirit back to its true historic mission. These men and these ideas, however, were forced aside by the main stream of development. Hence, in the traditional picture of history, they have been given only an insignificant place, or indeed no place at all. We must now take up the search for the wasted opportunities. Where possible, the Germans must now turn their own neglected traditions to the forces upon which to rebuild their life and their state. They must learn again to see that alongside and within the Prussian-German historical stream, there was also a German historical stream. This was so even though the German stream became increasingly an undercurrent, more and more swallowed up by the main current. They must once again bring up into their historical awareness the fact that there operated, beside the authoritarian, power-oriented current of forces, also liberal and democratic forces which merely did not have the historical chance to survive. They will then cease to be victim of the idea that, in the liberal, democratic, political and historical thinking something alien is being forced upon them.

CHAPTER ELEVEN

MISFORTUNE AND MORAL DECISIONS IN GERMAN HISTORY

by Hajo Holborn

Hajo Holborn was born in Germany in 1902. After studying at Berlin University briefly under Meinecke, he taught history at the University of Heidelberg from 1926 to 1931 and was Carnegie Professor of History and International Relations at the Berlin School of Politics and lecturer in history at Berlin University from 1931 to 1934. Since he has come to the United States, he has been professor of history at Yale University, where he now occupies the Randolph W. Townsend, Jr., chair.

Among the books which he published in Germany were: *Bismarcks Europäische Politik zu Beginn der siebziger Jahre und die Mission Radowitz* (Berlin, 1924); *Deutschland und die Türkei, 1878–90* (Berlin, 1925) and *Ulrich von Hutten* (Leipzig, 1929). Since he has come to America, he has published, among other books, *Ulrich von Hutten and the German Reformation* (Yale University Press, New Haven, 1937) and *The Political Collapse of Europe* (Alfred A. Knopf, New York, 1951).

The following essay appeared first in the monthly, *Der Monat*, as a contribution to a discussion on 'Irrwege der deutschen Geschichte', with an introductory article by Friedrich Meinecke.

By the events of the year 1945, the Germans again came into possession of their own history. The Hitler régime deprived the Germans of the right freely to interpret their great and rich past. The National-Socialist 'historical myth', a thin disguise for naked ideals of power, was an attempt to throttle completely the freedom of historical research, which is in fact one of the proudest achievements of modern German intellectual life. Essentially in order to cut off the Germans from the full inheritance of their own history, National-Socialism tried to prevent the critical understanding of German history. Only those events and ideas might be considered—and then only under artificial stage lighting—which could serve to prepare and to enhance Hitler's dictatorship and world rule. But, as a result, German history thereby was brought fundamentally into sharp contradiction with Western Christian development, of which it is but a part.

The freedom to take hold of the meaningful substance of German history through critical understanding and evaluation exists again, and it is the task of a new generation to make the best use of this opportunity. It is of the greatest interest that, in this opening stage, we should take heed of the voice of the revered and greatest living master of German historical research. I am pleased to accept an invitation to take part in the discussion opened by Friedrich Meinecke with an article in the October number of this magazine.

It is understandable that German historians, on beginning reconstruction of the concept of German history, should be concerned lest their revision of historical valuations be taken for opportunistic adaptation to the new political powers of the hour, and therefore for renewed political submissiveness (*Gleichschaltung*). It is also understandable that precisely those who, in view of the aberrations of the Third Reich, continued to think critically concerning the course of German history, should, at the present moment, wish to avoid making a self-righteous show of their own foresight. After Hitler's war, like a mighty earthquake, ruined the German scene and the lives of millions of persons, it would be presumptuous for a single individual to come forward to prove how right he had been in the past.

If, however, one wishes to achieve a new interpretation of the major forces of German history one must not go too far in being concerned about appearing to be a new 'joiner' ('*Gleichschalter*'). Any self-righteousness with reference to past differences of opinion is certainly out of place these days, but a radical historical criticism is one of the most urgent of national tasks to make it possible for the German people to understand its present lot and to devote its energy to the achievement of future objectives in keeping with the highest ideals of the German past. It is in this sense that a new awareness of historical continuity between Germany's past and present must be re-established. But this does not at all mean that we have to exculpate in any way the Germany of yesterday—Hitler's Germany—or the Germany of the day before yesterday—Bismarck's and William II's Germany. For in the thousand years of German history, each of these epochs constitutes still but a brief watch in the night.

Few speak directly of Nazi Germany, and few of the Weimar Republic either. The Empire of Bismarck and William II has become the centre of discussion. Obviously, many see in the Third Reich an absolute perversion of the ideas on which

Bismarck's Empire was founded. There is certainly some truth in this explanation. To a certain degree, Hitler did represent the intrusion of a foreigner into German history. He was indeed in a sense more distinctly a foreigner than the Corsican Napoleon was in France. Hitler's original political ideas, above all his racist theory, developed on the barren soil of the disintegrating Hapsburg Empire. But he experienced for the first and only time a sense of belonging in the German army during the First World War, and in the disintegration of German society after the war he was able to make himself the master of German destiny.

For that reason it is not possible after all to consider Hitler as a 'non-German' event, and Friedrich Meinecke, as a matter of fact, has always strictly avoided doing so. But it is also not right to see in the Third Reich the result of tragic accidents of an individual and a general kind. Tragedy certainly was not lacking, for it is always present in history, particularly at the great turning-points. For all that, Hitler's success in Germany between 1930 and 1943 would not have been possible without the acclamation, voluntary at first, which he received particularly from the German bourgeoisie. It was Bismarck who maintained the Prussian-German army above the constitution and prepared the German bourgeoisie to follow autocrats. It actually means little that the army, or more exactly the generals, eventually fared badly under Hitler, since hardly any one was more responsible for the victory of the authoritarian over the popular conception of the state in Germany than the leaders of the Reichswehr. And there can be no question that the traditions of the Bismarckian Empire were the principal factor contributing to the destruction of the Weimar Republic.

Any historical contemplation of the past must begin with the assumption that the course of past history was determined by causes and motives which make this course explicable. If we did not believe in such logical explanations of history, historical research would cease to have meaning. But the recognition of the causes for the victory of one or another state which we may discover by retrospective analysis, should not prevent us from understanding history as the struggle between necessity and freedom. Ranke described freedom in history in these words, 'We see before us a series of events following upon and determining each other. When I say, "determine", I do not mean, to be sure, by absolute necessity. The great thing is rather that everywhere human freedom is presupposed. History studies the scenes of freedom. This is its greatest appeal. But freedom is joined by force, indeed elemental force; without it, freedom would come to an end in secular events as well as in the world of ideas. At any moment again, something novel may originate that could be traced back only to the first and common source of all human action and inaction. Nothing exists merely for the sake of something else; nothing is wholly subsumed in the reality of something else. . . .'

Ranke was convinced that the free moral decision as well as intellectual and religious creativity of the single individual or people constituted fundamental elements of history. At many points in his work, Ranke reminded his readers that events might have taken another course had other factors come into play or other decisions been taken. On the other hand, Ranke did not hesitate to recognize a nemesis in history. We know that Ranke was very cautious in passing moral judgment and tended in general to harmonize the sharp conflicts of historical life. But he never questioned fundamentally the freedom of human action in the struggle with historical necessity.

If we were to consider by itself Friedrich Meinecke's article on 'Wrong Paths in our History', and forget his critical observations elsewhere on German history, it would seem that he can see fundamentally few truly wrong paths, but essentially only paths of tragic misfortune in German history. The word 'tragic' is in this case used in a very superficial sense as denoting the influence of external forces rather than the struggle of human hearts. Tragic guilt is not mentioned. The course of German history since 1648 is depicted as more or less inevitable. 'It was the geopolitical position of Germany in the centre of Europe which forced upon us the alternative either to remain a low pressure area or to become a power state', Meinecke declares in the decisive passage.

Now this is certainly true in the sense that Germany had a right to obtain the means of self-preservation, and it must also be admitted that in the eighteenth century this could only take place within the forms of despotism. I cannot see that Frederick the Great deserves the accusations made against him, particularly outside of Germany, though it must not be forgotten that they are to a large degree the result of the misuse of Old Fritz by modern German patriotism.

The first question which must be asked, in my opinion, is whether the power won by Germany since the days of Frederick was really used for simple self-preservation and for the pacification

14

of Europe. Here it must be said that, since the middle of the
nineteenth century, the feeling of common responsibility for
Europe as a whole has been in rapid decline everywhere in Europe,
but most particularly in Germany, that one would think as the
central country had a very special interest in the peaceful progress
of the Continent. The central position of Germany, however, was
utilized almost exclusively to justify power politics. Bismarck,
who could speak with real scorn of Europe as a 'mere geographic
name', did show, for all that, some feeling for the prosperity of the
whole European community of states. But the annexation of
Alsace-Lorraine created lasting French-German tension, and Bismarck's peacefully intended alliance policy was accompanied by
bellicose language and constant increase of armaments. Under
William II, Germany turned quickly to the open sea of world
politics. In the First World War, the leaders of German militarism and heavy industry found themselves easily joined in
adventurous expansionist plans, and the forces of moderate
opposition were repressed without great difficulty by them.

This brings us directly to the second problem, which is the
domestic leadership of the state in modern Germany, or the vain
struggle for genuine liberalization and democratization of German
political forms. I hear two principal objections to this thesis,
first, that the democratic movement of 1848–49 might have
become more nationalist than the authoritarian governments, and
second, that a democratic government would have sapped the
power of German self-preservation. It cannot be questioned that
modern mass democracy carries within it all the elements of
radical nationalism. Jingoism and chauvinism have always raised
their heads anew in Western democracy, but also have always
been thrust back within bounds by the American, English and
French nations. And the greatest democratic movement of
Germany, the old Social-Democracy, did not prove to be a
chauvinist force in German history.

With regard to the argument that German foreign policy
required monarchist leadership in order successfully to represent
German interests, I simply do not know what is left to say after
the loss of two world wars and the constant decline of German
power and welfare. It is hard to see how Germany could have
fared worse under a popular government than she did under
William II, Tirpitz, Ludendorff and Hitler. In all probability,
Germany on the whole would have had greater strength and less

internal dissension; she would have been more in accord with her own European past and had greater harmony among her social classes. Again, it was Bismarck who in public speeches always repeated his incitement to the Germans to make a stand against Europe and against those fellow citizens he was pleased to brand 'enemies of the Empire'.

But the Germans could have found greater unity between their cultural and political life than they were able to achieve after 1850. Friedrich Meinecke's distinction between cultural values and political values seems to be still strongly influenced by the theories of those liberals who, in seeking to conceive of the world of politics as the realm of tragic necessity, but of philosophy, ideology, science and art as the realm of true freedom, endeavoured to justify philosophically their resigned renunciation of establishing political liberty, accepting instead German national unity which Bismarck created through sheer power with the aid of the Prussian army. Meinecke is too much the historical realist ever to have understood this opposition as absolute. In his *Weltbürgertum und Nationalstaat*, he felt he could still overcome the contradiction between German cultural and political values. In his *Idee der Staatsräson*, written after the First World War, he threw the tension into bold relief, whereas in his most recent article, cultural values stand far above political values, but in such a way that a certain sympathy still shines over political events.

In Germany under William II, the doctrine of the difference between individual and general, historical and absolute values, found its leading philosophical advocate in Heinrich Rickert. Wilhelm Dilthey, whom not only Germany but also the world is learning to admire as one of the great German thinkers, declared that Rickert was upholding 'an indemonstrable and indeed one-sided definition of the meaning and purpose of history'. He added, 'This is much too amiable and benevolent a conception of human nature, in which the dark instincts of mutual repression and destruction play a very considerable role.' Dilthey was convinced that the power of spiritual ideas was proved by their capacity to conquer the totality of life, just as in turn this totality is the expression of the unity of that infinite-finite being, man.

Almost at the same time as Dilthey penned his criticism of Rickert, Hugo von Hofmannsthal wrote his *Briefe des Zurückgekehrten* (Letters on My Return) (1901), in which he cites as the highest wisdom of the formation of personality the simple

statement of a Scotsman, 'The whole man must move at once.' But
Hofmannsthal judged, 'that is what Germans are not these days.
. . . The thoughts in their heads do not fit the thoughts in their
hearts, nor the thoughts of their officials the thoughts of their
scholars; the façades of their homes do not fit the backstairs, nor
their enterprises their temperament, their public their private
life. . . .' At the same time, another great German, Theodor
Mommsen, made a moving personal confession in his testament,
poignantly expressing the destructive conflict between the
political and spiritual-moral natures of Germany at the beginning
of the new century.

One of the preconditions for the formulation of a new German
concept of history and new forms of social and political organization is the recognition of the unity of life. The state is not just
power. It has also the task to realize moral objectives. On the
other hand, even the loftiest of ideas do not refute the finite and
time-bound character of human nature. Human freedom may be
greater in the world of ideas than in political and social action,
but, if freedom does not prove itself to be a moral force in the
hard conflict with the realities of history, does it have more than
an abstract philosophical value? Mere idealism in practical action
deserves even less praise. Meinecke's statement that no one
should 'lecture' a tragic hero 'for having taken a wrong path, if,
filled with the proud sentiment "*In hoc signo vinces*", he performs
deeds which first carry him to the heights of victory and finally
plunge him into the abyss', seems to me wholly untenable. For,
in my opinion, the essential difference lies in whether he fights
under the sign of the cross, the star symbol of the Prussian Guard,
or the swastika. Moreover, the memory of what irreparable
wounds were inflicted not only on his own people, but on other
peoples, in the course of such events, should indeed never be
forgotten. The history of the last fifty years will appear to future
historians not only as the history of German defeats, but principally as the history of the political collapse of Europe.

It seems to me that a critical historical evaluation of the last
150 years of German history can contribute significantly not only
to the inner freedom and unity of the German people, but also to
the development of a new general European consciousness which,
in the present state of the world, is a practical necessity. It is at
the same time an ideal demand in harmony with the profound
forces and yearnings of German history.

BIBLIOGRAPHY

In this supplementary and selected bibliography the following abbreviations are used: *Dt.R.* for *Deutsche Rundschau*; *F.H.* for *Frankfurter Hefte*; *G.W.U.* for *Geschichte in Wissenschaft und Unterricht*; *H.Z.* for *Historische Zeitschrift*; *N.A.* for *Neues Abendland*; *W.a.G.* for *Die Welt als Geschichte*; *Z.g.St.W.* for *Zeitschrift für die gesamte Staatswissenschaft*; *Z.R.G.* for *Zeitschrift für Religions- und Geistesgeschichte*.

Antz, Josef. 'Bismarck und seine Wirkung auf das deutsche Volk', *F.H.*, II (1947), no. 1, pp. 38–46.

Bauer, A. 'Der Einbruch des Antisemitismus im deutschen Denken', *Aufbau*, II (1946), pp. 152–64.

Baumgardt, Rudolf. *Bismarck: Licht und Schatten eines Genius*, Munich and Vienna, Andermann, 1951.

Benz, Ernst. 'Franz von Baader über den Proletair. Zur Geschichte des vormarxistischen Sozialismus', *Z.R.G.*, I (1948), no. 2, pp. 97–124.

'Franz von Baader und der abendländische Nihilismus', *Archiv für Philosophie*, III (1949), no. 1, pp. 27–52.

'Kirchengeschichte als Universalgeschichte', *Saeculum*, I (1950), no. 4, pp. 487–507 (review of Kenneth Scott Latourette, *A History of the Expansion of Christianity*).

Besser, Joachim. 'Neuwertung der Vergangenheit. Die deutschen Zeitschriften im Kampf um ein neues Geschichtsbild', *Die Sammlung*, II (1947), pp. 574–84.

'Die Vorgeschichte des Nationalsozialismus in neuem Licht', *Die Pforte*, II (Urach, 1950), nos. 21–22, pp. 763–84.

Bing, Harold F. 'The Study and Teaching of History in Post-War Germany', *History*, XXXVI (London, 1951), pp. 92–107.

Bismarck. See the discussion in *Der Monat*, II (1950), no. 19, pp. 49–61; no. 20, pp. 215–18; no. 24, pp. 604–607; no. 26, pp. 222–23.

Brunschwig, Henri. 'L'Allemagne au XIXᵉ siècle. Thèses et synthèses', *Revue Historique*, LXXVI (1952), no. 207, pp. 49–59.

Buchheim, Karl. 'Macht und Missbrauch des politischen Berufungsgedankens', *Hochland*, XLI (1949), no. 5, pp. 477 ff.

'Entstehung und Eigenart des Nationalismus in Deutschland', *N.A.*, VI (1951), pp. 401–10.

Bülow, Franz. 'Hegel, der Historismus und die Dialektik', *Schmollers Jahrbuch*, LXIX (1949), no. 1, pp. 283–318.

Busch, Ernst. *Das Problem eines neuen Geschichtsunterrichts*. Bonn: Ferd. Dümmler, 1948.

Carré, Jean-Marie. *Les écrivains français et le mirage allemand*. Paris: Boivin, 1947.

Carroll, E. Malcolm. 'Recent German Publications and German

Foreign Policy, 1933–45', *The American Political Science Review*, XLVI (June 1952), no. 2, pp. 525–41.

Conze, Werner (ed.). *Deutschland und Europa*, Historische Studien zur Völker- und Staatenordnung des Abendlandes (Festschrift for the 60th anniversary of Hans Rothfels). Düsseldorf: Droste Verlag, 1951.

Degkwitz, Rudolf. *Das alte und das neue Deutschland*. Hamburg: Claassen & Goverts, 1946.

Dehio, Ludwig. 'Ranke und der deutsche Imperialismus', *H.Z.*, CLXX (1950), pp. 307–28.

'Gedanken über die deutsche Sendung 1900–18', *ibid.*, CLXXIV (October 1952), no. 2, pp. 479–502.

Denderlein, Ernst. 'Preussen oder Europe', *N.A.*, II(1947), pp. 265–69.

'Preussens geistiges Vordringen in Bayern', *ibid.*, I (1946), pp. 17–24.

Ellwein, Thomas, and Brückmann, Waldemar. 'Friedrich der Grosse im Spiegel der Nachwelt', *Z.R.G.*, I (1948), no. 3, pp. 222–44.

Eyck, Erich. *Das persönliche Regiment Wilhelms II*. Politische Geschichte des deutschen Kaiserreiches, 1890–1914. Zurich: Rentsch, 1948.

Foerster, Friedrich Wilhelm. *Christus und das menschliche Leben*. Recklinghausen: Paulus-Verlag, 1951.

Franzel, Emil. *Geschichte unserer Zeit 1870–1950*. Munich: Oldenbourg, 1951.

'Verfehlte Geschichtsrevision. Um die historischen Grundlagen der deutschen Aussenpolitik', *N.A.*, IV (1949), pp. 97–99.

'Unser Geschichtsbild und unser Weg', *ibid.* (1949), pp. 270–73.

'Das Bismarckbild in unserer Zeit', *ibid.*, V (1950), pp. 223–30.

Freund, Michael. 'Adolf Hitler. Versuch eines Porträts', *Gegenwart*, VI (1951), no. 15, pp. 7–9.

Friedensburg, F. *Die Weimarer Republik*. Berlin: Carl Habel, 1946. See review by Fritz Hartung, *Deutsche Literaturzeitung*, LXIX (1948), no. 3, pp. 112–14.

Gablentz, Otto Heinrich, v.d. 'Die Tragik des Preussentums', *Dt.R.*, LXIX (1946), no. 2, pp. 99–120.

'Um die Idee des Nationalsozialismus', *ibid.*, (1946), no. 4, pp. 100–104.

Gollwitzer, Heinz. *Europabild und Europagedanke*. Beiträge zur deutschen Geistesgeschichte des 18. und 19. Jahrhunderts. Munich: Beck, 1951.

Görlitz, Walter. *Der deutsche Generalstab, Geschichte und Gestalt 1657–1945*. Frankfurt: F.H., 1950.

'Wallensteins Lager 1920–38. Das Verhältnis der deutschen Generalität zur Republik und zum Nationalsozialismus', *F.H.*, III (1948), no. 5, pp. 414–24 and *ibid.*, no. 6, pp. 519–26.

'Die deutsche Militäropposition', *ibid.*, IV (1949), no. 3, pp. 230-37.

Gustav Stresemann. Heidelberg: Ahren-Verlag, 1947.

Görres Gesellschaft. *Historisches Jahrbuch*, ed. by Johannes Spörl. Freiburg and Munich: Karl Alber, 1951.

'Wissenschaft auf neuen Wegen.' Zur diesjährigen Tagung der General-Versammlung der Görres-Gesellschaft vom 13.–16. Okt. in München. *N.A.*, VI (1951), pp. 653–57.

Griewank, Karl. 'Ursachen und Folgen des Scheiterns der deutschen Revolution von 1848', *H.Z.*, CLXX (1950), pp. 495–523.

Guttmann, Bernhard. *Schattenrisse einer Generation*. Stuttgart: Koehler, 1950.

Haerdter, R. 'Der Mensch und der Staat', *Gegenwart*, II (1947), nos. 13–14, pp. 23–26.

'Metamorphose des Staates', *ibid.* (1947), nos. 9–10, pp. 12–14.

Hagen, R. von dem. 'Rousseau und die Problematik der Demokratie', *Dt.R.*, LXXVI (1950), no. 3, pp. 157–66.

Hallgarten, George W. F. 'Heinrich von Treitschke: The Role of the Outsider in German Political Thought', *History*, XXXVI (London, 1951), no. 128, pp. 227–43.

Imperialismus vor 1914. Die soziologischen Grundlagen der Aussenpolitik europäischer Grossmächte vor dem ersten Weltkrieg. 2 vols. Munich: C. H. Beck, 1951.

Harnack, Axel von. 'Die deutsche Revolution von 1848/49 als Aufgabe für den Geschichtsschreiber', *Die Sammlung*, III (1948), pp. 150–60.

'Gedanken über Memoiren und Tagebücher', *W.a.G.*, X (1950), pp. 28–38.

Heffter, Heinrich. *Die deutsche Selbstverwaltung im 19. Jahrhundert*. Geschichte der Ideen und Institutionen. Stuttgart: Deutsche Verlagsanstalt, 1950.

'Forschungsprobleme der Geschichte des Nationalsozialismus', *G.W.U.*, III (April 1952), no. 4, pp. 197–215.

Heimpel, Hermann. 'Der Mensch in seiner Gegenwart', *Die Sammlung* (1951), no. 9.

Hemmerle, Eduard. 'Das Rheinland im preussischen Staat', *N.A.*, II (1947), pp. 140–43.

Hermersdorf, Herbert (ed.). *Gegenwartskunde*. Bonn: Johannes Borgmeyer, 1952.

Herrfahrdt, H. 'Politische Wissenschaft als politische Aufgabe', *Dt.R.*, LXXI (1948), no. 4, pp. 15–23.

Herzfeld, Hans. *Die moderne Welt 1789–1945*. Pt. I: Die Epoche des bürgerlichen Nationalstaates. Braunschweig: Westermann, 1950.

Hippel, E. v. 'Rousseaus Staatslehre als Mystik des Materialismus', *N.A.*, VI (1951), no. 7, pp. 337–45.

Hofer, Walther. 'Wege und Irrwege geschichtlichen Denkens', *Schweizer Monatshefte*, XXX (1950), no. 4, pp. 238–45.

Hofer, Walther. 'Die Vorgeschichte der Nachkriegszeit', *Kontakte*, no. 15. (Berlin: August 1952.)

    'H. von Srbiks letztes Werk', *H.Z.*, CLXXV (February 1953), no. 1, pp. 55–66.

Hoffmann, Martin. 'Zur Vorgeschichte des Faschismus', *Aufbau*, (1946), no. 12, pp. 1187–98.

Holborn, Hajo. 'Der deutsche Idealismus in sozialgeschichtlicher Bedeutung', *H.Z.*, CLXXIV (October 1952), no. 2, pp. 359–84.

Holldack, Heinz. *Was wirklich geschah*. Die diplomatischen Hintergründe der deutschen Kriegspolitik. Munich: Nymphenburger Verlag, 1949.

    'Zur Geschichte des zweiten Weltkrieges', *Hochland*, XLI (1948/49), pp. 334–51.

Hubatsch, Walther (ed.). *Schicksalswege deutscher Vergangenheit*. Beiträge zur geschichtlichen Deutung der letzten 150 Jahre. (Festschrift for the 65th anniversary of Siegfried Kaehler.) Düsseldorf: Droste-Verlag, 1950.

Hübinger, Paul Egon. 'Um ein neues deutsches Geschichtsbild', *G.W.U.* (October 1950), pp. 385–401.

Huhn, Willy. 'Militaristischer Sozialismus', *Aufbau* (1946), no. 4, pp. 368–81.

Hylander, Franz Josef. *Universalismus und Föderalismus*. Munich: Schnell & Steiner, 1946. He calls the Third Reich 'Summe aller vorausgegangenen Fehlentscheidungen der deutschen Geschichte'.

Internationales Jahrbuch für Geschichtsunterricht, ed. by Arbeitsgemeinschaft deutscher Lehrerverbände, vol. 1. Braunschweig: Albert Lindbach, 1951.

Jaspers, Karl. 'Thesen über die politische Freiheit', *Die Wandlung*, 1 (1945/46), no. 4, pp. 460–65.

    Die Schuldfrage. Zürich: Artemis-Verlag, 1946. See review by Waldemar Gurian in *Erasmus*, 1 (1947), no. 8, pp. 505–508.

    'Volk und Universität', *Die Wandlung*, II (1947), no. 1, pp. 54–64.

Kaehler, Siegfried G. 'Vom dunkeln Rätsel deutscher Geschichte', *Die Sammlung*, 1 (1945/46), pp. 140–53.

    'Neuere Geschichtslegenden und ihre Widerlegung', *ibid.* (1945/46), pp. 140–53.

Klepper, Otto. 'Das Ende der deutschen Republik', *Gegenwart*, II (1947), nos. 42/43, pp. 20–22. See the replies by Otto Braun and Karl Swering, *ibid.*, III (1948), nos. 7/8, pp. 17–19.

Kleist, Peter. *Zwischen Hitler und Stalin 1939–45*. Bonn: Athenäum-Verlag, 1950.

Kogon, Eugen. 'Das dritte Reich und die preussisch-deutsche Geschichte', *F.H.*, 1 (1946), no. 3, pp. 44–51.

Köhler, Gustav. 'Idealismus und Geschichtlichkeit', *Die Sammlung*, II (1951), no. 1, pp. 122–51.

Kordt, Erich (and Karl-Heinz Abshagen). *Wahn und Wirklichkeit*. Die Aussenpolitik des 3. Reiches. 2nd ed. Stuttgart: Deutsche Verlagsanstalt, 1948. See review by Oscar J. Hammen, *The Journal of Modern History*, XXII (1950), no. 1, pp. 82–83.

Kramer, F. A. *Vor den Ruinen Deutschlands*. Koblenz: Historisch Politischer Verlag, 1946.

Krauss, Werner. 'Nationalismus und Chauvinismus. Eine Nation in der Selbstentfremdung', *Aufbau* (1946), no. 5, pp. 443–56.

Kuhn, Hugo. *Die verfälschte Wirklichkeit*. Stuttgart: Deutsche Verlagsanstalt, 1946.

Kühn, Johannes. 'Geschichtsphilosophie und Utopie', *W.a.G.*, I (1951), pp. 1–11.

Leisegang, Hans. 'Der Geist des Marxismus', *Schweizer Monatshefte*, III (1951), no. 11, pp. 680–89.

Lemberg, Eugen. *Geschichte des Nationalismus in Europa*. Stuttgart: Kurt E. Schwab, 1950. See review by Hans Kohn in *American Historical Review*, XVII (October 1951), no. 1, pp. 153 ff.

Lewalter, Christian. 'Metamorphose des Marxismus', *Merkur*, III (1949), no. 3, pp. 209–28.
'Das Vakuum Europas', *ibid.* (1949), no. 7, pp. 690–702.
'Preussen als Mythos und Realität', *ibid.*, IV (1950), no. 7, pp. 887–98.
'Die Faszination des Marxismus', *ibid.*, V (1951), pp. 680–83.

Litt, Theodor. 'Das Problem der politischen Erziehung', *G.W.U.*, III (1952), no. 4, pp. 193 ff.
'Die Geschichte und das Übergeschichtliche', *Die Sammlung*, V (1950), no. 1, pp. 6–19.

Löwith, Karl. 'Christentum und Geschichte', *Merkur*, IV (1950), pp. 1241–52.
'Natur und Geschichte', *Neue Rundschau*, LXII (1951), no. 1, pp. 65–79.

Luckner, Gertrud (ed.). *Beiträge zur christlichen Betrachtung der Judenfrage*. Freiburg i.B.: Deutscher Caritas-Verband, 1951.

Lukacz, Georg. 'Die Nazis und Hegel', *Aufbau* (1946), no. 3, pp. 278–89.

Mayer, Anton. *Probleme, Ziele und Grenzen der Geschichtsrevision*. Nürnberg: Glock & Lutz, 1947.

Meinecke, Friedrich. *Schaffender Spiegel*. Studien zur deutschen Geschichtsschreibung und Geschichtsauffassung. Stuttgart: K. F. Koehler, 1948.

Messner, J. *Das Naturrecht. Handbuch der Gesellschaftsethik, Staatsethik und Wirtschaftsethik*. Innsbruck, Wien, 1950. See review by Adolf Weber in *Z.g.St.W.*, CVI (1950), pp. 550–55.

Meissner, Erich. *Zwiespalt im Abendland*, ein Kommentar zur deutschen Geschichte 1517–1939. Stuttgart: Deutsche Verlagsanstalt, 1949.

Mendelssohn, Peter de. 'Die verhinderten Hochverräter', *Der Monat*, XXIX (1951), pp. 495–509.
See also reply *ibid.*, no. 31, pp. 102–106.

Mommsen, Wilhelm. 'Der Kampf um das Bismarckbild', *Universitas*, v (1950), no. 3, pp. 277–80.

Muhs, K. 'Die Dialektik der Geschichte und die gegenwärtige Situation des abendländischen Geistes', *Z.g.St.W.*, CV (1949), pp. 709–36.

Nadolny, Rudolf. 'Sinn und Tragik Preussens', *Aussenpolitik*, II (1951), no. 6, pp. 418–25.

Niekisch, Ernst. 'Nihilismus', *Die Umschau*, II (1948), no. 2, pp. 193–206.

Philipp, Werner. 'Gibt es ein Gespräch zwischen Russland und Westeuropa? Eine historische Betrachtung', *Die Wandlung*, III (1948), no. 5, pp. 441–62.

Pick, G. 'Julius Ficker und die deutsche Frage', *N.A.*, November 1946, pp. 21–23; December 1946, pp. 12–16.

Pollmüller, J. H. 'Die Rolle der Reichswehr von 1918–33', *F.H.*, I (1946), no. 8, pp. 745–53 and no. 9, pp. 833–43.

Proesler, Hans. *Hauptprobleme der Sozialgeschichte*. Erlangen: Palm & Enke, 1951.

Prussia. On the problem of Prussia see the discussions in *N.A.*, I (1946), no. 5, pp. 29–30; *Gegenwart*, II (1947), nos. 5/6, pp. 7–9 and *ibid.*, (1947), nos. 11/12, p. 24; *N.A.*, II (1947), pp. 152–55; *ibid.*, I (1946), no. 4, pp. 24–26 and *ibid.*, II (1947), pp. 53–54.

Rantzau, Johann Albrecht von. 'Geschichte und Politik im deutschen Denken', *Die Sammlung*, I (1945–46), pp. 544–54.
'Das deutsche Geschichtsdenken der Gegenwart und die Nachwirkungen Rankes', *G.W.U.* (December 1950), pp. 514–24.

Rassow, Peter. 'Schlieffen und Holstein', *H.Z.*, CLXXIII (1952), no. 2, pp. 297–313.
'Nationalgeschichte und Universalgeschichte', *G.W.U.*, II (1951), pp. 513–21.

Richter, Werner. 'Das Bild Bismarcks', *Neue Rundschau*, LXIII (1952), no. 1, pp. 42–63.

Ritter, Emil. *Radowitz, ein katholischer Staatsmann in Preussen*. Cologne: J. P. Bachem, 1948. See review by Hans Joachim Schoeps, *Z.R.G.*, II (1949), no. 2, pp. 87–88.

Ritter, Gerhard. 'Ursprung und Wesen der Menschenrechte', *H.Z.*, CLXIX (1949), pp. 233–63.
Europa und die deutsche Frage. Betrachtungen über die geschichtliche Eigenart des deutschen Staatsdenkens. Munich: Bruckmann, 1948.

Ritter, Gethard. 'Die Fälschung des deutschen Geschichtsbildes im Hitlerreich', *Dt.R.*, LXX (1947), no. 4, pp. 11–20.

'The German Professors in the Third Reich', *Review of Politics*, VIII (1946), no. 2, pp. 242–54.

'Der neue Geschichtsunterricht. Entwurf von Richtlinien für die Neugestaltung des Geschichtsunterrichts an höheren Schulen', *Die Sammlung*, II (1947), no. 8, pp. 442–62.

Rossi, A. *Deux ans d'alliance germano-soviétique*. Paris: Libr. Arthème Fayard, 1949.

Rothfels, Hans. 'Vom Primat der Aussenpolitik', *Aussenpolitik*, I (1950), no. 4, pp. 274–83.

Rüstow, A. 'Politik und Moral', *Z.g.St.W.*, CV (1949), pp. 575–90.

Schaffstein, Friedrich. *Wilhelm von Humboldt. Ein Lebensbild*. Frankfurt a.M.: Klostermann, 1952.

Schnabel, Franz. 'Was bedeutet uns heute der Freiherr vom Stein?' *Die Schule*, II (Hannover, 1947), nos. 6/7, pp. 4–8.

Schultz, Klaus-Peter. 'Verhängnisvolle Geschichtsschreibung', *Dt.R.*, LXXVII (1951), no. 9, pp. 796–804.

Sell, Friedrich C. *Die Tragödie des deutschen Liberalismus*. Stuttgart: Deutsche Verlagsanstalt, 1953.

Selle, Erich von. 'Sabotage?' *Dt.R.*, LXXVI (1950), no. 5, pp. 333–42.

Silberschmidt, Max. 'Wirtschaftshistorische Aspekte der neueren Geschichte. Die atlantische Gesellschaft', *H.Z.*, CLXXI (1951), pp. 245–61.

Smolka, Georg. 'Die deutsche Revolution 1848', *F.H.* (1948), no. 4, pp. 401–14.

Spranger, Eduard. 'Zur Frage der Erneuerung des Naturrechts', *Universitas*, V (1948), pp. 405–20.

Stadelmann, Rudolf. 'Das Jahr 1848 und die deutsche Geschichte', *Dt.R.*, LXXI (1948), pp. 99–110.

Soziale und politische Geschichte der Revolution 1848. Munich: Bruckmann, 1948.

'Die Romantik und die Geschichte', in *Romantik, ein Zyklus Tübinger Vorlesungen*. Tübingen: Mohr, 1948, pp. 151–75.

Deutschland und Westeuropa. Schloss Laupheim, Wuerttemberg: Ulrich Steiner, 1948.

Stadtmüller, G. 'Der Weg in die deutsche Katastrophe 1933–45', *N.A.*, VI (1951), pp. 65–74.

'Geschichtsbild und Geschichtsunterricht', *Saeculum*, II (1951), no. 1, pp. 1–9.

Steefel, Lawrence D. 'Bismarck', *Journal of Modern History*, II (1930), pp. 74–75.

Stöcker, Jacob. *Männer des deutschen Schicksals*. Von Wilhelm II bis Adolf Hitler. Berlin: Oswald Arnold Verlag, 1949.

Thieme, Karl. *Das Schicksal des Deutschen*. Basel: Koberscher Verlag, 1945.

    Gott und die Geschichte. Freiburg i.B.: Herder, 1948.

Traber, Theodor. 'Raimund Friedrich Kaindl (1866–1930)', *N.A.*, II (1947), pp. 174–78.

    'Die Paulskirche und die deutsche Frage', *ibid.*, III (1948), pp. 4–8.

Veit, Otto. 'Die geistesgeschichtliche Situation des Naturrechts', *Merkur*, I (1947), no. 3, pp. 390–405.

Vogt, Josef. 'Dämonie der Macht und Weisheit der Antike', *W.a.G.*, X (1950), no. 1, pp. 1–17. See Gerhard Ritter's reply, *ibid.*, pp. 81–85.

Weber, Alfred. *Abschied von der bisherigen Geschichte*. Hamburg: E. Claassen, 1946.

    'Der vierte Mensch oder der Zusammenbruch der geschichtlichen Kultur', *Die Wandlung*, III (1948), no. 4, pp. 283–95.

Weinzierl, H. 'Ein Klassiker des Föderalismus—Josef Edmund Jörg', *N.A.*, V (1950), no. 4, pp. 143–50.

Wenger, P. W. 'Die demokratisch-föderative Tradition des deutschen Südwestens', *Die Sammlung*, II (1947), pp. 65–68. See the discussion, *ibid.*, pp. 470–74 and 596–97.

Weniger, Erich. *Neue Wege im Geschichtsunterricht* (with contributions by Hermann Hämpel and Hermann Körner). Frankfurt a.M.: G. Schulte-Bulmke, 1949.

Wittmann, Reinhold. 'Geschichtsauffassung und Wahrheitsfrage', *Die Sammlung*, II (1947), pp. 89–104.

    'Das Interesse an der Geschichte', *W.a.G.*, XII (1952), no. 1, pp. 1–16.

Zeeden, Ernst Walter. 'Der Historiker als Kritiker und Prophet. Die Kritik des 19. Jahrhunderts im Urteil Jacob Burckhardts', *W.a.G.*, XI (1951), no. 3, pp. 154–73.

Ziegenfuss, W. 'Bemerkungen über Geist und Geschichte', *Kölner Zeitschrift für Soziologie*, II (1949/50), no. 1, pp. 1–21.

INDEX